A MINORITY IN BRITAIN

A
MINORITY
IN BRITAIN

SOCIAL STUDIES OF THE ANGLO-JEWISH COMMUNITY

Edited by

Maurice Freedman, M.A.

✡

JAMES PARKES, M.A., D.Phil., Hon. D.H.L.

HANNAH NEUSTATTER, Dr.Oec.Publ.(Munich), F.S.S.

HOWARD M. BROTZ, M.A., Ph.D.

MAURICE FREEDMAN, M.A.

VALLENTINE, MITCHELL & CO., LTD.
LONDON

CONTENTS

CONTENTS

PUBLISHERS' FOREWORD

THIS book owes its origin and inspiration—in fact its existence—to *The Jewish Chronicle*. For a long while the Directors of that paper had been acutely conscious of the lack of any serious sociological study which would enable the observer, either within or outside of Jewish circles, to examine the position of the community in its relationship to the general population of these islands. It is hoped that this collection of essays will help to fill the gap. As Mr. Freedman has emphasised in his introduction, this book is not to be regarded as a definitive work but as a preliminary study, which it is hoped will point the way to more profound research.

A Minority in Britain appears at a time when the Jewish community has reached a turning-point in its history. The early formative years gave way to a period of consolidation, which was followed by the years of rapid expansion when immigration from the Continent occurred—in waves of varying size—on a considerable scale. Now, for various reasons, the pressure from abroad has relaxed and, once again, as in the middle of the nineteenth century, the Jewish community finds itself faced with the necessity of relying on its own resources. The present is, therefore, an opportune moment to take stock of the situation and for all those who are interested in the position of the Anglo-Jewish community to try to estimate the direction in which it is going.

The compilation of this book would have been impossible without the assistance of a large number of friends whose names are too numerous to mention individually, and it is hoped that they will accept this informal expression of the publishers' thanks as a mark of their sincere gratitude for the assistance which has been unstintingly rendered. There are, however, certain among them whom it would be ungracious not to mention by name: Professor Morris Ginsberg, Professor D. V. Glass, Mr. David Mellows, Mr. Wilfrid Samuel, Dr. Eliot Slater, Mr. Joshua Podro, Mr. Henry Shaw, Mr. S. J. Prais, Miss Judith Djamour, Mr. D. G. MacRae, Mr. Julius Gould, and Mr. Basil Yamey.

PUBLISHERS' FOREWORD

The Association of Jewish Ex-Service Men and Women, the Jewish Representative Councils of Hull and Sheffield and the London Jewish Hospital worked diligently in the distribution of the questionnaire (A.J.S.-2) on which many of the statistical data were based. Valuable help was also rendered by the following institutions: The Registrar-General's Office, Census Department ; the Eugenics Society ; the Embassy of Israel in London ; the Board of Deputies of British Jews; the Jewish Board of Guardians; the United Synagogue (especially the Burial Committee) ; the Federation of Synagogues ; Jews' College ; the Jewish Memorial Council ; Patwa ; the Association of Refugees from Germany and Austria ; the Wiener Library ; the Library of the Royal Statistical Society ; and the Trades Advisory Council.

INTRODUCTION

IN introducing this book to the reader I must begin by saying
that it does not give an exhaustive account of Jewish society in
Britain. It is the earnest hope of the contributors to this volume
that their, as it were, prefaces to the sociology of Anglo-Jewry may
have brought the possibility of a scientific study of Jewish social
life in this country closer to realisation ; but the writers cannot
claim that they have, in any way, presented a rounded picture of
the phenomena which a sociology of Anglo-Jewry must embrace.

In Britain we have a distinguished body of historians of Anglo-
Jewry, a sizeable Jewish population, not a few Jewish social
scientists, and very little in the way of a sociology of the Jews. This
lack, which the present volume emphasises rather than remedies,
probably reflects, to some extent, the weakness of scientific concern
with problems of minority groups in Britain ; but, on a more
cheerful reading of its significance, it may be said to result from the
fact that, in recent times, Jews in Britain do not seem to have
presented any important practical problems to society at large. If,
of course, the study of the Jewish minority really is contingent upon
there being a Jewish ' problem ' we may well hope for the continued
frustration of the sociology of Anglo-Jewry. However, there are
good grounds for looking forward to this sociology without antici-
pating trouble.

The first of these—and it is the most important—is the light
which a study of Jews in Britain throws on the working of British
society. There are many problems in the fields of assimilation and
of what is often loosely called ' group relations ' which could be
illuminated by a comparative study of minorities in Britain. In the
second place, a dispassionate study of Jews is good for Jews ; not
because it can necessarily solve any of their practical problems as
they see them, but because it can both set their problems for them in
a wider perspective and help them rid themselves of systematised
illusions (pleasant and unpleasant) about their position. Finally, a
case can be made for the scientific study of Jewish life on the ground
that it could help furnish the vague world which the Jews call

Gentile with a factual basis for the exercise of its intelligent understanding.

The essays in this book are a tentative first approach to the general subject. They approximate to the requirements of a full treatment of the sociology of Anglo-Jewry only in respect of their (at least attempted) coolness and detachment. Although three of the writers are Jewish, none of them is concerned with grinding a communal—or for that matter, non-communal—axe. None of them is here for or against 'assimilation,' the Board of Deputies, the kasher meat system, religious Orthodoxy, or any of the other questions which burn so brightly in the pages of Anglo-Jewish literature. They have perhaps all made mistakes, but the reader may assure himself that the mistakes have not been engineered to make a case for this or that side in any stock controversy. The necessity for stressing this point has been imposed upon me by the duty I have towards my colleagues of preventing their work passing out as yet another piece of parochial politics.

While I am to emphasise that each essay in the book is the sole responsibility of its author, there is a sense, I hope, in which all four contributions, despite their differences in outlook and approach, hang together as an initial treatment of the subject. The form of the book was originally designed to present four major themes: the social history of Anglo-Jewry as a background to the understanding of modern conditions; a compilation and analysis of demographic and other quantitative material as a factual foundation; an analysis of the internal structure of the Jewish community in Britain; and a discussion of problems in the field of the relationships between Jews and non-Jews. As it has turned out, these four general topics have not been treated with exactly equal weight, but they have provided the book with four dimensions which, the contributors hope, have made it a more or less integrated piece of work.

Of the four contributions and their authors I need say least, for obvious reasons, of the first. Dr. Parkes's essay bears the stamp of his authority as an historian of Jewry and scholar in Jewish affairs. In tracing the development of Jewish social life in Britain and the course of Jewish relations with the wider society, he has given roots to the more contemporary studies that follow. Despite much work that has been done in the field of Anglo-Jewish history, to which Dr. Lipman's recent book, *Social History of the Jews in England 1850-1950*, is an important contribution, there is still need for more institutional analysis of a kind which historians of Anglo-Jewry will no doubt develop.

Dr. Neustatter, who has been of all the contributors the longest associated with the project of which this book is the outcome, has, over a long period of time, put together all the available quantitative material bearing on the topics she treats. I should perhaps say that her essay was finished some considerable time ago, and that, while she has made every effort to keep her material up to date, there may be some respects in which her information does not exactly apply to conditions in 1955. Her essay illustrates the difficulty of writing a full and coherent account of Jewish society in Britain in the present state of our knowledge. If she is diffident about the statistics she presents it is because much demographic, economic, and social data on Anglo-Jewry have yet to be gathered systematically. On a population of which we do not know even the exact size we can as yet make only general statements. On the other hand, using material she has herself collected and data from published sources, Dr. Neustatter has been able to offer future workers on Anglo-Jewish statistics an appraisal of what is known and a set of problems for investigation.

In the third essay we have the work of an American sociologist who has been able to look at Jews in Britain with some of the detachment of the outsider. Dr. Brotz's analysis, furthermore, has been based on a piece of field research on Jews in a London area and has the distinction of being a pioneer study. As far as I am aware, no other sociological field study of Jewish life in this country has been published. Because he breaks new ground Dr. Brotz is able to throw up a multitude of problems for study in the realm of the social relationships which form the nexus of Anglo-Jewish society. He shows us how Jews think of the sub-system within which they live, how they fall into patterns of residence, and how the leading characteristics of Jewry as a minority in a free and fluid society affect such things as leadership and social stratification.

The last essay takes up some of the themes discussed by the other writers and attempts to offer some reflections on the nature of the relations between Jews and their neighbours. I cannot claim to have made any contribution to the knowledge of Anglo-Jewish affairs, but I have tried to look at the Jewish position somewhat after the manner of a social anthropologist examining, in a preliminary way, certain problems of prejudice, assimilation, and minority status in a Western society. (Perhaps it is important to say that for the anthropologist it is Western society which is, in a sense, exotic.)

It would be impertinent of the authors of this book to assume that what they have written will determine the shape of a future sociology of Anglo-Jewry. But if the book is to make a contribution towards this much-desired research then it ought to indicate some of the morals which its compilation has pointed. I have thought it worthwhile, therefore, to set out briefly my own views of this matter.

Many readers, and those Jews who live in the provinces especially, will be bound to regret the emphasis on London Jewry which is apparent at least in the last two essays. This preoccupation with the metropolis arises, of course, from personal biases and limitations on experience rather than from a conscious claim to represent importance by scale of treatment ; but at least this lack of balance will serve to show how ignorant we are of the varieties of Jewish social life throughout the country. It is too easy to fall into the error of dismissing the provincial settlements as smaller replicas of what is to be found in London or of generalising about them as though they fell into a common extra-metropolitan mould. Indeed, it is precisely in the smaller Jewish local communities that organised field research could most profitably begin.

There are reasons of theory and method for this. A whole and rounded view of what constitutes Jewish communal life in Britain can most easily be obtained from the study of a group whose small size makes it possible for the observer to cover it as a limited field. I am prompted by the prejudices of my profession to urge that the field methods associated with social anthropology are likely to make suitable tools for the intensive study of local Jewish communities. Such a study, in taking a comprehensive view of a local situation, should be able to set out for us in clear detail the nature of the forces making for both cohesion and disintegration in Anglo-

Jewish society. Comparative study of a series of such local communities would help us towards making general propositions on the social processes at work in Anglo-Jewry.

An initial approach of this order would have the advantage of suggesting what general themes could most usefully be made the subject of investigation on a broader front. Intermarriage, family and kinship organisation (a particularly striking gap in our present knowledge), occupational structure, social mobility, religious change, voluntary associations, Zionism, and education are clearly all themes which could guide concurrent study in a number of different physical settings. On the basis of an intensive study of them in a few particular local communities we should be able the better to approach them individually over a wider geographical field. Once we have some clues, for example, to the functioning of voluntary associations in particular local groups, we can then, with the aid of survey techniques, match our intensive knowledge of the situation in one area with information gathered over a large part of the country.

A series of studies of local communities might help us to build up a typology of Jewish settlements in Britain. In a general way we know, of course, that Jewish settlements in resort towns differ from those in industrial towns, and that the smaller settlements seem to have narrower ranges of occupation and wealth than the larger. But there is a great number of criteria which could be used—economic, residential, religious—to erect a useful series of types of Jewish communal life.

The analysis of local communities and general social processes in Anglo-Jewry leaves out of account the interesting set of institutions which seek to co-ordinate the Jews of Britain as a whole. However nebulous it may at times appear, there is certainly a comprehensive system of power and leadership within Anglo-Jewry as a whole, and the distributions of this power and the structure of this leadership are matters of great theoretical interest, quite apart from any practical implications they may have for Jews themselves. Up to what point of integration into the wider society, by political, cultural, and social ' assimilation,' can a minority, such as the Jews form, maintain a distinct structure of leadership and sanctions? What in effect are the functions of representative bodies, lay and religious, in the maintenance of the widest communal solidarity? What general changes in the recruitment of leaders follow from shifts in economic power and ideological emphasis?

The last field of study to which I should like to direct attention is that of antisemitism. In the course of preparing my contribution to this book I have been much struck not only by the obvious vagueness of the concept for which antisemitism is the label, but also by the hiatus between Jewish thought on the subject and what non-Jews appear to believe. It is not simply a question of concern on the part of Jews and, generally, indifference on the part of non-Jews; when both groups think of antisemitism they do not necessarily think of the same thing. It is evident that we need some careful and systematic studies of antisemitic attitudes and actions in the general population and of the perception of antisemitism by Jews, such as J. H. Robb's *Working Class Anti-Semite*. And we need, as a corollary to these investigations, an intensive analysis of Jewish defence activities and an assessment of their effect.

I have tried very briefly to suggest the significance of a few possible lines of inquiry. In the essays that follow the reader will himself be able to pick out problems that call for closer examination and see the gaps in our knowledge which can be filled only by hard and scholarly work. It may well be many years before work of this kind comes to fruition and before we have a comprehensive sociology of Anglo-Jewry. One may hope that both Jewish and non-Jewish resources of goodwill and talent will quickly be brought into use.

MAURICE FREEDMAN.

London School of Economics
   and Political Science,
      London, W.C.2.

March, 1955.

PART ONE

The History of the Anglo-Jewish Community

JAMES PARKES, M.A., D.Phil., Hon. D.H.L.

The History of the Anglo-Jewish Community

The Nature of the Jewish People

TO the question: *What is a Jew?* there is no single answer, if what is desired is some easy definition which can be applied objectively to every possible case. There is no clear criterion on which it can be based. Hence the Nazi Government, after all its pompous declarations about ineradicable racial distinctions, could get no further in practice than the statement, ridiculous from a 'racial' point of view, that a Jew was one, a certain proportion of whose grandparents were Jews. Hence also contemporary sociologists, dealing with the contemporary situation, have to content themselves with the statement that they mean 'everyone who, when asked if he is a Jew, says "yes."' For the study of living Jewish communities this gives an adequate basis. But its limitations are obvious. In certain situations the question at issue might be the position of one who, for personal reasons, strenuously dissociated himself from the Jewish community to which, in fact, he had belonged. In others the person in question might either be a member of one of various Protestant sects which have adopted the name, or a convert to Judaism. In all such cases, the denial or the affirmation would involve special considerations not covered by the question of the sociologist.

Nevertheless, if it be impossible *to define a Jew,* it still remains true that from an historical point of view it is perfectly easy *to identify the Jews*; and this identification will, at the same time, explain why a single definition covering every Jew is unattainable. For the root from which the Jews have grown is the experience of a nation, as much and as little homogeneous as any other nation, in Palestine during a period which terminated nearly two thousand years ago; and the trunk which joins the present branches to that root is the experience of a religion which held the Jews together when the geographical unity of the nation perished. As this

3

combination is unique, neither element can be used by itself to define the Jews. For a definition obtains its clarity only by allowing of accurate comparison with other similar phenomena, and comparisons with other religions or other nations are misleading. We need a more general term, and the most satisfactory is to describe Jewry as a civilisation, having its roots in the experience of the Jews in Palestine, and owing its survival to the nature of rabbinic Judaism. A civilisation can manifest itself in many different forms, and can exist simultaneously at many different levels. And of no civilisation is it possible to draw such clear-cut frontiers that we can say that this man is just outside those frontiers and that man is just within them. This remains true although at times historical accidents have imposed such clear-cut segregation between communities that a definition of the group would be identical with the definition of each member within it. Such was the situation of Jews in the millets of the Arab and Turkish empires and the ghettoes of medieval and post-medieval Europe. How recently it was applicable to important sections of the Jewish people can be read in *Life is with People*,[1] the recently published study of the Jewish culture of the small town of Eastern Europe.

Jewry is a civilisation. It is not a homogeneous racial group, either in the sense that all Jews have the same racial origin, or in the sense that there is any single racial stock all of whose members either are, or have been, members of the Jewish people. From their first emergence in the history of the Middle East the Jewish stock has been mingled with that of their neighbours, not all of whom were of semitic origin, whether we define semitic in terms of language or racial affinity. In their passage through Europe, Africa, and Asia, Jewish communities have drawn in members of the local peoples, Mongols and Tartars in Eastern Europe ; Nordics and Mediterraneans in Central and Western Europe ; Hittite, Dravidian, and Chinese in Asia ; Berber, Arab, and various African peoples of dark skins in Africa, and so on.[2]

---

[1] *Life is with People.* The Jewish Little-town of Eastern Europe. Mark Zborowski and Elizabeth Herzog. International Universities Press. New York, 1952.

[2] The best description of all these ' peripheral ' Jewish communities is (in spite of its irrelevant title) *The Lost Tribes : A Myth*, by Allen H. Godbey, Duke University Press, 1930.

There is not even an original racial stock all of whose members have been partakers in Jewish history. The fact that it is often (though by no means always) possible in England to identify a Jew with a fair degree of certainty may seem to contradict this statement. But all that this identification means is that *in England* it is unusual to meet members of some particular racial stock (or racial mixture) except among Jews. If it be an Eastern European stock, then it ceases to provide an identification of a Jew in Eastern Europe. If it is one of the many stocks of the Eastern Mediterranean, then it will not identify a Jew in the region where the majority of the indigenous population also belong to the stock in question, however much it may help identification in England. There is, however, a certain measure of agreement between anthropologists that there are matters of gesture, of deportment, or of carriage which enable a local inhabitant to sense a difference and identify a Jew of his locality. Some anthropologists call this an ' ethnic ' expression. But the phrase must be used with caution ; for it does not imply that, for example, a Central European who will usually be accurate in spotting a Central European Jew will as easily distinguish a Jewish from a non-Jewish Englishman or American.

On the other hand, we are on sure ground in identifying, in the complex tapestry of human societies, a Jewish society which, though subjected like all others to innumerable influences from outside, has yet maintained and developed into many different channels a culture and a tradition which are peculiarly its own. Its origin we know, and its development we can trace with certainty across the pages of history.

The First Jewish Community in England

The extension of the frontiers of the Roman Empire to the Rhine and the Danube allowed the peoples of the Mediterranean to extend their migrations and their trading interests into Northern and Western Europe. Jews were but one of the peoples who took advantage of this opportunity ; and nothing particularly distinguished them from other such migrants and travellers until they came to be the only non-Christian communities in a continent which had come to accept Christianity as the basis of communal life. As

Romans the Jews had been citizens since the beginning of the third century. But as Roman law began to give way to various codes of Germanic origin, they found themselves 'foreigners' and in need of special protection from the princes under whom they lived, or through whose territories they wished to travel. The earliest examples of the special privileges which came to form the basis of every medieval Jewish community took the form of 'passports' issued by Louis the Pious in the ninth century either to individuals or to groups of individuals, allowing them to travel freely through his dominions.[1] By the time that medieval society was fully developed the Jews had been allocated the status of 'servi cameræ,' by which was understood that they were completely the property of their prince, on a par with his castles or his hounds. As their owner, he could exercise possession over all their property, did he so desire ; he could banish or admit them ; he could even order their forcible baptism or pronounce sentence of death for no reason against them ; and against his actions they had no appeal.[2]

The extension of the control of Islam over the Mediterranean seaboard intensified the peculiar position of the Jewish people. For they alone among the inhabitants of North-Western Europe could travel relatively freely between Islam and Christendom, and maintained at least a trickle of the wares of the east into the markets of the west. Hence the development in their status already described accompanied the growth in North-Western Europe of an urban economy, a policy of expansion, and a general rise in prosperity. For such a society had a place within it for a merchant class, and was prepared to pay for its encouragement. Thus, when in 1084 Rudiger Huotzmann, Bishop of Speyer, desired to extend the boundaries of his cathedral city with a new suburb, he explained that 'he would amplify a thousand times its dignity if he persuaded Jews to settle in it.'[3] The example of Rudiger was soon followed by other princes ; and there was even keen competition among the rulers of North-Western Europe to secure a Jewish community.

[1] Parkes, *The Jew in the Medieval Community*, pp. 158ff. and 391.
[2] *Ibid.*, Chapter iv: "The Jew as Private Property."
[3] *Ibid.*, pp. 160ff. The text of a similar charter, granted by the Emperor, Henry IV, in 1090, is given on p. 392. The text of the charter of Rudiger is given in Aronius, *Regesten zur Geschichte der Juden in Deutschland*, Berlin, 1902, p. 69.

The rapid expansion of the English economy which followed the Norman conquest, and its close integration into the economy of the adjacent areas of the continent, adequately explain the appearance in Norman England of a Jewish community which expanded with similar rapidity. The charters which must have formed the original basis for its establishment have not survived, and the earliest English charter dates from the end of the twelfth century.[1] By that time the financial value of a Jewish community to the prince who owned it had become well known ; and the Jews of England were no exception in finding that their protection and privileges depended entirely on their usefulness to the crown. As this diminished, so the kings found it more useful to transfer their favour to the Churchmen, who hated them as subversive unbelievers, and to their rivals among the Christian financiers, who disposed of far greater resources.

The most characteristic activity of the Jewish communities of this period was the making of short-term loans to the prince and his subjects. These loans covered the whole field of the expanding economy of the period, and they could be a rich source of immediate profit, since the terms on which they were granted were extremely high. But Jews were not the only money-lenders, and the oft-repeated statement that 'money-lending was in the hands of the Jews because the church forbad usury' is completely misleading. Money was always a scarce commodity at the time and it was lent for profit by all those who had it—monasteries who received it as donations from pilgrims and other visitors to their shrines, tax collectors, through whose hands it passed on its way to the king's coffers, and merchants who needed it for their transactions. It was as members of the last class that Jews became involved in the occupation ; and their peculiar status in it arose from the fact that, unlike Christian merchants, they were the private property of the princes, who could, and did, assess their rates of interest by the needs of the royal treasury and collect the profits which had accumulated in Jewish coffers whenever they were in particular need of cash. In addition, the princes imposed on them a multitude

[1] *Ibid.*, pp. 168ff. and 393ff. The reference to an additional clause in the charter of John at the end of the first paragraph on p. 170 is erroneous. See also Cecil Roth, *History*, Chapter II.

7

of financial exactions to accompany almost every act of their lives. The system of money-lending practised by Jews was (in medieval terminology) that of ' usury.' This means that a fixed charge on the loan had to be paid weekly, usually a penny or twopence per £. This system was judged unlawful by the Church ; but this did not mean that Christians did not lend money for profit. The scholastics evolved an alternative system, which was held to be lawful. A Christian should not make profit from a loan ; but equally he should not incur a loss from his generosity! His loss (*i.e.*, the amount by which his position differed [*quod interest*] from what it would have been had he kept the money) he might add to the loan as a lump sum, provided it was not repaid within a period (always so calculated as to preclude payment) for which no charge would be made. Once that period had elapsed, every kind of additional charge might be invented and added. It is not surprising if the medieval borrower preferred the straightforward, though onerous, system of the Jews. It was, nevertheless, a system which was economically disastrous for those subjected to it. The royal appetite inevitably grew ; and likewise the hostility of the populace to the resulting increase of Jewish demands ; and in England the extent of royal power made it possible for there to be an efficient central organisation of Jewry under strict control, such as could not be achieved on the continent. Hence a single century witnessed the establishment, rise, and ruin of the Jewish community. The second century of their existence, before their expulsion in 1290, was a century of poverty, of almost continuous royal exaction, of increasing public hostility and violence, until Edward I judged them no further use to him and could make an easy gesture of respect to the Church by expelling them from his dominions. He was also heavily in debt to their Christian rivals, the Italian money-lenders.

The Re-establishment of a Jewish Community in the Seventeenth Century

For two hundred and fifty years after the expulsion of 1290 there was no Jewish community in England, though from time to time individual Jews penetrated into the country. But a new situation was created by the great expansion of trade in the sixteenth century.

In 1492 and 1496 all those Jews who would not accept baptism had been expelled from the Iberian peninsula. Those who remained were known as 'new Christians,' popularly 'Marranos,' and since the authenticity of their 'conversion' was inevitably doubtful, they were viewed with great suspicion by the Inquisition. Numbers sought safety in flight and established themselves in the more hospitable ports of the Atlantic seaboard, where expanding trade gave them an opportunity to re-establish themselves. Antwerp was their chief centre, and from Antwerp small groups came to London and Bristol, and there established secret Jewish communities which lived a somewhat insecure existence throughout the sixteenth century. Officially they were either 'Portuguese' or else 'Protestants'; but that in fact they were Jewish was well known to the authorities—when they needed to make use of the knowledge. In 1609 they were expelled from the country, largely as a result of a quarrel within the community in which one party had denounced the other to the authorities for Judaising practices. It was half a century before they recovered the lost ground, though some crept back in the next decades, and even opposed the more formal recognition of their existence implicit in the mission of Manasseh ben Israel.

The situation which led to their formal re-establishment bore many resemblances to that in which the first community had come into being after the Norman conquest. England had become more closely integrated into the life of the continent, both political and economic; and it was a period of rising prosperity when the absorption of a new element in the population could be the more easily accepted. There were, however, other factors which were peculiar to the times.

Of these, the most important was the change in religious attitude among Englishmen of the period. The widespread reading of the Bible had led to a new veneration for Biblical customs from the Old Testament as well as from the New. Side by side with such movements as that of the Presbyterians, who sought to model their church on that of apostolic times, were others which demanded the reintroduction of the Sabbath, of distinctions of meats, and even of circumcision. The latter came inevitably to look with a new interest at the Jewish people. Moreover, the religious excitement

9

of the times, and the wide variety of ways in which it was expressed, led to a new movement for toleration. It was not so much that any of the Protestant sects were in themselves tolerant ; but that, so long as no single one had any chance of dominating the whole religious life of the nation, their own survival depended on others tolerating them! Only a few outstanding men believed in tolerance for its own sake. Nevertheless, the question of tolerance of differences was in the air ; and, once it was discussed, it gave rise to the question of what should be the limits of toleration. Here the interest in the Bible was of advantage to the Jews, the people who accepted the Old Testament, more than, for example, the Roman Catholics, who were held to have departed entirely from Biblical Christianity.

The discussion of toleration led to no practical result. Once it passed from the stage of pamphleteering to that of political consideration, it encountered too many obstacles. But just at this moment a fresh approach was made to the question. Manasseh ben Israel, a Dutch rabbi and the outstanding Jewish apologist of his time, published in 1650 a work entitled *The Hope of Israel*, in which he put forward the thesis that the Messianic Age could not come until the dispersion of the Jews was complete. Some of the lost tribes had just been 'identified' in America, and now England remained the only land from which they were excluded. If they were readmitted to England, the conditions for the coming of the Messiah would be fulfilled. In the spate of pamphlets which followed *The Hope of Israel*, the discussion shifted from the apocalyptic to the political, and led to an examination of the conditions on which a Jewish community might be allowed to establish itself in the country.

So the matter smouldered for five years, when Manasseh came to England and laid before Cromwell himself his plea for the readmission of the Jews. A judicial committee pronounced that there was no law in the statute book which made it impossible for Jews to reside in the country ; but when it came to the practical discussion of what actually should be allowed, all the opposition forces raised their heads and made a formal decision impossible. That Cromwell desired their readmission is certain ; though his motives were political and economic rather than messianic. But he was unwilling to force the issue by over-riding the opposition. In consequence, the eloquent plea of Manasseh received no formal answer, and he returned home to Amsterdam to die, a disappointed man.

The Jewish community not only received no legal document stating the conditions on which they would be formally permitted to establish themselves and maintain their religion, but they do not seem to have even received any written statement from the Protector that they would be permitted to remain in the country, or would be protected against malicious persecution in the courts. Nevertheless, he gave them to understand that the best thing they could do would be to go on as they were, to remain inconspicuous, and to trust to his favour. To the Jews of that day it was a disappointing result of their hopes and endeavours. In fact, it turned out a blessing. Not merely the Christian pamphleteers, but Manasseh and the Jewish leaders themselves, had always assumed that a licensed resettlement would be on stringent conditions. They expected to have to pay special taxes, and that these would be substantial; they expected a narrow definition of such rights and opportunities as the law would allow them. They expected the establishment of a ghetto. In fact, no special taxes, no rights and opportunities, no area of residence, were ever defined. Disputable issues were allowed to await decision until they arose out of actual cases.

The fact that there had been no formal law passed under the Commonwealth which could be repealed at the Restoration emphasised the value of their uncertain status. Charles II, tolerant by nature, refused to take any steps against them just as he refused to grant them any formal rights. In consequence the English Jews of the seventeenth century had to discover step by step what they could, and what they could not, do. A Jew had already been admitted a broker of the City of London in 1656, and he was soon followed by others. Parliament had allowed Jews to contract for supplying the army during the Civil War; and they continued to secure public contracts. The property of a Jew who was nominally a 'Portuguese' was exempted from confiscation when war broke out with Spain, which still considered Portugal to be a kingdom under the Spanish monarchy. Legal decisions soon followed. In 1667 a Jew was permitted in the Court of King's Bench to take the oath on the Old Testament. In 1677 a case was postponed so

11

that a Jew should not have to give evidence on his Sabbath. In 1682 it was ruled that the religion of a Jewish plaintiff was no bar to his bringing an action. By such imperceptible means was the re-establishment of the Jewish community made a fact, without it even being subjected to the dangerous possibilities of parliamentary debate. In fact, the earliest written authority for their existence in the country was an almost casual minute of Charles II in 1664 on a secondary issue that Jews might ' promise themselves the effect of the same favour as formerly they have had, so long as they demeane themselves peaceably and quietly with due obedience to his Maties Lawes and without scandall to his Government.'

It was said at the beginning of this section that there were both parallels and differences between the first and second establishments of a Jewish community in England. One final difference remains to be treated. While the coming of a restricted number of mainly prosperous Jews of Spanish and Portuguese origin (known as Sephardim) parallels the coming of a similar group of Norman and French Jewish merchants in the eleventh century, in the seventeenth there was a further factor which began to affect the Jewish community from the first years of its settlement.

During the later Middle Ages the general trend of Jewish migration had been eastwards towards the Kingdom of Poland, where they lived in large numbers and in relative security and prosperity. This security and prosperity of centuries was rudely shattered between 1648 and 1651 by the rebellion against the Polish King of the Cossack leader, Bogdan Chmielnitzki. In the rebellion Jews, who were regarded as the main instruments of Polish rule and extortion, were the first object of the hatred of Chmielnitzki's forces. Thousands were massacred. Thousands began a flight westwards which filled the new centres of Jewish life in Western Europe with penniless refugees. Some few reached the shores of England, and before the end of the seventeenth century they may even have become more numerous than the Sephardim. Known as the Ashkenazim, and having some prosperous members of their community, their economic and religious needs justified them in seeking a separate existence, an existence which the Sephardim were the more ready to recognise in that it relieved them of sole responsibility for an enormous burden of charity. By the end of the century two clearly defined groups were accepted as 'Jews,' and they remain distinct to this day. One was the community of Sephardim, consisting mainly of Jews of Spanish and Portuguese origin. The other were the Ashkenazim, from Central and Eastern Europe.

The Basis of its Existence

For the Jews to re-enter England in the seventeenth century it was a certain British attitude which was necessary, and that was found in the medley of religious, political, and economic arguments which led to the resettlement. But for them to remain in the country and prosper, it was necessary for them to find a niche for themselves in the general economy of the country ; and this niche had to have certain peculiar characteristics. For it was not merely an affair of individual immigrants seeking, each for himself, some occupation congenial to his talents from which he could earn a living. Not only would such a development have brought about a good deal of hostility and suspicion ; for Jews could not conceal that they were 'foreigners,' and foreigners were objects of suspicion to the middle and lower-class English way of thinking. But it would also have been alien to the Jewish way of thinking. It is the normal characteristic of a Jewish migration that it seeks to establish in the new country a somewhat close-knit communal and social organisation ; for only so can the Jewish way of life be preserved in a Gentile environment. This was not merely a question of religion. Prudence compelled Jews to extend to social and economic matters a communal control or influence which had its roots not only in the strong emphasis on mutual solidarity and responsibility in rabbinic Judaism, but also in the recognition that the reputation of each individual Jew affected the security and well-being of all his fellows. Jews could not avoid being responsible for each other.

A great asset of the original Sephardi immigrants under Cromwell, Charles II, and William III was their membership of a widespread commercial community, often closely linked by family associations, whose trading activities and experience could make a solid contribution to a nation which was itself rapidly expanding its commerce to every quarter of the globe, and was steadily increasing in domestic wealth and prosperity. That such a contribution would

13

also provoke hostility, especially among commercial rivals, is to be expected ; and the early story of the Jewish community faithfully reflects both elements, approval at the national level, and with the national government, and hostility among the merchants of the City of London and the Christian rivals in enterprises in which Jews became prominent.

All the main activities in which we find London Jews engaged in the seventeenth century reflect the value of this membership of this far larger association. England was engaged in widespread and expensive military enterprises abroad. These involved vast operations to feed and equip troops. Here was a field in which Englishmen had had few opportunities to gain experience. But it was a normal activity of the ' Court Jews ' who were to be found in every principality of Germany ; and it was familiar to all the great Jewish banking and trading firms of the continent. Gold was also needed in these activities, as in the expanding demands on the national exchequer. The close link between the Jews of London and of Amsterdam, the main centre of the bullion trade of Western Europe, gave them considerable advantages in this field.

Equally solid were the advantages which they enjoyed in the immense expansion of trade beyond Europe which had been growing since the Elizabethan era. The expulsions from Spain and Portugal had led to the establishment of Jewish communities in all the commercial centres of the Mediterranean and the Levant ; and the extension of the Inquisition to the American possessions of Spain and Portugal across the Atlantic led to a flight of Marranos already settled in the Americas from these Roman Catholic communities to the Protestant freedom of the colonies of Holland and England, whither they took their commercial experience and often their wealth. In addition to the trade in gold and colonial wares, they had a special place in the trade in diamonds and precious stones, objects obtainable from lands with which they were usually more familiar than the native-born Englishman.

When all these advantages are put together it is not surprising to find that the small group of leading Jewish families were exceedingly wealthy. They are said to have brought £1,500,000 in specie with them on their arrival, and to have had an annual turnover amounting to one-twelfth of the total overseas commerce

14

of the country. Their contributions, voluntary or involuntary, to public loans reflect the same wealth ; and Sir Solomon de Medina, who was the chief purveyor to Marlborough during his campaigns, found the operation sufficiently remunerative to allow the Duke himself an annual *douceur* of £5,000 on his profits.

The community, however, did not consist exclusively of merchants of substance, whose centre of operations was almost wholly limited to London. Even among the Sephardi Jews there were inevitably a certain number of people who were destitute and incapable of working, or were humble artisans or shopkeepers. But in addition to these, there was, from the beginning, an influx of those Jews from Central and Eastern Europe, almost all of them in humble circumstances, and many completely penniless, who were in due course to found the Ashkenazi community. The presence of these various groups of poorer Jews created a problem from various points of view. City magnates, who were prepared to give a grudging recognition to the solid services rendered to the nation by the contributions of wealthy Jewish merchants, were quick to demand action when it seemed possible that an immigration of Jewish paupers might increase the burdens on the parish vestries ; and English artisans and shopkeepers viewed with open hostility the possibility of Jewish rivals for their humble living. In the City of London Jews could not establish shops ; for the retail trade was confined to freemen of the city. Jews had but limited and ill-defined rights, and certainly lacked the privilege of this freedom. Hence, while some Jews established themselves in the boroughs and villages around the City, the general policy of the leaders of the community was to seek openings for their poorer brethren at a distance from the capital.

The most obvious centres where Jews might find opportunities for earning a living were in the seaports ; for both the naval and the trading activities of the country were continually increasing. Already before the end of the seventeenth century it is probable that individual Jewish tradesmen or pedlars were widely scattered round the coasts, but they were not in a position to acquire property and found communities, and the records of their activities have perished. It is only with the eighteenth century that we find substantial traces of fully established Jewish communities outside London.

15

and formal records scarcely begin before the second half of the century. By that time we find communities existing at such ports as Portsmouth, King's Lynn, Plymouth, Bristol, Ipswich, and Liverpool, as well as in inland centres such as Birmingham, Canterbury, and Norwich, while records of individual Jews are to be found in almost every town of any size throughout the country.[1]

In all these centres Jews were mostly retailers and artisans ; few families achieved more than a modest prosperity. The centre of Jewish wealth remained in London. To a considerable extent this fact was due to the difficulty which Jews found in entering directly into the rising field of industry. Many factors made it difficult for them to create factories or to become extensive employers of labour. It is only from the Napoleonic wars onwards that they began to enter this field ; and they only achieved prominence in any sections of it in the era following the immigration from Russia in the 1880s. Until that time banking and international trade were their main sources of wealth, and peddling, retailing, and crafts such as silversmith or working jeweller the main occupations of the humbler classes.

The Synagogal Structure of Anglo-Jewry

THE SEPHARDI CONGREGATION

In all negotiations for their return to England Jews envisaged the formal grant of such conditions as would lead to the establishment of an autonomous community under their own officials, and that these officials would have a recognised status guaranteed by law. This was necessary in their eyes because Jews required more than freedom of worship. The Jewish way of life involved communal authority over many other matters. In this there was nothing new. The conception of a Jewish community living under its own laws goes right back to the Roman Empire and to Sassanid Persia. It was accepted by the Christian rulers of the Middle Ages and by the rulers of the Islamic world alike. It was the basis of innumerable charters ; and it was, in fact, a settlement under charter which Jews sought from Cromwell in the seventeenth century.

[1] Roth. *Provincial Jewry, passim.*

It has already been said that no such formal basis for their readmission was ever granted, and that in the long run this proved an immense advantage to Anglo-Jewry. But at the time it was the subject of bitter disappointment. For each step had to be taken tentatively and by negotiation ; and Jews had to find out by experience how they might practise their own way of life among the mass of strict and restrictive legislation which defined the religious practices open to the English people.

The first needs for a community were a synagogue and a cemetery. In the uncertain circumstances of their lives Jews could not own land or buildings. Their first cemetery and their first synagogue were alike leased from Christian owners. The latter was a house in Cree Lane acquired in December, 1656, the former a field at Mile End. The next question concerned the government and finances of the community, and communal statutes, modelled on those of Amsterdam, were issued in 1663. They had no sanction other than the willingness of members to accept their authority and to pay the substantial dues demanded. In the following year arrangements were made for the religious education of the sons of members. With these five institutions—synagogue, cemetery, governing body, communal taxes, and school—the community could be considered fully established. But a host of subsidiary institutions soon followed.

Though the synagogue was to remain for almost two hundred years the exclusive centre of the life of the community, this does not mean that Jewish life was ruled by the rabbis. The government of the community, and of the synagogue itself, was in the hands of a council of laymen, the Mahamad, and the functions and authority of the rabbi were relatively constricted. The activities of the Mahamad paralleled those of the parish vestry in the days before Poor Law reform and the extension of local government had robbed it of most of its functions. They did not therefore seem unusual to the Englishmen of the seventeenth century. But they were more extensive and involved greater financial commitments on the part of members than did a parish vestry ; and, unlike the commitments of the vestry, they were entered into voluntarily by men who had already paid their parish rates and accepted their normal liabilities as residents in London.

17

c

At the end of the seventeenth century the synagogue in Cree Lane, in spite of extensions and adjustments, had become too small. A new site was acquired in Plough Lane, Bevis Marks, in 1699. It was still obtained on lease, though a Jew was able to acquire the freehold later and presented it to the community. On this site was erected the present synagogue of Bevis Marks, and it still retains all the essential dignity and comeliness of its period.

To become a full member of the Sephardi community involved the acceptance of a considerable financial burden. The community had to provide not only for its place of worship and its minister, but for the maintenance of its poor and the education of its children. In addition, it was part of a wider community of Jewry and had to contribute to the needs of Jews elsewhere. Funds for the ransoming of captives and for the assistance of Jews in the Holy Land involved more than token payments. For the Mediterranean trade was exposed to many dangers from the local pirates of the African coast, and the Jews of the Holy Land were unable to create for themselves a solid economic basis of life in a country constantly ravaged by local feuds, Bedouin raids, and the extortion of Turkish governors.

To meet the costs involved in all these responsibilities the Mahamad financed itself not only by 'pew-rents' but by an elaborate system of fines. The heaviest fines were attached to the refusal to share in the burdens of the community by accepting office. Candidates were not asked for their agreement before election; and the records of the Congregation show that there was a constant attempt to evade the responsibilities of office—the consequent fine was £25, a considerable sum in those days. There were also substantial fines for such offences as buying meat which had not paid the ritual slaughter tax, taking part in the admission of a proselyte, and similar offences.

As the community established itself, it extended its organisations. In 1703 provision was made for the support of widows and orphans. In 1730 a school was opened for girls. In 1748 a hospital for the sick was established. Money was also needed continuously for the relief of poverty. Though the leaders of Sephardi Jewry were wealthy, there were inevitably some poor Jews who managed to escape from their Marrano existence to the freedom of England.

18

But by far the largest problem arose from the constant arrival of refugees from Northern Europe, and there was at first no Ashkenazi community which could look after them or even share the burden. Most of the difficulties encountered by the Jews in their relations with the Christian authorities arose from fears and hostility aroused by this stream of refugees, and the Sephardi Jews were as anxious as anyone to reduce the problem. They were more ready to pay for these unfortunate creatures to be returned to the continent than they were to find means for their support in this country. It was not that they were exclusive and niggardly, but that the burden continually threatened to become more than they could bear.

The constant drain on their resources entailed in providing for the poor led the community to make the most stringent regulations to prevent Jewish settlers from evading the responsibilities inherent in synagogue membership. While the establishment of an Ashkenazi synagogue was welcomed, no Sephardi worship other than at Bevis Marks was allowed within six miles of that building ; and a group of Jews who concluded a festival in their own homes with an act of worship were actually fined for doing so. Their effort to maintain their position led to the Mahamad of the eighteenth century becoming an increasingly narrow and tyrannical oligarchy, but the only consequence was that they were engaged in a continual struggle to maintain an impossible position. Even marriage outside the community involved heavy financial punishment, a ridiculous provision when they were powerless to enforce their views if the insulted suitor simply left their community for another.

The nineteenth century witnessed considerable changes. The movement for reform led to a bitter conflict and the final establishment of a new synagogue (see p. 29). But the dispersal of the members of the congregation also led to revolutionary action. Originally all the Sephardim had lived in London. When economic opportunities led to the formation of communities in Dublin, Manchester, or other cities the establishment of a synagogue could scarcely be opposed, and such provincial synagogues gladly saw themselves as daughter congregations. But in London also Jews had moved away from the district of Bevis Marks, and the synagogue became inaccessible to those who lived in the new western and north-western suburbs. In 1861 a branch synagogue was opened in Bryanston Street (it had a temporary predecessor in Wigmore Street) ; but before the end of the century the situation had so changed that a proposal was actually passed unanimously by the congregation to abandon altogether the historic site of Bevis Marks, demolish the venerable synagogue, and rebuild, both for worship and for congregational purposes, either further east among the Jewish poor of the East End or further west among the prosperous Jews of the West End. Today the effective centre of the community is in Lauderdale Road, Maida Vale, but Bevis Marks enjoys the dignity of an historic monument and is the scene of all the formal occasions in the life of the community.

The story of the Sephardi community during the three centuries of its existence is one, not so much of continual decline, but of increasing aloofness from the main stream of Anglo-Jewish life. Already by the middle of the eighteenth century they had to share the public representation of Jewry with the Ashkenazim. During the nineteenth century their conservatism and continual difficulties in securing suitable religious leadership greatly reduced their importance, though not their dignity or influence in the City. Their oldest families disappeared by intermarriage, later Sephardi immigrants lacked the wealth and family pride of their predecessors, some intermarriage with the Ashkenazim took place, and the community was often in debt. As the new conflicts over nationalism and Zionism began to agitate and confuse Anglo-Jewry, they were increasingly out of touch with the Jewish masses ; so that their rôle came to be that of the conservation of a culture rather than communal leadership. Even the Presidency of the Board of Deputies, which had been almost a prerogative of their community right up to the time of the Second World War, has passed from them ; and today their influence in communal affairs is too often little more than that of a neglected minority.

THE ASHKENAZI COMMUNITY

Ashkenazi Jews, that is, Jews from Germany and Eastern Europe, began to come into England at the same time as the Sephardim. But they were too poor and their existence was too uncertain for them to be able to form a community for a number of decades.

Almost the only exception was Benjamin Levy, a wealthy Jewish merchant of Hamburg, and he had been accepted as a member of the Sephardi community.

As they were unable to organise or support themselves, the whole burden of relief and maintenance fell on the Sephardim ; and many of the difficulties which were encountered with the authorities arose from the constant influx of these Central and Eastern European Jews. Every effort was made to ship them back to Europe, or even to find openings for them in the expanding English colonies of the New World. But such efforts could not act as more than palliatives, for the stream was continuous. By the end of the seventeenth century, when a small number of Ashkenazim had succeeded in establishing themselves in permanent occupations and in achieving a modest competence, the time was ripe for them to establish a community of their own and to accept responsibility for their members. This was a ' split ' which could only be welcomed by the older community ; and there is evidence that actually there were two synagogues following the German rite by the year 1690. All trace of one of them has perished. But the main Ashkenazi community possessed a synagogue covering at least part of the site of the Great Synagogue in Duke's Place as early as that year. Six years later they acquired, through the generosity of Benjamin Levy, a cemetery of their own near the Sephardi cemetery at Mile End. The fact that they waited so long for a cemetery, and then only obtained it by the generosity of one man, reflects their poverty in these early years.

The first fifty years of the Ashkenazi community is difficult to trace in detail, as its records have perished. What survives is the story of continual controversies and secessions, which usually took a violently personal character, and which led to the permanent establishment of three Ashkenazi synagogues in the capital—the Great Synagogue, in Duke's Place, the Hambro Synagogue, so called from its following the rite of Hamburg, whence most of its founders had come, and a third which had arisen out of one of the personal quarrels, but which has not survived.

In fairness it must be said that the continual growth of numbers would have made a number of synagogues necessary anyhow ; but the schisms prevented the growth of a common leadership and a common policy. This was a matter of importance, since the security of the whole of Anglo-Jewry depended on its good relationship with the non-Jewish authorities and population. Hence the community of the Great Synagogue was prepared to ask, and able to receive, the help of the still older Sephardi community in its attempts to suppress its rivals and to prevent activities, such as the reception of proselytes from Christianity, or the exposure to the public of private scandals, which imperilled the position and reputation of all Jews alike.

In 1744 the Ashkenazim took the initiative in an action which was to be the first of many interventions by Anglo-Jewry on behalf of less fortunate Jews in other countries. In that year the Jews of Bohemia, including the ancient community of Prague, had been expelled by order of Maria Theresa, Empress of Austria. They appealed to Jews elsewhere to help them, and the Wardens of the Great Synagogue petitioned George II to receive a deputation. With the Wardens came a leading member of the Sephardim ; and, as a result of the King's sympathy, diplomatic action was taken by the British Ambassador in Vienna. Sixteen years later, on the other hand, they were not consulted when the Sephardim offered their congratulations on the accession of George III in 1760. Their vigorous protest was recognised as reasonable, and it was agreed that in future when any public matter engaged the attention of ' the two nations,' consultation should take place and common action be secured. Thus was founded the ' London Committee of Deputies of British Jews,' soon to be known as ' The Board of Deputies of British Jews,' and to become the central body of Anglo-Jewry.

While the Sephardi community remained relatively stationary, events in Central and Eastern Europe ensured that all through the eighteenth century Ashkenazi immigration should continue without cease. In consequence, it was a perpetual problem for the Jewish authorities to discover new livelihoods for immigrants. One obvious solution was the dispersal of the newcomers into new centres ; and this century witnessed the permanent establishment of many provincial communities, fully equipped with their own synagogue, burial ground, and local charities and centres of study. But there were still more semi-permanent groups, based on travelling pedlars and artisans, and centring in a small core of more permanent shopkeepers and craftsmen. Unlike most such communities in the countries whence the immigrants had come, these new communities were not wholly independent. They were usually not able to afford a rabbi of their own, and they lacked the knowledge which would help them in relations with the Christian community and the authorities, and the scholarship which would enable them to settle their own problems, smooth out their difficulties, and deal with such matters as the registration of marriage and divorce. Hence they grew up with an organic link with the London community and with an acknowledged dependence on the authority of its rabbis.

The conflicts between rival synagogues in London had, thus, repercussions throughout the whole community, for a provincial community might prefer one rabbi to another, or a London candidate for office seek to win support in the provinces against his rival. By the middle of the century the quarrel between the Great Synagogue and the Hambro was, at least usually, buried. But in 1761 yet another synagogue was opened in the City and came to be known as the New Synagogue. Yet the three could not afford three separate rabbis ; and there were constant difficulties as to which rabbis should be acknowledged by which synagogue, and which rabbi's authority should be recognised by the provincial communities. Gradually, however, the Great Synagogue in Duke's Place, twice enlarged and rebuilt during the century, assumed the position of predominance which it subsequently enjoyed in the Ashkenazi community in the country, and even beyond in the colonies to which English Jews migrated.

In consequence, it was around the Great Synagogue that clustered all the multifarious social and charitable organisations of a Jewish community, centres of study, schools, help to the sick and needy, homes for orphans, training for apprentices, burial of paupers, provision of ritually clean meat, and, at Passover, flour, as well as, at times, stern action for the protection of the Jewish reputation with the non-Jewish authorities and population. These activities mostly had a somewhat chequered career in the eighteenth century, for the community was continually hard-pressed for money, and was never free from the cost of coping with penniless immigrants and its own poor. These alone cost it something like £1,000 a year. The organisations which gradually crystallised out of many false starts and temporary alleviations were numerous, and the more important are dealt with in subsequent sections of this chapter. It is with the synagogue itself that we are here concerned.

In the opening years of the nineteenth century the leaders of the community came to recognise a change which had been gradually taking place in the preceding decades. As a community they had ceased to be, or to think of themselves as, foreigners. They were English. Nearly all their leaders had been born in the country and English was their mother tongue. They had various rights and were entering on the final battle for full political emancipation. Hence it became increasingly anomalous that their rabbi should be noticeably a ' foreigner,' able to address them only in Hebrew or Yiddish, languages which a diminishing minority of the leaders understood.

The last of the old type of rabbi of the Great Synagogue was, curiously enough, actually of English birth. For Solomon Hirschell had been born while his father, Hart Lyon, had for a brief while occupied the same position. Nevertheless, his sermons were usually in Yiddish and his communications in Hebrew, and in spite of forty years' rabbinate his English remained defective to the end. He was the first who could be said to have been ' chief rabbi ' of all the Ashkenazi Jews in the country, for his authority was recognised not only by the three synagogues in London, but also by the provincial communities.

Although none of Hirschell's successors, until the present holder of the office (Israel Brodie), were actually born in the country, the successor to Hirschell was born in Hanover at a time when it formed part of the patrimony of the British Crown. Dr. Nathan Marcus Adler was to preside over the Great Synagogue for forty-five years, and under his régime an immense reorganisation and anglicisation took place. In 1870 this reorganisation found statutory expression in the establishment of the ' United Synagogue.'

THE UNITED SYNAGOGUE AND THE CHIEF RABBINATE

The formation of the United Synagogue and the definition of the office of Chief Rabbi, while closely connected historically, need to be kept distinct. For their present scope is not identical. The

United Synagogue is, in the main, a group of synagogues of London Jews following the orthodox Ashkenazi ritual. The Chief Rabbi is not only their religious head, but extends his jurisdiction not only to the provinces, but even to Jewish communities beyond these islands in the British Commonwealth.

Two matters led to their emergence in the nineteenth century. From the very beginning of their organised religious life the Ashkenazi Jews found it impossible always to maintain a rabbi for each of the separate synagogues in which the community met and worshipped. In consequence it was not unknown for a rabbi appointed to serve one synagogue to be accepted as their rabbinical authority by another. Nevertheless, until the 1860s it was not found possible to come to any permanent arrangement regarding these rabbinical posts. The second historical reason for the discussions of the '60s lay in the field of communal, and especially charitable organisation. It has already been said that from the beginning of the story one of the most burdensome charges on Ashkenazi Jewry arose from the constant flight of Jews from less fortunate circumstances in Central and Eastern Europe to the freedom of these Isles. Throughout the eighteenth and nineteenth centuries London always possessed a fluctuating mass of indigent Jews, many of whom never found a satisfactory living in their new surroundings, and still more of whom needed help in getting started, special assistance if misfortune overtook them, and care in sickness and old age. In such circumstances it was the height of folly to allow mutual jealousies and the overlapping of organisations to raise still further the cost of charity, relief, and assistance.

In 1805 a formal compact was made between the Great, the Hambro, and the New Synagogues by which they pooled their charitable activities in a joint budget to which the Great contributed one-half and the others one-quarter each. This arrangement was extended in 1834 and worked satisfactorily. But the steady move of residence to the western districts of London, and the emptying of the three City synagogues of their wealthier and more prosperous members, made fresh arrangements necessary. As long as the joint budget for communal charity was arrived at by separate fixed contributions from the City synagogues, each one inevitably sought jealously to preserve its membership and to prevent ' poaching '; and all three were united in hostility to the appearance of any new congregation, even though it was established in the actual place where the congregants lived. These jealousies were intensified by the fact that, by this period, each synagogue had extensive endowments and invested funds.

In 1866 the Chief Rabbi, Dr. Adler, called together the leaders of the three City synagogues and their two branches (the Portland Street and Bayswater congregations) to suggest a pooling of all their separate organisations, endowments, and institutions into a single ' United Synagogue ' under his leadership. The scheme was accepted in principle, but the existence of the endowments and funds meant that such a pooling would have to be accepted by the Charity Commissioners and embodied in an Act of Parliament. A common plan had been ratified by all members by 1868, and in 1870 the Royal Assent was given to a Bill embodying the scheme and allowing for further synagogues to become constituent members. The Act of Parliament deals with the endowments. It makes no attempt to regulate the religious life of the United Synagogue or to define the religious authority of the Chief Rabbi. Those remain matters for adjustment by the constituent synagogues ; and, since its formation, various modifications of ancient ritual have been adopted in particular synagogues, in agreement with the Chief Rabbi.

By the end of the century the United Synagogue comprised fourteen synagogues ; for there was no longer any reason why a Jewish community in a new district of London should not have its own house of worship, now that this involved no subdivision of charitable activities, or possible jealousy. Today it numbers twenty-four metropolitan synagogues, together with nineteen District synagogues, mostly in the new suburbs, and thirty-one Affiliated synagogues further out or in the provinces.

The Chief Rabbi, while he is the head of the United Synagogue, has, by tradition, a wider jurisdiction. The orthodox synagogues of the great provincial centres, such as Birmingham or Manchester, are not members of the United Synagogue. They accept, however, the jurisdiction of the Chief Rabbi and the authority of the Beth Din. They also participate in his election and in the financial support of his office, though the total voting strength and financial contribution of the provinces are considerably less than that of the London synagogues. It has already been said that small provincial communities had become accustomed to consulting the London rabbinate during the eighteenth century. English Jews who left to settle in British Colonies and Dominions naturally followed the same practice. Thus the Chief Rabbinate came to exercise a world-wide influence, no less real for being largely undefined. Today ease and speed of travel have made this influence a reality, and both the present Chief Rabbi and his predecessor, Dr. Hertz, have personally visited Jewish communities in the Dominions and elsewhere.

Associated with the Chief Rabbinate is the Ecclesiastical Court or Beth Din. Its jurisdiction not only extends to the members of the United Synagogue and 'the United Hebrew Congregations,' which contribute to the office of the Chief Rabbi, but is also asked for by orthodox Hebrew congregations outside his official jurisdiction. Its status was recognised by English courts of law as authoritative in Jewish matters as early as the eighteenth century. For in 1793 Lord Stowell accepted its decision as to whether what was claimed to be a marriage between two professing Jews was, in fact, valid.

OTHER ASHKENAZI ORTHODOX RELIGIOUS BODIES

By the end of the nineteenth century the orthodoxy of the United Synagogue had inevitably come to assume a somewhat 'anglicised' and modernised air. Changes in services had been authorised by successive Chief Rabbis ; sermons were in English, services had been shortened and synagogue worship came to possess a 'foreign' air of coldness and decorum to Jews coming from Eastern Europe. It was typical of the divergence of temperament between the newcomers and the old-established congregations that the United Synagogue conceived the grandiose scheme of building a single vast synagogue in East London to accommodate the masses of refugees who began to flow into the district in the '80s. But Russian and other East European Jews preferred either to build large synagogues which were independent, or to frequent smaller but cosier houses of worship, often in rooms of private houses, in which a multitude of diverse rites. Chassidic or otherwise, could be followed.

The result was inevitably a full measure of confusion, with many undesirable features. For not all who claimed spiritual leadership were fitted for it. In 1887, therefore, Mr. Samuel Montagu (afterwards Lord Swaythling) called together a number of leaders from the different synagogues which had come into existence, and a Federation of Synagogues was formed, originally with sixteen and now with some sixty congregations. It was not founded in opposition to the United Synagogue, for its founder, and its first President, Lord Rothschild, were prominent members of that body.

The Federation was able to guarantee to its members the services of rabbis and ecclesiastical judges (*dayanim*) whose orthodoxy was unimpeachable, and it set out to secure for this new Jewish population adequate representation on the Board of Guardians and the Board of Deputies, as well as adequate protection in the dispensation and receipt of charity, education, and relief in distress. In addition, it helped the new arrivals to adjust themselves to Anglo-Jewish life. Each synagogue remained autonomous and no attempt was made to introduce uniformity into their worship or restrict their practices.

To some extent the Federation has led a difficult life, since from the social point of view ' the East End ' is a transitional stage in Jewish life in England. In one or two generations the older immigrants become absorbed into English life, move, according to the prosperity which they have achieved, to other parts of London, and begin, as previous generations have done, to leaven their orthodoxy, where they do not abandon it, with diverse ' anglicisations ' which are frowned upon by those who seek to maintain unimpaired the traditional orthodoxy of the Eastern European ghetto.

To many of the more religious-minded Jews in the Federation, the United Synagogue was tainted with progressive ideas. In 1927 they, in turn, appeared insufficiently orthodox to the extremists, and yet a new orthodox body came into existence, the Union of Orthodox Hebrew Congregations, with over forty synagogues in London, and provincial synagogues in some of the larger Jewish centres.

The orthodox synagogues in the provinces are usually independent congregations, and such is, indeed, the Jewish tradition. In centres such as Liverpool, Leeds, Manchester, or Birmingham, where a number of orthodox synagogues exist, various forms of co-ordination have been adopted. In Manchester there is a Communal Rabbi, elsewhere there are various forms of communal council or co-ordinating committee ; but there is no standard organisation. and religious Jewry remains an essentially congregational body under the general leadership of the Chief Rabbi.

THE MOVEMENT FOR REFORM AND PROGRESSIVE JUDAISM

The gradual anglicisation of London Jewry, to which reference has already been made, led at the very beginning of the nineteenth century to voices being raised for change and modification in the services of the synagogue. It was among the Sephardim that the demand was first heard—probably because they remained the most tradition-loving and unyielding congregation. As an example of their determined conservatism it may be quoted that, although Portuguese had long been a dead language among them, it was only in 1819 that thc Mahamad consented to keeping its minutes in English, and it was not until 1848 that Portuguese was wholly abandoned for synagogal announcements.

In 1803 Mr. Jacob Mocatta asked the Elders for some very moderate changes which would increase the decorum of services. From then onwards the demand for change took an ever-widening range, until the central question came to be the opening of a branch synagogue in West London, where most of the congregants lived, and some shortening and modification of the services to be held in this new synagogue. But the Mahamad remained adamant, and finally, in 1840, eighteen members of the congregation withdrew to form their own synagogue.

Similar, though less determined, voices had been raised within the Ashkenazi community, and these eighteen were joined by six Ashkenazim. To avoid the distinction, now largely meaningless, between the two 'nations' they decided to call themselves the 'West London Synagogue of British Jews.' In 1842 they opened their synagogue and announced the changes they proposed to make. Moderate as they were, the orthodox of both communities proclaimed that they constituted a desertion of the oral law, and that those who adhered to them would be excommunicated. This involved more than religious penalties. It excluded members of the congregation from the charitable and educational work of the community, and also from membership of the Board of Deputies.

Such an all-embracing exclusion was impossible to maintain. In many charitable and other public activities members of the West London Synagogue took an increasing part. In 1869, while the proposals which led to the formation of the United Synagogue were under discussion, there was for a time a hope that there might be a religious reconciliation. This failed, but in 1871 they joined the newly formed Anglo-Jewish Association without any objections being raised by the orthodox, and in 1876 they were at last admitted to membership of the Board of Deputies.

In 1902 a further development took place within the progressive movement. In that year a group of Jews, largely of progressive views, decided to make some attempt to stem the defections from the community, and reduce the number of open conversions to Christianity which were taking place. They had, at the time, no intention of forming a separate congregation. They wanted only to experiment with simpler forms of worship and teaching, such as might attract those who had abandoned membership of the synagogue, and who were not likely to be regained by the more formal and traditional worship of Bevis Marks or the United Synagogue. They freely asked orthodox leaders to join them in the endeavour, and they were prepared to hold their services in any of the existing synagogues.

The radical nature of the innovations in synagogue worship which they proposed made a united effort to win back lost members impracticable. The more orthodox withdrew, and in 1902 the 'Jewish Religious Union' came into existence under the leadership of Claude Montefiore, Israel Abrahams, and the Hon. Lily Montagu. To find a suitable rabbi it was necessary to look to the United States, where alone progressive training was available, and in 1912 Dr. Mattuck was invited to lead the congregation, which, after some years in temporary quarters, in 1924 built itself a synagogue in St. John's Wood Road. Today, the Jewish Religious

Union contains not only a number of other London congregations, but also several synagogues in the main provincial communities. In 1942 the reform congregations, led by the West London Synagogue, also united in an Association of Synagogues in Great Britain. It is more conservative than the ' liberal ' World Union.

Secular Institutions of the Jewish Community

It is a common feature of Jewish life everywhere that a Jewish community possesses almost as many institutions as it possesses members ; and there are few issues of interest to Jews on which there are not at least two institutions reflecting each shade of opinion. Even to list the multifarious questions on which organisations have grown up in the three hundred years of Anglo-Jewish life since the resettlement would be impossible. Women, students, refugees, ex-servicemen, all have their organisations. Friendly societies abound, and around every synagogue are a multitude of social, charitable, and educational activities. In the present section only four types of organisation will be treated, the general representation of the community, its charitable activities, its religious education, and its links with the wider Jewish world.

Undoubtedly the most important, as well as the most ancient, organisation is the Board of Deputies. From the very beginning of resettlement the community had to tackle day-to-day issues of relationships with the Gentile environment. By the middle of the eighteenth century the Sephardim and the Ashkenazim had both had occasion to make contacts with the highest British authorities in the interests of their own community, or of Jewish communities elsewhere. In 1760 the Sephardim sent a deputation to congratulate George III on his accession. The Ashkenazim were indignant that they had not been invited. The Sephardim promised to discuss future actions of a similar kind ; and out of this beginning the Board came into existence. For the next sixty years the meetings were rare and irregular ; on most occasions there seem to have been no Ashkenazim present.

By the 1820s regular meetings had become the rule. There were twenty-two deputies, from Bevis Marks, the Great, the Hambro,

31

and the New Synagogues. The only provincial community represented was Liverpool. In 1835 a formal constitution was adopted,
and in 1836 the Board received official recognition by being named
in the appropriate Act of Parliament as the Jewish body whose
President should certify the marriage secretaries of synagogues, who
would thereby become entitled to register marriages.

It was the period in which Anglo-Jewry was beginning to look
for full political emancipation. The actual struggle was mainly
carried on by individuals ; but the Board was inevitably interested,
and its leaders gave their full support, and sometimes the financial
backing of the Board, to the efforts which were being made to
secure the abolition of all Jewish disabilities. This activity of the
Board passed into the background when the final stronghold of
Parliament was stormed ; but still survives in the watchful eye that
the Law and Parliamentary Committee of the Board keeps on
legislation which might affect Jews.

In place of this concern with their own affairs, from 1840
onwards the Board effectively represented the concern of the
increasingly secure and prosperous Anglo-Jewish community in the
affairs of their brethren in less fortunate circumstances. In that year
the ritual murder accusation was raised at Damascus, then under
Egyptian rule. Moses Montefiore, President of the Board, went on
its behalf to interview the authorities concerned, secured from the
Porte a *ferman* denouncing as false the blood libel, saw the arrested
Jews released, and returned to England having made the name of
'The Board' famous throughout the Jewish world. From then
onwards it was constantly in foreign affairs ; and when the Anglo-
Jewish Association was formed in 1871 the two bodies worked in a
Joint Foreign Committee which became almost a Foreign Office
for Jewish Affairs.

As Anglo-Jewry grew and expanded its organisations so the
Board also grew from its original twenty-two members to over four
hundred, including a number of important, but not synagogal,
institutions. Until the Second World War the Board had neither
parties nor rivals. But in that period two changes in the community
affected the membership of the Board and threatened for some
time to put its unique authority into jeopardy. In 1943 elections
were, for the first time, fought on a Zionist or non-Zionist ticket ;

and in the same year the pressure of the more nationalist politics of the World Jewish Congress put an end to the long period of co-operation between the Board and the Anglo-Jewish Association. This change, however much it may be regretted, was inevitable, if the Board was faithfully to mirror the community. For the division between Zionist and non-Zionist, nationalist and assimilationist, runs right through contemporary Jewish life, and a representative Board could not but reflect it—or return to the authoritarianism of eighteenth-century Sephardim.

In previous sections mention has constantly been made of the perennial problems of the indigent immigrant, and of the effort made at the beginning of the nineteenth century by the three Ashkenazi synagogues to work together for their relief. Wise though the move was, it produced some absurd results. The dole handed out to the Jewish pauper amounted to one shilling per week. To get this he had, after the scheme of co-operation had been adopted, to visit the Great Synagogue, which gave him sixpence, and then the Hambro and the New, each of which gave him threepence!

In 1859 an arrangement was agreed by which a Board of Guardians was established, with a budget based on these proportions and amounting to less than £500 per annum. The Board soon found this administration of a dole but the least of its activities. Under wise and far-seeing management it set out from the first to prevent rather than alleviate poverty. One scheme after another was adopted, by which the poor might earn their own livings, their children might be properly apprenticed, their sick nursed back to health, and their old people looked after with dignity. By the end of the century the annual budget of the Board of Guardians for the Relief of the Jewish Poor had grown to £40,000 ; and was still rising rapidly. For 1906 income stood at over £137,000 and expenditure at over £147,500. Loan funds, educational schemes, convalescent homes, almshouses, and innumerable other social activities, all came under its management, and it played a central rôle in the immense problem of adjusting to English life a Jewish population which grew within decades from a few tens to hundreds of thousands. The Board of Guardians does not, of course, entirely replace the social activities of synagogues and friendly societies, the schools and hospital wards, the burial societies, and other groupings which are inherent in the Jewish way

D

of life. But it has unchallengeable authority as the main instrument of social policy in Anglo-Jewry.

The history of Jewish education follows lines similar to that of Jewish charity. During the eighteenth century there was a multiplicity of Talmud Torahs and other schools, mostly ill-kept and providing a very indifferent education. With the nineteenth century reform began. It was accepted that children needed to be educated in English as well as Hebrew, and given 'modern' as well as traditional learning. The Jews' Free School in East London was founded in 1817, and by the end of the century was educating over two thousand boys and a thousand girls. With other Jewish schools in the metropolis it catered for about one third of the Jewish children of London. In the provinces a similar situation reigned. While the majority of Jewish children thus went to non-Jewish schools, the vigilance of the Board of Deputies saw that in each successive Education Act provision was made to secure for Jewish children appropriate exemptions in regard to religious education and the observance of Sabbath and the Festivals.

In the eighteenth and early nineteenth century the community was too small to hope to be able to educate its own rabbis and religious leaders ; and this position still remains true for the Sephardim. But as the Ashkenazi community grew in numbers, it became both possible and desirable for it to educate men for its own ministry. After several years of discussion Jews' College was opened in 1855. The present Chief Rabbi is the first to occupy that post who is himself a graduate of the College.

While the main emphasis of the institutions so far discussed has been on aspects of the life of Anglo-Jewry, there has always been a concern among British Jews for the Jewish world outside. That this came to occupy an important part in the work of the Board of Deputies has already been described ; and until full emancipation had been secured in this country it was difficult for such work to be done by anyone except the recognised leadership of the community. With full emancipation won in 1858, it was possible to devote more attention to foreign affairs. At that time the main Jewish institution dealing with the Jewish world as a whole was that led by French Jewry, the Alliance Israélite Universelle. The defeat of France by Prussia in 1870 reduced the influence of the

Alliance, and in 1871 the Anglo-Jewish Association was formed, not as a rival, but to carry on and supplement the work of the Alliance wherever Jews were in distress, or wherever fresh religious and educational facilities could be offered a Jewish community from outside. The field of need was so vast that there was ample room for both organisations ; and together with the Joint Foreign Committee of the Board of Deputies and the Anglo-Jewish Association, they covered the field satisfactorily up to the end of the First World War.

The Versailles Conference revealed, however, that there were three streams within Jewry seeking recognition in the reordering of the world by the statesmen of Versailles. The Joint Foreign Committee and the Alliance represented the older 'assimilationist' point of view. They sought equal rights for Jews individually in the countries where they lived, and they regarded the Balfour Declaration, and the promise of a National Home in Palestine, as almost a minor matter, intended to cope with the problem of Jews who could not be adequately protected in their present homes. These views were shared neither by the Zionists nor by those who sought full corporate minority rights for Jews in Central and Eastern Europe. In consequence, several conflicting Jewish points of view were constantly being pressed at Versailles, and these different points of view led in the inter-war years to the growth of new bodies dealing with ' Jewish Foreign Affairs.'

The Zionist Federation of Great Britain, feeling itself in a position of special importance as the Federation in the country which exercised the Mandate over Palestine, became a powerful political organisation independent of the Board, which normally represented a 'non-Zionist' position. In the '30s yet another body came into existence, the World Jewish Congress, whose British Section was opened in 1936, and which again represented an attitude to the affairs of the community very different from the tradition of the Board.

All three were ' democratic ' movements in that they were subject to the changing atmosphere and interests of the community. By and large it would be true to say that the Board represented the standpoint of pre-Russian immigration Jewry, but the Zionist Federation and the British Section of the World Jewish Congress reflected the more nationalist attitude of those who had immigrated since

1881. This state of affairs was not uniquely Anglo-Jewish. The same struggle existed in American Jewry between the American Jewish Committee and the American Jewish Congress ; and it was to be found on the Continent of Europe also. Since the time when those representing the more nationalist attitude captured the Board itself, a struggle has ensued between those who desire the independence of the Board, as exclusively representing Anglo-Jewry, and those who see it primarily as the British section of a world Jewish interest, either Zionist or Nationalist. In this issue, still undetermined, the Board effectively represents the present dilemma of the Jewish world.

The rise of Nazism affected Anglo-Jewry in many ways. The most obvious was the creation of the Central British Fund, and the tremendous financial burden accepted by Anglo-Jewry for the relief and assistance of refugees from Hitler's Germany, and ultimately Hitler's Europe. But two other aspects of the new situation deserve mention. With the spread of fascist doctrines to England under the leadership of Sir Oswald Mosley, the community was compelled to develop a defence organisation, expressed in the Defence Committee of the Board with its own staff, the Trades Advisory Council, and other similar organisations. In addition, those refugees who established themselves in this country brought their own contribution to Jewish life, developed their own social and charitable organisations, and in the Wiener Institute and Library brought to this country an institution of world-wide significance in the general struggle against authoritarianism of all kinds.

The scope, the variety, and the limitations of the organisations which have been described in this section effectively reflect the unique position of Jewry, and the impossibility of fitting it into the conventional picture of either ' a religion ' or ' a nation.' For if, on the one hand, these organisations go beyond what we are familiar with in the religious field, on the other, none of the organisations mentioned, not even the Board itself, has any legislative or financial powers over the Jewish community. All support of them is voluntarily given, all their finances are voluntarily raised from British citizens who have in addition paid their full rates and taxes to the general expenses of the community, and none of their decisions is binding on any individual Jew who is not willing to accept them.

The Status of the Jews since the Resettlement

Those Jews who entered England at the Resettlement, and those who followed them for many generations, suffered from two main disabilities. They were resident aliens, subject to such disabilities as affected all foreign-born inhabitants of these islands ; and they were Jews, subject to all such disabilities as befell those others of the King's subjects who were not members of the dominant religion. In their passage to the full status of equal citizens they were, therefore, liable to be affected not only by public opinion or legislative measures directly aimed at their relief or repression as Jews, but also by all measures or opinions which tended to make life easier or more difficult for either foreigners or dissenters. Jews born in England must in some sense have been the King's subjects. But in the seventeenth century this involved no clear definition of rights, especially for those who *as a community* were long regarded as ' foreigners '—as indeed they were in language, customs, and religion. Foreign and native-born both had to advance tentatively and step by step.

The absence of any charter defining their terms of residence meant that in the beginning they were very chary of laying claim to any rights which might involve public comment or controversy. But the nature of their community made two privileges essential. If they were subjected to the laws enforcing religious conformity they could have no synagogue services ; and if they were subjected to the prohibitive embargoes laid on the participation of foreigners in the import and export trade through British ports, their economic foundations would be shattered. There was, however, a way out of this impasse. As to the first, the Sovereign, when necessary, forbad interference with this worship ; and, as to the second, it was possible for him (for a suitable gratification) to issue a Patent of Denization (or Endenization), by which a foreign-born resident was given the rights of an English-born subject in such matters. For these Patents the wealthier immigrants applied, and a number were granted almost from the beginning of the Resettlement.

A further essential step depended not on the Crown, but on the Lord Mayor of London. That was the right to conduct the business of broker in the City of London. This also they obtained for substantial payments, but for a limited number of brokers. Up to 1826 the Lord Mayor continued to receive a fee, amounting to between one and two thousand guineas, for the issue of a broker's medal.

It has already been said that at the beginning even the cemetery and the religious buildings of the community were only held on lease from Christian owners. The right to acquire land, individually or communally, was only slowly and tentatively acquired. When in 1723 the oath of abjuration was extended to land-holders, Jews were allowed to omit ' on the true faith of a Christian.' This could be held to imply that Jews could be landowners. But when a couple of decades later the wealthy Jewish merchant, Sampson Gideon, purchased an estate, he secured a special Act of Parliament confirming his ownership ; and as late as 1830 the Solicitor-General, a known authority on real property, considered that legislation was necessary to make it clear that Jews could own land.[1]

Jews certainly voted in Parliamentary elections long before the abolition of the oath of abjuration for Parliamentary electors ; but they could only do so, so long as no one challenged them to take the oath. So the story could be repeated in almost every department of social and public life. It was only by experiment that Jews found out what they could and what they could not do. Irritating as this situation was, experience showed that it was often wiser than to attempt to secure legislation, comprehensive or detailed, to regularise their position. In 1753 a very modest attempt was made to grant them a very limited privilege. The Naturalisation Bill of 1753 made it easier for foreign-born Jews to acquire denization, up to then a very costly and arbitrary privilege. Nevertheless, the storm which it aroused, the fantastic speculations to which it gave rise, the fears expressed that the Jews would flood the country and dominate its religious, political, and social life, were all such that the same government withdrew the Bill in the following year[2] and did not dare to raise the subject again.

The story of the petty pinpricks and administrative absurdities from which the Anglo-Jewish community, or its members, were

[1] H. S. Q. Henriques. *The Jews and the English Law*, p. 193.
[2] Cf. R. J. Robson. *The Oxfordshire Election of 1754, passim.*

liable to suffer is a very long one ; but it is, fortunately, never in the centre of the picture, and it has to be balanced by the more important fact that all through the eighteenth century, and in the following half century which preceded their full and open emancipation, they enjoyed many of the realities of security and respect, if without their legal foundations. Jews advised Prime Ministers before they could be Parliamentary back-benchers. They financed the Government before they could open a retail shop in the City. They could write the letters F.R.S. after their name before that of B.A. A Jew held the office of Sheriff of the City of London before he could be admitted to the lesser dignity of Alderman ; and Jews administered and endowed the most remarkable public social services before it was certain whether a bequest for a Jewish religious purpose was not against the public interest in a Christian country.

While Jews, corporately and individually, were anxious at any moment to secure such extensions of their lives and activities as circumstances might render possible, their eyes were naturally set all the time on the ultimate destination of full citizenship in the country of their birth or residence. To understand why this struggle took so long and was not crowned with final victory before the second half of the nineteenth century in what was generally considered one of the most liberal and progressive countries of the world, we have to study not the particular situation of the Jews, but the general development of political thought in England. For the struggle for political emancipation was, almost wholly, the struggle over the form of oath to be administered to anyone occupying a position of power or importance in the country.

The medieval conception of Christendom lasted long after the disappearance of the Middle Ages. The England of the Stuarts, the Commonwealth, and the Hanoverians still considered itself a Christian country. Moreover, only slowly was it accepted that within the definition ' Christian ' more than the State Church could be intended. Those Protestants who accepted the doctrine of the Trinity were included within the possibility of State toleration in 1689. But Protestant Unitarians were accepted only in 1813 and Roman Catholics in 1832. Foreigners who wished to become English citizens had to take the Sacrament of the Lord's Supper from a minister of the Anglican Church as late as 1825. Any Englishman who sought public office, local or national, or any place of profit under the crown had to take the Sacrament within three months of entering on his office up to 1828, although before that certain reliefs had become customary for Protestant Dissenters. Even then the idea itself was not abandoned. For the Sacrament was substituted a declaration ' on the faith of a Christian.' And these are but some of the main restrictions in a whole mass of legislation designed to keep England a Christian and Protestant country.

On the other side was the conception of the secular State which had grown out of the doctrines of eighteenth-century philosophers, and which was more consonant with the ethos of the increasingly powerful industrial and middle class of nineteenth-century England, but which had to meet the ingrained conservatism and fear of revolution which were as characteristic of those classes as was their determination to secure political advantage for themselves.

In this situation Jews had to walk warily. If they might find allies at almost any point in a fluctuating and evolving situation, they might likewise encounter enemies in the most unexpected places. In 1830 a Bill was first put before Parliament for repealing the civil disabilities of the Jews. It was twenty-eight years before it was passed in such a form that Jews became eligible for the House of Commons, and eight more years were to pass before a Jewish peer could take his seat in the House of Lords. In this long struggle Archbishops and leading Churchmen, Tory and Whig statesmen, lawyers and political philosophers appeared on both sides of the contest, not according to their like or dislike of Jews, but according as to whether they sought to retain the old conception of a Christian polity or whether they had adopted the new political philosophy of the secular State, extending its toleration to all who would obey its laws and advance its interests.

The full story of this struggle for emancipation has been told again and again.[1] Its piquant incidents, such as the election of Lionel de Rothschild (who held the Austrian title of Baron) by the City of London when his electors knew he could not sit, or the audacity of David Salomons sitting and voting when he had been

[1] See James Picciotto, *Sketches of Anglo-Jewish History*. Chapters lii and liii.

elected but had been refused permission to make the statutory declaration in the form which would be binding on his conscience, without which he could neither sit nor vote, are familiar. In the end the battle could only end in one way. The Commons had accepted the principle of Jewish elected members as early as 1833. In 1858 the Lords allowed them to have their way and to administer their oath as they liked. But they still refused to admit Jews to their own House. In 1866 they, too, gave way, and admitted in principle that a peer need not take the oath on the true faith of a Christian. But it was not until 1885 that the son of Baron Lionel de Rothschild, who had himself for twenty years been a member of the Lower House, took his seat as the first Jewish peer. In 1867 and 1868 the whole medley of oaths and declarations was finally reduced to order and Jewish citizens found every office and position open to them to which their talents or the votes of their fellow-countrymen entitled them.

This long-drawn-out struggle had not been without its effects upon the Jewish community itself. It is true of Jews, as of other men, that circumstances will arise in which an individual will prefer the career to which opportunity or choice entices him to loyalty to his religion which would bar him from entering it. During the eighteenth century a number of Jews entered both the army and navy, careers which would have to have been preceded by baptism. Moreover, there was a steady passage from the richest section of the community into the class of hereditary landowners. In some cases the father remained loyal to Judaism, but baptized his sons in infancy. In others he cheerfully married his daughters into the peerage and his sons followed their footsteps. In fact, it is sometimes easier to find today descendants of the great names of the seventeenth and early eighteenth century in Debrett than in the records of the contemporary synagogue.

While the foregoing paragraph applies but to a minority, the long struggle for emancipation was inevitably also a struggle to show the non-Jewish neighbour that the Jew was a good Englishman. It was a struggle for assimilation. From the moment when doors began to open, the path to social assimilation was likewise opened. During the whole period under review the almost universal tendency was to regard a Jew as an Englishman whose only distinction from his fellows was that his religion was Judaism. The modern nationalist movement was not born until the immigration from Russia, which began in the '80s, had found its feet and begun to express itself as a part of the Anglo-Jewish community.

The Social and Economic Life of Anglo-Jewry

The Jewish community has passed through several clearly defined stages in its passage from the seventeenth century to the twentieth. During the first hundred years there is little to consider except the single London community, in which rich and poor lived largely in the same district on the eastern boundaries of the City. Then follows a century of almost continual crisis. Apart from the healthy growth of provincial communities, the picture is a gloomy one. The London community, still containing the overwhelming proportion of Anglo-Jewry, loses its unity, a good deal of its solidarity, and much of its economic basis. In the last hundred years widespread reform at the beginning happily enabled the community to meet successfully the unexpected challenge of the flood of refugees from Eastern Europe which began in the '80s and led to the establishment of the firmly grounded contemporary situation.

The Jewish community from 1653 to 1750 had a very narrow economic basis. Its main support came from the financial operations and foreign trade of a group of substantial merchants, some of whom were men of very great wealth. These merchants, in spite of local jealousy and opposition, filled a valuable niche in the national economy and could count on the benevolent assistance of the Government when anything threatened to make their situation intolerable. Most of them still lived in the neighbourhood of the City synagogues, and to a large extent they shared the general social conditions of their own poor. They could, therefore, cope with the problem of new arrivals, distribute them with reasonable success into the openings which were available to Jews, mainly within the London community itself, so that the burden, though undoubtedly very great, was not absolutely intolerable. The charities, schools, and funds which each synagogue possessed could be stretched to cover their needs ; and the wealthier members of the community could give natural opportunities of employment to the poorer. No doubt to those who were perpetually haunted by the never-ceasing stream of refugees this picture would appear rosy. There *was* a great deal of poverty and the economic openings available for Jews were very restricted. But, looking back, we can see that the situation was infinitely better than that in the following period.

✝ The period from 1750 to 1850 is the period in which a real geographical and spiritual schism took place between the rich and the poor. The more prosperous members of the community deserted the narrow confines of the City to live in the more pleasant districts of Western London or even took villas in the outskirts. In both situations they now lived among Christians of comparable economic standards and so came to share their cultural and social life. Their needs were those of the English middle and upper classes ; their main ambition was that they should no longer be felt or thought to be ' foreign.' In these circumstances they were not of the slightest economic use to the Jewish poor still herded in the narrow alleys of the East End. They could give them no employment, either about their persons and in their houses, or as tradesmen and shopkeepers. For Eastern and Central European Jews had neither the skills nor the personal standards which would fit them for such occupations. They were primitive and uncouth. They were unfamiliar with the food, the dress, the furnishings, the valeting, and domestic service customary in Christian houses of the middle and upper classes of the eighteenth century, that century where ' polite manners ' were the essential basis of life. And these had now become the standards of every Jew who had managed to reach a comparable income.

Hence, the Jewish poor sank into deeper and deeper distress. For them there were no ready openings among their Christian neighbours, who still viewed them with suspicion and dislike. The purveying of old clothes was almost the only livelihood available apart from the generosity of their fellow-Jews who were as poor as themselves, or communal charity. They had little interest in being apprenticed to skilled trades—even where such was open to them—as they had no field in which to exercise the skill they would acquire.[1] And still the situation in this country seemed so

[1] See the complaints of Levy Alexander in A. Cohen, *An Anglo-Jewish Scrap-Book*, 1600-1840, p. 237f.

preferable to Jews from Central and Eastern Europe that immigrants continued to come in. It is not surprising that this is the period of Anglo-Jewish history in which there are legitimate complaints of the number of Jewish beggars and petty criminals, even of Jewish highwaymen.

The one hopeful aspect of the situation was the establishment and growth of the provincial communities ; and the one constructive activity of the London leaders was the support which they gave to the movement of Jews out of the metropolis and its suburbs. In the provincial towns, especially the seaports, to which Jews migrated, there was nothing comparable to the social problem which existed in London. There would be few or no Jewish families seeking to ape the manners of the upper class, for the English upper classes did not live in such towns. Moreover, the Jewish community was dependent on its Christian neighbours, not for manners and customs, but for a livelihood. There was no mass of indigent Jews inevitably living apart from the common community, but a small group of tradesmen, artisans, and dealers, who lived by trading, not with each other, but with the local population. In his *Rise of Provincial Jewry* Dr. Roth quotes the first seven Jewish families of Plymouth as being ' two dealers in naval stores, two silversmiths, a grocer, a general merchant, and a slop-dealer.' The date is 1740.[1] A community built up in this way was a natural and healthy unit, and found its feet without undue difficulty in local life. Around it were probably a certain number of pedlars and travelling artisans, and they in their turn would settle down and either extend an existing community or found a new one where they found conditions propitious. In this way Jewish life would tend, imperceptibly and naturally, to gain a broader economic basis ; and Jews would discover by trial and error where new openings were available, either in the increasing economic prosperity of the times or in the increasing laxity with regard to outworn restrictions. It is typical that Jews first seem to have turned to industrial activities in the provinces, where we hear of glass makers at Bristol and Birmingham before the end of the eighteenth century. In the provinces also lived the first Jew to hold a public office, Mr. Phineas Levi, of Devonport, who was a Navy Agent in 1830, at a time when, strictly speaking,

[1] Cecil Roth. *Provincial Jewry*, p. 91.

he ought to have had to make a declaration on the true faith of a Christian!

There is an abundant mass of evidence for the disorder of London Jewry at the turn of the century, and it took some decades for reforms to be accepted and made to work. But by the middle of the century the Board of Guardians had opened a new chapter in the treatment of the Jewish poor and the contemporary completion of the long struggle for emancipation meant that all openings were henceforth accessible to Jews. The result of the constructive work of the Guardians and the opening of new careers meant that it was a solidly and broadly based community which faced the new strains which began in the '80s and continued almost down to the First World War, though the stream dwindled after the Aliens Immigration Act of 1905.

The flight from Russia brought in a population as widely separated from the Anglo-Jewish norm of the period in standard and outlook of life as it is possible to imagine. They came straight from the ghettoes of the Russian Empire and from the cruel conditions imposed by Russian law and administration. They were accustomed to live at a level which the English workman would find intolerable, their standards of housing and sanitation were deplorable, and they possessed, on arrival, almost no mechanical or industrial skill which would fit them to earn a living. The inevitable result was that they were tempted to do shoddy work for sweated wages, and their arrival in thousands and tens of thousands contained all the elements necessary for a flare-up of antisemitic feeling and boisterous xenophobia. That no such outbreak took place, and that reactions were confined to the relatively minor facts set out in the next section, were due to a variety of causes.

In the first place must be set the fact that Anglo-Jewry was at this time very well equipped to receive them. It was a prosperous period and Jews were not the least prosperous section of the population. The very large sums which were needed to help the newcomers on their first arrival were available through the Board of Guardians. The experience which would help to provide them with the minimum education and equipment to allow them to adapt themselves, not to English, but to 'English-ghetto' life had already been won. In the second place the general opinion, though it looked with very little favour on the immigrants themselves, was not in favour of refusing them or of imposing restrictions on their life. The ordinary workingman had just reached the situation where he could say with pride: ' it's a free country,' and he was prepared to endure a certain amount of annoyance or difficulty to go on saying it.

Nevertheless, when these external factors have been given their weight, the main reason for their absorption lay with the newcomers themselves. Whatever their limitations, they were astonishingly adaptable. Whatever their faults, they were a law-abiding and peaceful community. And whatever competition they may have caused, basically they introduced new industrial processes which did not compete with the native workman. Nor were they incapable of looking after themselves. They were very ready to criticise, and even reject, the help offered them ; and they had no intention of falling into the abyss inevitable to their predecessors a hundred years previously, and accepting the position of permanent paupers sustained by the charity of the community.

A third of all the newcomers found work in two branches of the tailoring industry, either in men's coats or in women's jackets and mantles. Here, although they worked under conditions of sweated labour, they did not compete with English workmen, but they did indirectly create various problems which affected others than themselves. The nature of the work made it desirable for them to live close to it ; and this produced appalling overcrowding and deplorable sanitary conditions in the East End, where whole streets came to be occupied by Jewish immigrants.[1] In these districts they forced up rents and, as many of the immigrant Jews themselves came to be landlords, they were not popular. Much of these conditions were gradually improved. The sweated labour situation was overcome partly by new labour regulations, partly by the fact that Jews were themselves keen bargainers for higher wages, once they had acquired the skill which justified them. The overcrowding and high rents took longer to deal with, and in places still existed when the Second World War destroyed whole streets in the area.

[1] See map in C. Russell and H. S. Lewis *The Jew in London : A Study of Racial Character and Present Day Conditions.*

The extensive concentration of Jews in the clothing industry led to Jews taking a prominent part in the extension of the clothing retail trade, both in multiple stores and in the provision of good-quality ready-made clothes for both men and women. Later they took a similar part in the making and selling of cheap furniture, in the extension of restaurants, and in other occupations which catered for the needs of the increasing section of the population with small but regular incomes.

The story of the expansion of the Jewish community and of its economic basis in London is repeated in the main provincial communities, such as Manchester, Leeds, and Liverpool. In all of them it is possible to see a certain pattern of expansion. Jews are not spread evenly over the whole economic life of the community, but are concentrated into a number of occupations where they had originally found a market which was not already exploited by their Gentile predecessors or contemporaries.

The last century has, of course, also witnessed an extension of Jewish participation in the professions, the civil service, the army and navy, and other occupations from which in pre-emancipation days they were excluded. While freedom has blurred the edges of the pattern, it is, however, still true to characterise them as a group within the whole society which is primarily urban, largely middle class, and with a special tendency to prefer self-employment or smaller economic units to work in large factories and other mass production.

Non-Jewish Reactions to the Jewish Community

Although in real life human motives are nearly always mixed, yet it is possible, for purposes of analysis, to consider reactions to the existence and growth of Anglo-Jewry under four main headings. First, there are those who have frankly welcomed the existence of the community ; then there are those who, equally frankly and for motives which they consider to be motives of principle, have opposed its establishment and the extension of its rights. Less honourable, but on the whole more clamorous have been those whose opposition has been factious and based on motives of malice or self-interest ; and at the lowest end of the scale must be set those who have deliberately exploited feelings of religion, of conservatism, or of loyalty to make use of unfavourable opinions of the Jews for partisan ends in which, in fact, the Jews played no rôle at all.

In the first category will come the great political liberals such as Macaulay ; in the second the sincere *laudatores temporis acti* such as the stalwart opponent of emancipation, Sir Robert Inglis. Lesser men will occupy places in the other categories, men such as the Earl of Berkshire, who tried to blackmail the Jews in the time of Charles II, or Sir Oswald Mosley, who used latent anti-semitism to advance the cause of fascism in England in our own day.

The basic fact which has governed the development of the Jewish community is that at no time have they had to encounter the serious hostility of His Majesty or Her Majesty's Government ; and that no municipal council or City Fathers set themselves the task of maintaining their city *judenrein*. Almost all that could be recorded under the heading of official hostility is one incident in the reign of William III, when he was temporarily persuaded that grants of denization ceased to be valid on the death of the Sovereign who granted them, and that a large sum in import duties was owing to him ; and a second when his namesake, William IV, became convinced that the admission of Jews to Parliament would destroy the Christian character of the country. Such personal actions of the Sovereign can be balanced by others on the opposite side. George II was so moved by the recital of the sufferings of the Jews who had been expelled from Prague by Maria Theresa that he ordered his ambassador to take the unprecedented step of inter-vening with the Empress on their behalf ; and Queen Victoria allowed Moses Montefiore, when she made him a baronet, to have supporters to his coat of arms (a privilege normally reserved for the peerage) and the succession of his baronetcy to pass to his nephew, because, it is said, of her admiration of his devoted work for his coreligionists in less happy lands.

Of more importance was the fact that Jews never had to count with the hostility of the Government in so far as the interests of Anglo-Jewry were concerned. This by no means implies that

Governments were always anxious to advance their interests ; but it is fair to say that the failure of the modest concessions of the Bill for the Naturalisation of the Jews in 1753, and the thirty years of struggle before full emancipation was won in the nineteenth century, stemmed more from the basic fact that the English are a conservative people than from any official hostility. A Government cannot move faster than public opinion will tolerate ; and it cannot always risk its authority on an issue which is secondary. What is true of the national government is likewise true of local government. From the beginning Jews were free to reside in any part of England which they might choose. The one exception which might be claimed was the City of London, which for long withheld the freedom from them, and with that refusal seriously restricted their economic opportunities. Yet it was in that same City that the Jewish community settled and developed into one of the freest and most prosperous in Europe, so that the restrictions imposed cannot have been unduly onerous in practice.

The reason given for the slowness with which full emancipation was achieved—the conservatism of the English—needs some further consideration. On the whole it must be said that the Jewish community was accepted because such acceptance was in accord with the English spirit of liberty, and not because there was any general affection for Jews as such. On the whole they were regarded with contempt, and the more ostentatiously religious continued to regard them with hostility as the enemies of the Christian faith well into the nineteenth century. At periods they were widely regarded with suspicion and dislike. The ease with which the cry ' no Jews, no wooden shoes ' was raised in 1753 shows that slumbering enmities could be aroused, and Mosley certainly won more popular interest when he started to attack the Jews than when he simply aped a continental dictator.

The complex of emotional reactions, prejudices, and a hard core of facts, or believed facts, which make up modern antisemitism have been the subject of frequent study. In so far as Anglo-Jewry is concerned, antisemitism only threatened to show itself at two periods, during the wave of immigration from Russia, when both in London and in provincial cities the newcomers were compelled by poverty to settle among the poorest and most ignorant

E

of the local population, and in the depression of the 1930s. In the first period their visible foreign-ness and the low wages for which they were prepared to work, easily aroused the fears and jealousies of neighbours who themselves lived on the border-line of poverty. It is interesting that a sharp distinction seems to have been made at this period between 'English' Jews, who were generally popular, and the 'foreigners,' who were the reverse.[1] But local hostility, unpleasant as it was for the Jews, and especially for their children, never reached dangerous proportions and proved a relatively short-lived phenomenon.

The second outbreak of antisemitism, that fostered by Mosley and his followers, differed in many respects from the first. The hostility which greeted the refugees from Russia was not artificially engineered. It was based on the estimate of an ignorant and depressed section of the populace of an actual menace to their security. In the 1930s there were millions of unemployed. But this was due to the world-wide slump, and in no wise to Jewish competition. For, including the many thousand refugees from Germany, Jews numbered less than one per cent of the population.

From the very beginning the new hostility *was* artificially engineered. This time there were no visible facts of a mass of poverty-stricken Jewish neighbours who might take away one's job. Facts did not enter in. Mosley's antisemitic propaganda relied on all the panoply of falsehoods, from the Protocols of the Elders of Zion to the sinister international Jewish financier, with which Goebbels had bedevilled the German people. In this it was more akin to the troubles of 1753 and the 'Jew Bill.'

Yet another important difference lay in the fact that the success which Mosley achieved by his anti-Jewish tactics constituted as much a problem for the whole nation as for the Jewish minority. For the Jews were but a smoke screen for an attack on the general democratic way of life of the Englishman. Hence, in organisations which they built up to combat his falsification, the Jewish community could rely on a considerable measure of support from the general public.

The establishment of a Council of Christians and Jews under the presidency of the Archbishop of Canterbury, the Moderator

[1] Russell and Lewis, pp. 24f.

of the Church of Scotland, the Cardinal Archbishop of Westminster, and the Moderator of the Free Church Council, together with the Chief Rabbi, was due largely to the desire of Christian leaders to align themselves with the Jewish community in opposition to fascist antisemitism.

In this action they could count on a considerable tradition in British public life. The flood of pamphlets which every particular incident in Anglo-Jewish history has provoked has produced as much literature in their defence as in the attack upon them. From the religious groups which supported their return in the seventeenth century up to modern times there has been a steady opinion which has seen in them ' the people of the Book ' rather than the deicides. Though it is no part of this study, it can be added that the same is true of the Balfour Declaration. It was no suddenly adopted attitude, but reflected opinions which had been expressed for at least a century. In the mood of liberalism which pervaded the nineteenth century, all these different favourable opinions combined to ensure for the Jewish community a position as favourable as any that they have experienced during their long story. In the twentieth century the refugees from Hitler found a door which, in view of the fact that they came during a period of depression and unemployment, must be called ' open.' Again, there are shadows on the picture. But they are not enough to reverse the general verdict that the Jew in England has found more kindness than hostility, more understanding than contempt, more opportunities than restriction. And in return he has proved an excellent citizen, and the country has profited in many fields from his citizenship.

PART TWO

Demographic and Other Statistical Aspects of Anglo-Jewry

HANNAH NEUSTATTER, Dr.Oec.Publ.(Munich), F.S.S.

Demographic and Other Statistical Aspects of Anglo-Jewry

Population Estimate

THE dispersion of modern Jewry into minorities scattered over most of the world is the end of a long history of forced and voluntary migration. The various pressures which have operated to produce this distribution—poverty and under-privilege, pogrom and less drastic forms of persecution—still show some of their effects in the forms of social and economic organisation, cultural traditions, and demographic structure of the present-day communities of the diaspora. No Jewish catastrophe stands so clearly in the public memory as the extermination of millions of Jews[1] during the Second World War, but the international redistribution of Jewish population to which this disaster also led is not generally understood. The losses to European Jewry and the movement of many of its survivors have brought considerable changes in the numerical size of a great number of Jewish minorities both within and without the actual area of destruction.

The Jewish population of Great Britain, which has felt some of the effects of this redistribution, must first of all be seen in numerical relation to world Jewry as a whole. *Whitaker's Almanack*, 1954, quotes a World Health Organisation estimate of world population for 1949 as 2,377,400,000. World Jewry is assessed in the *Jewish Year Book*, 1950, at 12,000,000 or about 0.5 per cent of the total estimated population of the globe. This approximate percentage must be kept in mind as a rough index of the numerical scale of the Jewish question as a whole. In a report published March 21, 1952, the New York office of the World Jewish Congress has provided us with figures of the present distribution of world Jewry and some comparable data for earlier periods. The following figures, showing

[1] G. Reitlinger, *The Final Solution*, London, 1953, p. 510, gives an estimate of between four and four and a half millions.

the change brought about in half a century, are of particular interest:

The Jewish Population of Selected Areas.

	1900	1951[1]
North and South America	1,200,000	6,000,000 (of whom 5,000,000 are in the U.S.A.)
Europe	8,900,000	2,700,000
Israel	35,000	1,400,000

The Institute of Jewish Affairs (of the World Jewish Congress) has estimated that the percentage of Jewish population in the Western Hemisphere increased from 10.9 per cent in 1900 to 52.9 per cent[2] in 1952. Of the 3.5 millions of European Jews, 2.5 millions live at the present time behind the ' Iron Curtain '; that is, over 70 per cent of all Jews in Europe.[3]

In a survey of the Jewish communities east of Germany and west and south of the Soviet frontiers, Leon Shapiro and Joshua Starr arrive at estimates which indicate that at least half of the Jews of Europe lived in that area in spring 1946.[4] The authors assume that

[1] Comparative figures for 1953 are—N. and S. America: 5,750,000 ; Europe: 3,500,000 ; Israel: 1,468,000.

[2] See Jacob Lestchinski, *The Jewish Population of the World Today*, cited in the World Jewish Congress Report.

[3] From the report of the World Jewish Congress cited above the following table is quoted as a summary picture of Jewish population movement by continent:

Continent	1900		1939		1951	
	No.	%	No.	%	No.	%
Europe ...	8,900,000	80.9	9,500,000	57.8	2,700,000	23.8
America ...	1,200,000	10.9	5,250,000	31.9	6,000,000	52.9
Asia (less Israel)	475,000	4.8	550,000	3.4	600,000	5.3
Israel ...	35,000	0.3	480,000	2.9	1,400,000	12.3
Africa ...	375,000	3.4	625,000	3.9	600,000	5.3
Australia ...	15,000	0.2	35,000	0.2	50,000	0.4
Totals ...	11,000,000	100.0	16,400,000	100.0	11,000,000*	100.0

* The figure of 11,000,000 for 1951 given by the report quoted is not the actual addition but obviously an estimated total.

It will be noted that the estimated total figure differs by a million from that given as the *Jewish Year Book* 1950 estimate. There is little need to stress the vagueness of all estimates of Jewish population.

[4] ' Recent Population Data Regarding the Jews in Europe,' *Jewish Social Studies*, vol. VIII, No. 2, April, 1946, p. 75 *et seq.*, and No. 4, October, 1946, p. 319 *et seq.*

within the few fateful years of the Second World War the Jewish population of the area in question had decreased from 3.5 millions to 700,000. Greece alone had lost around 85 per cent of its Jews. Enormous as this loss is, the redistribution within the country is even more striking. While in 1940 Salonika was the place of residence of 50,000 of the 72,000 Greek Jews, by 1946 it held only 2,000 of the surviving 10,000 Jews in the country. Only Athens could show an increase in its Jewish population (from 2,500 to 4,880), while the rest of the Jews of Greece lived in twenty-two different communities which varied in size from 6 to 731. This radical change speaks, of course, for the loss of organised communal life for a great number of the survivors. In Yugoslavia the same feature is especially impressive. About 9,000 Jews living there in 1946 were spread over 102 localities, only 53 of which had some form of Jewish community. In Czechoslovakia, where the pre-war Jewish population had been reduced by three quarters, the remaining 51,000 to 55,000 Jews lived in larger and smaller centres, 53 of which had about thirty members each. The general picture for the whole area is the same. The disasters of war years led to the dispersion of the surviving Jews into small and unorganised settlements.

A particularly interesting fact emerges from the notes on Rumania,[1] where before the war a natural decrease in the population had already heavily reduced the size of the Jewish community. Between 1930 and 1941 alone the Jewish population declined by one sixth. In 1942 over 40 per cent of all Jewish households consisted of one or two persons each. In addition, conversion to Christianity made inroads upon Rumanian Jewry. 1.71 per cent were lost in this way during the period 1930-41, nearly three quarters of whom had been converted before the introduction of the racial laws of 1940. Since 1939 Rumania has lost more than 60 per cent of its Jewish population. In the same time Hungary has suffered a similar reduction of 92 per cent. One may doubt whether the old Eastern European centres of Jewry could again supply the west even if unhindered movement were possible. Certainly in present circumstances Western European Jewry cannot draw from its former chief source of population increase.

The Second World War has, of course, also severely reduced

[1] See Note 4, p. 56.

the Jewish population of Western Europe. The Jews of Holland declined by 83 per cent, Belgium by 60 per cent, and Italy by 45 per cent. France alone among all Continental Western European countries with sizeable Jewish groups preserved a high proportion (90 per cent) of its Jews. But even here the figure is deceptive since the total today includes many post-war immigrants who settled in France after the liberation. The position of Great Britain in this respect is unique. Not only was there no decline in its Jewish population between 1939 and 1951, but there was in fact a remarkable increase during the six years preceding the outbreak of the Second World War. Again, however, we have to make use of figures from different sources, which are estimates based on information of very different significance.

The total population of Great Britain according to *Whitaker's Almanack*, 1954, was 53,327,000, while the *Jewish Year Book*, 1952, estimates the number of Jews in the country during that year at 450,000, or between 0.8 and 0.9 per cent of the total population. According to *The Jewish Year Book*, the proportion of Jews in the population of Great Britain fluctuated in the following manner during this century[1]:

1901	1911	1921	1931	1936	1951
0.4%	0.5%	0.6%	0.6%	0.7%	0.8%

Taking 1931 as a basis, these figures show the important fact that, while the proportion of Jews in the world population dropped from 0.8 per cent in 1931 to 0.5 per cent in 1950 (or by almost 40 per cent), the proportion of Jews in this country increased during the same years by about 40 per cent. At a glance these figures show how the storm of destruction passed over Europe but left the Jews in Britain intact.

At this point it must be noted that the new State of Israel has not attracted many immigrants from Great Britain. Since 1948, when immigration into Israel was open to any Jew who wished

[1] *The Jewish Year Book*, 1901-2, 1912, 1922, 1929 (quoted in 1932), 1937 and 1952.
[2] But figures given by Louis Rosenberg, *Canada's Jews, A Social and Economic Study of the Jews in Canada*. Canadian Jewish Congress, 1939, p. 3, Table 3, are 1901, 0.6 per cent; 1911, 0.6 per cent; 1921, 0.6 per cent; 1931, 0.5 per cent; 1936, 0.7 per cent.

to go there, up to September 1953, 2,470 Jews left this country to take up permanent residence there. The greatest number in any one year, and more than half of the total, went during the first eight months of the period. Clearly many of these emigrants had been waiting for some time to obtain entry permits. It seems therefore fairly safe to assume that no mass emigration from this country to Israel can be expected to take place in the near future and that population loss through emigration to Israel can be disregarded in estimating trends in the Anglo-Jewish population.[1]

On the other hand, emigration to Israel is not likely to be substantially exceeded by immigration from other countries, at least as long as movement from countries beyond the 'Iron Curtain' remains as difficult as it is today. It is perhaps idle to speculate whether, if these difficulties were removed, one could expect Great Britain to exercise the same attraction to Jewish immigrants as it did before the creation of the State of Israel. All that can be said is that in present-day circumstances the development of Anglo-Jewry rests on the population stock now within the frontiers of this country.

All these facts make it an attractive proposition to collect and analyse all the demographic data concerning the minority group of Anglo-Jewry which, small as it is, is the largest of its kind in Western Europe. The group which contributed so much to the growth of organised Zionism and the issue of the Balfour Declaration, which can look back on a history of steady social and political progress for centuries, is certainly worthy of a serious review of its vital possibilities and prospects.

Attractive as the task of compiling demographic data of Anglo-Jewry appears to be, there are many reasons why it is extremely difficult to carry out. The Registrar General does not inquire into the religion of residents in this country, nor is there any general consensus as to what constitutes an unambiguous definition of a Jew. In fact, even within the minority which outsiders would normally classify as Jewish, there are differences of opinion concerning the manner in which the line is to be drawn to mark off Jew from non-Jew.

[1] Immigration into Israel from Britain fell from 580 in 1950 to 140 in 1953. See *The Jewish Chronicle*, 25/6/54.

Definition

A definition[1] might be based on Jewish origin, but this would unfairly claim for the Jewish community people who of their own free will have not only severed connection with the religion of their forbears, but who would strongly deny any feeling of solidarity and any identification with the community. Such persons might very well be in a position to stress the fact that other people do not regard them as Jews either. If, to go to the other extreme, we were to define as Jews only such people as those who profess Judaism by being members of synagogues, or the immediate dependents of such persons, we should exclude from our survey many individuals who regard themselves as Jews, and so limit the size of Anglo-Jewry to the scale of a small religious sect. Certainly, a rigid definition on religious lines would not accord with the pragmatic definition, however vague, of the mass of the general population of the country.

A century ago, on the other hand, the differentiation between Jew and Gentile in Great Britain was not fraught with the same difficulties. Then, Jews were still a distinct group within the general population by being of Jewish extraction, by professing their own religion, by the observance of the Sabbath and dietary laws, and by their affiliation to synagogues and specifically Jewish organisations. The tradition which makes a religious service possible only by the participation of a male quorum of ten adult Jews (the *minyan*), and which makes it necessary for a Jew to live within walking distance of his synagogue,[2] has also to some extent accounted for the clustering together of Jews in certain residential areas. Furthermore, at that time most Jews preferred to live and work in a district where they could provide themselves with the special food prescribed both by religious law and secular tradition. The congregation of the mass of the Jews in certain quarters, their economic specialisation, and certain overt cultural traits, made it possible for Jews and non-Jews alike to identify the members of the minority.

The definition of a Jew chosen in this essay is essentially one

---

[1] See pp. 3-5, 150-153, 201-203.
[2] Strict observance of Jewish law forbids the use of transport on the Sabbath and on Holy-days.

involving self-identification. It follows the same principle as that adopted by officialdom in countries where the inquiry into religion is included in census forms. Every individual who, when asked, would call himself a Jew, should be counted a Jew by our terms of reference, and no other person should be so called. This, of course, is an ideal definition from our point of view. Nobody in this country is in a position to ask the relevant question of all possible candidates. However, the difficulty in applying this ideal definition to demographically unsatisfactory material does not rob it of all utility, for the progress of assimilation and 'emancipation' would make any other definition still more unrealistic. Jews are as much affected by modern indifference to religion as other sections of the population. For some time it was assumed that Jews, however negligent of religious duty, desired to be buried by traditional rites. It was on this assumption that the estimates by H. L. Trachtenberg, 1933, and Miron Kantorowitsch, 1936, were made of the Jewish population of Greater London[1] (to which reference will be made again later). But even this last tie with organised Jewry no longer seems to be so effective. A pillar of the Jewish community exclaimed to me in the course of an interview carried out in connection with this survey : ' What kind of Jews are these who never in their lifetime come near a synagogue and who, when they die, are not buried in a Jewish cemetery ! '' And yet, despite his distaste for such assimilationists, my informant himself acknowledged their Jewishness and claimed for Jewry many of them who were socially prominent, though they themselves might very well have been doubtful of their exact status as Jews. This was by no means confined to Jews who were converts or who were married to non-Jews and were bringing up their children in another religion.

On the other hand, of course, the definition chosen in this study leaves out of account individuals typified by such outstanding personalities as Disraeli and Heinrich Heine who are commonly regarded as Jews. These considerations are important. They prove from the very beginning that the following exposé does not really deal with concrete facts and that it does not claim to be a genuinely

[1] H. L. Trachtenberg, 'Estimate of the Jewish Population of London,' 1929. *Journal of Royal Statistical Society,* vol. XCVI, Part I, 1933. M. Kantorowitsch, 'Estimate of the Jewish Population of London,' 1929-1933, *Journal of Royal Statistical Society.* vol. XCIX, Part II, 1936.

statistical survey in spite of its figures, its tables, and its statistical glosses. But then it must be borne in mind that this essay is not intended to be more than an initial exploration of a difficult field.

Even the very first item in a demographic statement, namely, the total Jewish population of this country, cannot be accurately established. Jews affiliated to Jewish organisations are only an unknown fraction of the total minority. Nor could the total membership of such organisations give the size of the inner core of Anglo-Jewry with any accuracy since there is an unknown degree of duplicated membership which obviously increases with the intensity of the attachment of individuals to communal values and activities. A mere glance through the *Jewish Year Book* would validate this statement. The same name often recurs on boards and committees of institutions apparently so far apart from one another as a Representative Council, a children's refugee organisation, a branch of the Friends of the Hebrew University, a local Talmud Torah (an institution concerned with religious education), the Kashrut Commission (which supervises the production and distribution of ritually proper food), a Zionist association, and so on. This is not an unfairly selected case, nor does the name belong to a paid communal worker. It is a reasonably typical example taken from the group of Jews who freely give their support to communal activities. There are even cases in which individuals duplicate their membership of synagogues. This occurs when people move out of the East End of London, for example, and still contribute to their original synagogue while they have become members of another synagogue in their new area of residence. Clearly, then, there is no way of assessing within any reasonable limits of accuracy the size of the Anglo-Jewish population on the basis of the membership of Jewish organisations.

It is not quite so difficult to lay down rules for describing individuals who, in theory, should be covered by a survey of Anglo-Jewry once the meaning of the term Jew is accepted. Such a survey should obviously deal with every Jewish citizen in the country who has achieved that status either by birth or by naturalisation. In addition, any permanent resident who has not acquired British nationality but who otherwise conforms with the terms laid down should be included. This latter category comprises a great variety of people who are nevertheless relatively small in number, *e.g.*, some foreign-born wives of British Jews, persons who have resided for many years in this country without acquiring British nationality, and a few who have not yet acquired the necessary residential qualifications for obtaining naturalisation. Among the bars to naturalisation perhaps the most interesting is lack of knowledge of the English language. As recently as 1911 it was considered necessary to issue for the population census 30,000 forms printed in Yiddish.[1] In 1951, of course, no such necessity was felt, but even then, the Board of Deputies opened advisory offices in large Jewish centres to help people fill in census schedules. It would seem then that even at the present time there is a need to assist a number of people whose command of English is so poor as to render them, without help, incapable of dealing with official documents.

Reverting to the problem of assessing the size of the Jewish population of Great Britain, we may repeat that we cannot rely on any official information. There is an exception to be made however in the case of Northern Ireland, where an inquiry into religion is made at each census. If, nevertheless, we venture to arrive at an estimate and to give at least some idea of the size of Anglo-Jewry, it is inevitable that such an attempt should suffer from the weakness inherent in drawing indirect conclusions from insecure assumptions.

Sources

Generally speaking it has been almost impossible to base this investigation on fresh material. Obviously no nation-wide private census could be carried out for both financial and technical reasons. The successful operation of such a private census could in fact hardly be expected in a community so loosely organised as that of Anglo-Jewry. The sources of information on which this survey

---

[1] See *General Report 1911 Census England and Wales*. At that time Redcliffe N. Salaman estimated the average size of the Jewish family to be approximately five, which means presumably that about 150,000 Jewish individuals were living in households of which at least the head was considered incapable of dealing with an English schedule. See 'Anglo-Jewish Vital Statistics.' *The Jewish Chronicle Supplement*, 1921, Nos. 4, 5, 6, 7, and 8.

is based are to a great extent already available in published form. What follows in the way of demographic data is based on the sources listed below:

1. Information provided by 55 provincial Jewish communities in response to a questionnaire (A.J.S.-1) sent out to 110 such communities for the purposes of this survey (1950).[1]

2. Replies obtained from 1,666 Jewish households to a questionnaire (A.J.S.-2),[2] of which 12,000 copies were distributed for the purposes of this survey (1950-52).

3. A check carried out on the names of persons naturalised in the period 1938-1948 in the records published by the Home Office.[3]

4. Figures for the size of Jewish communities in a number of centres as collected by the *Jewish Year Book* during the past thirty years.

5. A calculation of the size of the Jewish population of Greater London, 1929-1933, made by Miron Kantorowitsch on the basis of burials registered at local Jewish burial societies.

6. A survey compiled in 1945 by the Jewish Refugee Committee under the title *Who are the Jewish Refugees?*

7. A population estimate for the year 1914 made by Dr. Redcliffe N. Salaman.

All of these sources are far from being dependable. One defect becomes clear when we consider that the figures obtained from most communities for the purposes of the *Jewish Year Book* comprise only members of synagogues or other communal organisations, while some may include, as far as one can tell, individuals who are not connected with any such body. No community, of course, is in a position to account for 'outsiders' who are not known locally. The larger the community the greater this unknown section is likely to be, while the number of individuals within it must have increased considerably during the past twenty years. It must also be remembered that Jews who have moved away from old Jewish centres into suburbs and the countryside where no communities have been formed are not covered by the *Jewish Year Book*. This trend away

[1] See Appendix, p. 245.
[2] See Appendix, pp. 246-47.
[3] For table of this analysis see Appendix, p. 248.

from the old Jewish centres has increased with the drift from strict religious observance. Progressive assimilation lessens the need for residential clustering ; dispersal over wide areas has become an accepted feature of Anglo-Jewish patterns of residence. It is almost impossible to trace Jews living in districts where no communal organisation has been formed.[1] For example, it is of interest to note that while there is reason to suppose that thirty Jews are resident in Salisbury, a place not covered by the *Jewish Year Book,* this publication does record twenty Jewish inhabitants of Exeter, where the community has been organised for many years.

A recent survey by the Inter-University Jewish Federation of Great Britain and Ireland also demonstrates the point. This survey attempted to provide information on a wide range of questions concerning the number of Jewish students in this country, their education, their religious affiliations, and their attitudes to various Jewish matters. From the start, however, the survey encountered the difficulty of tracing the so-called Jewish students. The organiser of the inquiry, Raymond V. Baron, in an article on the first results of his survey, had to admit that ' as far as can be discovered, there were 3,000 Jewish students in Great Britain and Ireland of whom 1,000 were members of their local Jewish societies.' That is to say, only one-third of the estimated number of Jewish University students formally associated with other Jewish students as such. Of the remaining 2,000 students, 1,000 could be traced by the secretaries of the local societies, and some of these even filled in the survey forms distributed to them. About 1,000 Jewish students (*i.e.,* 33 per cent of the estimated total number) could not be contacted at all and lived unidentified in the general body of students.[2] In the case of the third largest Jewish community in the country, that of Leeds, the lack of reliable figures in estimates of Jewish population is likewise shown. Since 1921 the community has assessed the total Jewish population consistently at 25,000. On the face of it, the unchanging figure is most improbable. In Belfast and Dublin,

---

[1] A Jewish community may be regarded as organised as soon as the common effort of local Jewish residents leads to the formation of some specifically Jewish institution. Frequently the first product of communal effort has been the provision of a Jewish burial ground.

[2] Raymond V. Baron, ' Jewish Students—A Survey,' *The Jewish Chronicle,* 16.2.51 and 23.2.51.

65

where the census gives separate figures for the Jewish inhabitants, there has been an increase of approximately 50 per cent in the same period.

JEWISH POPULATION

	1921	1950
Belfast	1,200	1,800
Dublin	3,500	5,311

The difficulties in the way of collecting basic numerical information are by no means solved by the questionnaires sent out in connection with this survey. In response to 110 questionnaires (A.J.S.-1) distributed among provincial communities, 55 forms were completed and returned. The forms inquired into the size of the local communities, the number of Jews not affiliated to any Jewish organisation, the number of births and deaths during the past five years, and so on. Many Jewish communities, the larger ones in particular, lack the administrative facilities to collect such information. Moreover, where various organisations were approached with the request for information concerning the same community, very different and conflicting figures were offered. The second questionnaire (A.J.S.-2) was distributed to 12,000 Jewish householders through the courtesy of the Representative Councils of Hull and Sheffield, while in the rest of the provinces this task was undertaken by the Association of Jewish Ex-Service Men and Women. The forms, which give some indication of age and sex structure, marital condition, nationality at birth and at the present time, etc., were duly completed by 1,666 householders, and cover 5,225 Jewish individuals. The uneven geographical distribution of the replies received make the results extremely doubtful. No replies were received from Manchester or Birmingham. London, where two-thirds of all Jews in the country are concentrated, is represented in the sample by 362 households covering 1,181 individuals ; and even this small sample was secured only by the co-operation of three different organisations, the Association of Jewish Ex-Service Men and Women, the London Jewish Hospital, and the staff of *The Jewish Chronicle*.

Miron Kantorowitsch's estimate of the Jewish population of Greater London suffers, first of all, from the inevitable flaw resulting from his method of calculating the population on the basis of deaths registered with local Jewish burial societies.[1] This is based on the assumption that the ratio between Jewish deaths and the Jewish population is the same as that between deaths and the population in general. That such an analogy is bound to give rather strange results is suggested by the table Mr. Kantorowitsch gives for the age-structure of the Jewish population during the years 1929 to 1933. In this table the Jewish age-groups 5-9 and 10-14 are about 20 per cent greater than the preceding age-group 0-4, a result which is in contrast to the age-structure of the general population. Even if one is justified in assuming that the decline of the Jewish birth rate exceeds that of the general population, this anomaly is difficult to understand unless the lower infantile mortality among Jews is also taken into account. This would mean that the age-group 0-4 is underrated by Kantorowitsch's method of estimating. It would also explain, at least partly, why the subsequent Jewish age-groups are stronger than those of the general population. On the other hand, this assumption would lead to the expectation of a higher proportion of males in the Jewish than in the general population, as mortality in the lower age-groups is higher among males than females. Yet Kantorowitsch comes to the conclusion that in the

[1] The same method was used by A. J. Jaffe in his article "The Use of Death Records to Determine Jewish Population Characteristics," *Jewish Social Studies*, April, 1939, vol. I, No. 2, pp. 143 *et seq*. Mr. Jaffe tries to estimate the total Jewish population of Chicago in the year 1930. He compares the population estimate arrived at by his method (265,000), which involves the application of death rates of the total population to Jewish burial figures, with that reached by the "Yom Kippur Method" (305,000) applied by W. A. Goldberg in 1931, which is based on the figure of school-children absent from school during the Holy-days correlated with children of the same age in the general population. He points out that there are shortcomings in both methods. 'Many but not all who would admit being Jewish would bury their dead according to the Jewish ritual and keep their children out of school on the Holy-days.' Later in the article the author states that there are two main difficulties in the use of the death record method: first, to obtain death records of *all* Jewish deaths, and, secondly, to obtain a death-rate applicable to Jews. In the same Journal, vol. vii, No. 2, April, 1945, Erich Rosenthal, in an article entitled ' The Size of the Jewish Population in Chicago, 1930,' points out that when applying differential rates to the ' Yom Kippur Method ' (the population of the age group prior to 15 years varied between 7.6 per cent and 29.3 per cent of the total population), one could estimate the total Jewish population of Chicago at 274,000, thus very closely approaching the result of the death certificate method (265,000). What these articles demonstrate most clearly is the uncertainty of population estimates reached by indirect methods of calculation.

age-groups 15-24 and 25-34 the number of Jewish females is higher than that of males by almost 40 per cent (males 31,623 and females 50,075).

There are good reasons for assuming that in the Jewish population there are more people in the higher age-groups than in the corresponding age-groups of the general population. The immigrants arriving in this country between the 1890s and the outbreak of the First World War, many of them single men, at that time expanded the age-groups over 15 and are now in the age-group of 55 and over. Consequently the death-rate among Jews should be higher than that of the population as a whole. In addition, the decreasing birth-rate should, as we shall point out below, be responsible for a greater proportion in the higher age-group. Kantorowitsch's table, however, gives quite a different, and in one respect questionable, picture.

Nevertheless, we have no means of replacing Kantorowitsch's estimate by a more reliable one. In accepting it as the best available we must presume that, despite its shortcomings, the final result is not too far off the mark. Some reservation has to be made in so far as it is more than probable that some Jewish deaths were not recorded in the registers of Jewish burial societies since the deceased had been cremated or buried in a non-Jewish cemetery. The total figure for the Greater London population is, therefore, likely to have been somewhat larger in 1933 than Mr. Kantorowitsch's estimate of 233,991±.

Natural Increase

If we take into consideration the various sources of information listed above we have still to account for the natural increase of the Jewish population and the impact of Jewish immigration after 1933. This has a special bearing on Greater London but is also relevant to the question of the actual size of the Jewish population of the United Kingdom.

All the indications are that, at least for the last two decades, natural increase has been negligible, if in fact there has been any at all. The Jewish population has certainly followed the general national trend as regards decrease in the birth-rate. Moreover, one is inclined to assume that the Jewish birth-rate has dropped even more rapidly than that of England and Wales generally. An excellent article, 'Anglo-Jewish Vital Statistics,' by Redcliffe N. Salaman,[1] demonstrates the fall of the Jewish birth-rate. He bases his conclusions on a cross-section of 370 families in West London in 1921, comprising several generations and including 1,600 children. All the families fell within the professional and better-off commercial classes. Dr. Salaman states that in the youngest generation the average number of children per family was 2.7, but this generation is still in the child-bearing age, with the consequence that the figure of 2.7 is on the low side. The parent generation in these families had 3.5 children, their grandparental and great-grandparental generations 5.6 and 7 children per family respectively. The average size of the Jewish family today, according to estimates given by 52 provincial communities in response to the relevant section of questionnaire A.J.S.-1, is 3.4.[2] These communities estimate the total Jewish population covered by them at 83,622. The communities of Cambridge, Merthyr Tydfil, and Plymouth (with a Jewish population between them of 748) who replied to other questions on the form, did not enter estimates of the average size of the family. London was not included in this inquiry, as the problem of distribution seemed insuperable. There is, however, no possible reason for assuming that the Jewish family in London is greater than its provincial counterpart. On the contrary, the larger the town the smaller, as a general rule, the average size of family ; although, as we shall see later, the size of the Jewish family seems not to be greatly influenced by the size of the town in which it lives.

The estimates of the average size of the family gathered by our questionnaire from 52 provincial communities are as follows:

PERSONS PER FAMILY					NUMBER OF AREAS
5	...	...	...	...	1
4	...	...	...	...	17
3.5	...	...	...	...	8
3	...	...	...	...	22
Under 3	...	...	...	...	4

[1] *The Jewish Chronicle Supplement*, 1921, Nos. 4, 5, 6, 7, and 8.
[2] See Appendix, Table III, p. 249.

Even though these figures, which imply that the average number of children per family was 1.4 in 1950, are only estimates, they are not necessarily impossible.

The Jewish family normally consisting of father, mother, and non-adult children, but with the occasional addition of children under 16 living in the same household as wards or foster-children, and childless married daughters, appears from our questionnaire A.J.S.-2 to be even smaller.[1] After eliminating visitors and lodgers, making an adequate allowance for householders who live by themselves, and excluding composite households, we find that the average size of the household-family is 3.0, or one child per family. The size of the private household (as distinct from institutions and boarding-houses) is slightly greater, namely, 3.1. This compares with the 1 per cent sample tables of the 1951 Census of Great Britain, which gives 3.3 persons per household as the average.

In our sample there was only one married woman under the age of twenty, and she had no children. The figure of one child per family may, of course, be somewhat lower than the actual figure, as the children who have left the household and formed family units on their own were not covered by our inquiry, while those temporarily absent at boarding-schools and universities or serving with H.M. Forces were. The strong representation of higher age-groups in our sample makes this inadequacy probably of especial importance. On the other hand, we did not differentiate between the natural issue and other children, such as wards and foster-children under the age of sixteen living in the same household, a fact which is important when the size of the family is used as an indication of natural increase and decrease in a population. To some extent these two inaccuracies cancel one another out, so that they may not prejudice too far our approximation to a population estimate.

While the average size of the family among manual workers is 4.49 persons or 2.49 children per family, the Report of the Royal Commission on Population (1949) gives the figure of 1.73 children per family among non-manual workers (for couples married 1925-29) for the country as a whole. This figure raises the question whether the decline of the Jewish birth-rate may have originated

[1] See Appendix, Table IV, p. 249.

from a general social and economic ascent by Jews in this country from the class of poorly-paid unskilled and semi-skilled workers to 'white-collar' employment and small businesses conducted independently. The ambition of such Jews was to be accepted in professional circles, and it is a well-known feature of Western Europe in modern times that the intelligentsia and professional classes breed at a low rate.

Another reason for the declining Jewish birth-rate may be found in the progressively diminishing influence of religious tradition in Anglo-Jewry. The Jewish religion, in common with many others, fosters a high birth-rate and regards fertility as a blessing; so much so that it recognises barrenness in women as a ground for divorce. The Jewish religious tradition of matrimony (*niddah*) encourages early marriage. As will be shown later, this habit has changed completely.

Urbanisation cannot be the reason for the decline in the size of the Jewish family. Jews were already clustered together in urban districts at a time when their birth-rate was high and are only now spreading in the rural areas. However, the new geographical distribution seems not to counteract the decline in the size of the Jewish family. On the contrary, this trend is strong among Jews and exceeds in extent and speed even that of the general population.

The interesting analysis of the Jewish population of Newcastle upon Tyne made by Mr. L. Olsover[1] estimates the average size of the family at 3.2 persons. Further reference to this analysis, which enjoys the advantage of being limited to a medium-sized and compact Jewish community, will be made in due course. However, it should be pointed out here that its results are especially significant, as the conditions of Newcastle upon Tyne allowed the application of methods which would be greatly misleading in larger communities.

A unique attempt has been made in Manchester by the Rev. Dr. I. W. Slotki to estimate the size of the Jewish population on the basis of Jewish schoolchildren, which is all the more important for dealing with a large community.[2] His method is far superior

---

[1] 'A Social Survey of Newcastle Jewry,' *The Watchman*, September, 1951.

[2] Israel W. Slotki, *Jewish Education in Manchester*, 1928, Manchester: Sherrat & Hughes, 1928, and 'The Jewish Population of Manchester,' *The Jewish Chronicle*, 3.11.1950.

to the 'Yom Kippur Method' applied by W. A. Goldberg (see p. 67). Through personal contacts Dr. Slotki collected data concerning every child of school age in the area, which will be realised to have been a remarkable achievement in view of the fact that Manchester's Jewish community is the second largest in the country and numbers well over 30,000. By applying the method of correlating the age-group between five and fourteen of the general population and the total population of Manchester in the middle of 1927, and multiplying the number of Jewish schoolchildren in the same age-group by the ratio so obtained, he comes to an estimated Jewish population of Manchester and Salford of between 33,000 and 34,300.

Dr. Slotki demonstrates the decreasing number of Jewish children, which is a fact already commented on in the present study and to which further reference will be made in connection with the question of Jewish birth-rate. He states that the number of Jewish schoolchildren in Manchester was between 4,500 and 5,000 in 1927-28. In 1943-44 their number had decreased to 3,053, although at the later date he had taken into account the trend of the Jewish population out into the suburbs and had covered the schools in Prestwich and Whitefield in addition to those in Manchester and Salford. This means that there has been a decrease of about one-third. The conclusion, however, which Dr. Slotki draws, namely, that the Jewish population in the area had decreased correspondingly from between 33,000 and 34,300 to 22,000 is somewhat erroneous. Taking the children of school age as a basis for estimating the total population in 1927-28, he compares them with the corresponding age-group of the total population and so arrives at his total. He then assumes that a decrease in that age-group of 33 per cent means a decrease in the total population of about 11,000. This inference is not conclusive. It may happen that, while the number of children decreases, the total population increases. This paradox is explained by a change in the age structure of the population, which may take place as soon as the birth-rate decreases steadily for some length of time and causes the population gradually to comprise more adults and elderly people and fewer children. This is precisely the case with the general population of the United

Kingdom and even more so with its Jewish element. The more numerous generations born before the First World War swelled the middle-aged groups in the '30s, while the decline of the birth-rate after the First World War reduced the ranks of the lower age-groups.

The population as a whole has nevertheless increased. The conclusion, therefore, that the decrease in the number of Jewish schoolchildren means a decrease in the Jewish population is open to question.

We may take as the basis for a tentative estimate of the size of Anglo-Jewry Dr. Redcliffe Salaman's figure of 300,000[1] for the year 1914. From his researches he further estimates the annual increase at that time at 5,000. If this rate had continued steadily, the population in 1950 would have been 300,000 plus 180,000 = 480,000 ; but such a calculation would ignore the fact that not all the children born in one year reach maturity and that, on the other hand, after a period of roughly twenty-five years, when children born in 1914 would have reached the age of marriage, the number of families would have increased. If each family had on the average the same number of children as in 1914, the total number of Jewish births would be higher. This, however, is not the case, since during the period the number of births has continually decreased. It seems justifiable to reduce the natural increase calculated above at 180,000 by a half and so to put it roughly at 90,000. This would bring the Jewish population in 1950 to 390,000. To this figure must be added the number of Jewish immigrants who settled in the country during the period. This figure may be estimated at approximately 60,000. The group consists of a great number of Russian immigrants who arrived in Britain between 1914 and 1930, the mass of Central European Jews who fled from Nazi persecution and those naturalised after 1948 whose numbers were swollen by releases from the Polish Resettlement Corps. This estimate of 60,000 for post-1914 Jewish immigrants seems conservative.[2]

[1] But cf. p. 262, Notes 11 and 12.
[2] An estimate of 80,000 is quoted in an article by D. Pela, *The Jewish Chronicle*, 22.2.52, entitled 'Storm over Refugee Report.' According to this source there are 46,000 pre-war refugees, *most* of whom are Jews, and a further 34,000 pre-war refugees who had become naturalised. We assume that part of the difference between the estimates is due to the inclusion of non-Jews in these figures.

The various estimates arrived at make the following statement:

Jewish residents in 1914	300,000
Natural increase up to 1950	90,000
Immigration	60,000
Total Jewish population of Great Britain in 1950	450,000

Here it is desirable to compile a population estimate based on other available sources for the purposes of comparison. Two points of general importance must once more be stressed. In the first place, the figures for places given in the *Jewish Year Book* (the same places have been covered by our questionnaire A.J.S.-1) do not account for Jews living scattered over the country outside these centres and not organised into communities. A drift from the larger towns to suburban areas and neighbouring rural districts has taken place during recent years. This movement has been partly the result of cheaper rents and better accommodation outside the towns, and improved travelling facilities. It has been accelerated by war-time conditions. One obstacle to the dispersion—the need for religious services and kasher food—as we have said earlier, has been partly removed with growing assimilation and the decline of interest in religious Judaism. In the second place, especially in London, but also elsewhere, a certain number of Jews who fall within our definition are untraceable. We estimate this section at 15 per cent. A table[1] is appended giving estimates of Jews not affiliated to any communal body submitted from forty-two areas which replied to the relevant question of our questionnaire A.J.S.-1.

We thus arrive at the following results:

London

1929-1933 estimate by Kantorowitsch 233,991 ± rounded off	234,000	
Immigration from Central Europe after 1933 (naturalised 1938-1948)	16,944	
	250,944	
Fifteen per cent not accounted for	37,641	
		288,585

[1] See Appendix, Table V, p. 250.

Manchester	30,000	
Immigration	1,138	
	31,138	
Fifteen per cent not accounted for	4,670	
		35,808
Leeds	25,000	
Immigration	569	
	25,569	
Fifteen per cent not accounted for	3,835	
		29,404
Glasgow	13,000	
Immigration	416	
	13,416	
Fifteen per cent not accounted for	2,012	
		15,428
Birmingham	6,300	
Immigration	604	
	6,904	
Fifteen per cent not accounted for	1,035	
		7,939
Liverpool	7,500	
Immigration—negligible	—	
Fifteen per cent not accounted for	1,125	
		8,625
Total all large communities		385,789

Smaller Communities in Other Large Towns

Newcastle upon Tyne	2,300	
Hull ... .,.	2,000	
Sheffield	1,850	
Belfast	1,800	
Edinburgh	1,500	
	9,450	
Fifteen per cent not accounted for	1,417	
		10,867

Smaller Towns ...	...	...	...	...	36,038	
Fifteen per cent not accounted for ...			...	...	5,406	
						41,444

Immigrants in Smaller Communities

Immigrants naturalised at all localities other than those with large communities	...	10,758	
Fifteen per cent not accounted for ...	...	1,614	
			12,372

Estimated Jewish Population, 1950 450,472

The total estimated figure of approximately 450,500 for the total Jewish population is based on figures from various initial sources,[1] plus the number of immigrants after 1933 estimated from the names taken to be Jewish in the naturalisation records published annually by the Home Office for the years 1938-1948,[2] plus fifteen per cent for those Jews not accounted for by this scrutiny of names, plus fifteen per cent for the respective sections in all other estimates here enumerated. This last percentage is the average of Jews not affiliated to any Jewish organisation in proportion to the local population estimates given by forty-two provincial centres in A.J.S.-1. It is clear that this proportion will increase with the size of the community. As the largest communities did not give the required information, fifteen per cent may be considered a very conservative estimate, the more so in that, apart from those Jews known not to be affiliated,[3] most probably there are Jews who are not accounted for. This population estimate closely approaches the estimate made on the basis of Dr. Salaman's figure of 300,000 for the year 1914, plus natural increase and immigration, but reduced in accordance with the general decline in birth figures during the '20s, '30s, and war years. It must, however be borne in mind that these estimates are very rough, since the basic figures are doubtful and such factors as intermarriage and conversion have been altogether neglected. But they are the best estimates which can be made.

[1] A.J.S.—1, *The Jewish Year Book,* Mr. Prais's estimate of Birmingham Jewry, Mr. Olsover's estimate of Newcastle Jewry, and Mr. Kantorowitsch's estimate of the Jewish population of Greater London.
[2] See Table II, p. 248.
[3] See Appendix, Table V, p. 250.

Demographic Data

The following paragraphs examine estimates of Jewish vital statistics, which are subject to the same limitations as those of the earlier population figures. In dealing with particular localities we must, of course, accept the information we have collected on them for a given point in time and neglect migration within the country. However, from a comparison of the population figures in the *Jewish Year Books* for 1921 and 1952 it can be seen that the Jewish population is as mobile as the general population. While the *Jewish Year Book* 1921 recorded seventy-seven areas as having organised communities, the edition of 1952 gave a corresponding figure of ninety-one. The total Jewish population in 1921 was estimated at 317,500 and in 1952 at 450,000. The following statement sets out for the same two years the larger concentrations of Jewish population:

	1921	1952
London	170,000	289,000
Manchester	32,000	36,000
Leeds	25,000	29,000
Glasgow	14,000	15,000
Liverpool	7,000	9,000
Birmingham	6,000	8,000
	254,000	386,000

These figures mean that in 1921[1] eighty per cent of all Jews in this country lived in the six largest Jewish centres, which were also the great concentrations of the general population; while in 1952 the corresponding percentage was eighty-six. Since emigration and immigration are likely to be negligible during the coming years, the question of internal migration merits our attention. In his article, 'A Demographic Revolution,'[2] Mr. Soref points out that the trend of Jewish migration within this country has worked in two different

[1] The total Jewish population in 1921 is calculated on the basis of Dr. Salaman's figure of 300,000, plus seven years' annual natural increase of 2,500, which equals 317,500.

[2] Harold Soref, 'A Demographic Revolution,' *The Jewish Chronicle*, 15.3.52.

directions. At the beginning of the twentieth century there were still distinct traces of the historic composition of Anglo-Jewry to be seen in their geographical distribution. Many Jews were settled in the seaports at which they had arrived from abroad, and in certain industrial centres from which they operated as pedlars in the surrounding countryside and to which they returned on the Sabbath and the Holy Days.

In the course of one generation a redistribution of Anglo-Jewry had begun which led them in increasing numbers from the smaller towns to the biggest Jewish centres. Many smaller communities disappeared during the process.[1] The next generation saw a trend in the opposite direction, although this did not mean a return to the traditionally smaller Jewish communities but rather a movement to other seaside places and smaller towns near the largest centres of Jewish population. As we have seen earlier, Jewish communities tend to begin their activities by acquiring a burial ground and they maintain this institution to the last.

War-time conditions greatly accelerated this migration, which was not reversed by a return to peace. On the contrary, the Anglo-Jewish trend towards settlement in rural districts and seaside places near the towns and in the suburbs still prevails.

The disintegration of such centres of Jewish life as the East End of London is due not only to the movement out of rising Jewish families in search of better residential districts and to the overflowing of an overcrowded population, but is also the result of a changed attitude towards Orthodox Judaism. As long as the dietary laws, observance of the Sabbath, and the presence of the quorum of ten for prayers were necessities in Jewish life, a scattered existence among non-Jews was an impossibility. When, in many places such as Manchester and Leeds, improved communications with the suburbs induced Jewish families to move away from the

[1] In an article, 'A Jewish Corner of Kent,' Prof. Norman Bentwich tells how in the course of this development the ancient community of Canterbury disappeared, leaving behind a secularised synagogue, a burial-ground, which, because it was filled to capacity, was no longer used, and an acre of the general cemetery which the community had acquired, but which held no Jewish graves, since there was no longer a Canterbury congregation. Dover was also a victim of the trend, but there the burial-ground is still maintained. Ramsgate has preserved some of its Jewish tradition, but 'Margate, the youngest congregation of these four, has become the most lively and vigorous of all of them.' (*The Jewish Chronicle*, 26.9.52.)

cities, they did so with some sacrifice of Jewish religious tradition. The Rev. Dr. I. W. Slotki has pointed out[1] that 'the Jewish population would probably have been much larger had not Jewish migration spread to such outlying places as Sale, Stratford, Timperley, Brooklands, Altrincham, Hale, and further afield localities which in past years had a few lonely Jews, or, more, often, none at all.'

In contrast with this trend a special form of urbanisation has taken place among Jews in this country during the past half century. There has been an influx into the biggest communities, leaving the smaller ones abandoned. In the process of this migration, for example, only one community—Belfast—survived in Northern Ireland.

Obviously, the two migration trends have contradictory consequences in the distribution of Jews over the country. Urbanisation, in its normal form, draws rural population into the town and has quite different effects from the migration trends which have prevailed among Jews during the last fifty years. We can hardly bring this special redistribution of Anglo-Jewry under the heading of urbanisation; certainly not to the extent of using it, as a form of urbanisation, to account for the decline in the average size of the Jewish family during the last three decades or so. We have already referred to this phenomenon in our attempt to estimate the natural increase of the Jewish population since 1914, but it is a topic important enough to need fuller investigation.

Size of Family

If we may draw inferences from trends prevailing in better surveyed Jewish populations abroad, we may assume that the size of the Jewish family everywhere decreased at a greater speed and to a greater extent than that of the general populations among whom they lived. In his model survey of Canadian Jewry, based on information furnished by the Registrar-General's office, Louis Rosenberg[2] provides interesting data on this question. He includes

[1] 'The Jewish Population of Manchester' (*The Jewish Chronicle*, 3.11.50).
[2] Louis Rosenberg, *op. cit.*

79

in Jewish birth figures all births to parents of whom one at least
is a Jew. From his material it becomes clear that during the decade
1926-1936 Jewish births fell from a crude rate per thousand of 15.3
to 13.6 (with an average of 14.2), while for the general population
the rate increased from 22.1 in 1926 to 24.6 in 1928 and dropped
to 22.1 again in 1936, 22.1 being also the average for the ten years.
The birth-rate per thousand married women 15-44 years old was
99.1 for Jews and 190.7 for women of all origins. It is therefore
clear that Canadian Jewry during the decade was considerably less
fertile than the general population.

In Germany we find that during half a century the Jewish
birth-rate dropped to a greater extent than that of the non-Jews.
Neumark[1] presents two interesting tables in an article on the
population structure of Germany, and points out that the reasons
for its shrinking Jewish element were the small influx of Jews from
the East and an especially strong decline in the birth-rate beginning
at an early date. These two tables taken together are as follows:

Year	Proportion of Jews in the total population	Proportion of Jews in the population of those large towns containing 70% of the total of Jewish inhabitants
	Per cent	Per cent
1880	1.1	4.1
1910	—	2.4
1913	0.9	—
1925	0.9	—
1933[2]	0.76	1.8

The same general situation holds in the Netherlands, as we may
see from Methorst's work.[3] His survey covers marriages contracted
between 1907 and 1911 and not dissolved (by death or divorce) up
to 1928. The 'urban' sample of the investigations embraced four
towns, Amsterdam, Rotterdam, Utrecht, and Dordrecht, with populations ranging from 56,000 to 757,000, while the 'rural' sample
consisted of 103 localities with between 4,000 and 10,000 inhabitants

[1] F. Neumark, 'Betrachtungun zur Gegenwaertigen Bevölkerungsgliederung Deutschlands,' *Population*, November, 1935.
[2] *I.e.*, up to the middle of 1933 and before the beginning of mass
emigration.
[3] M. H. W. Methorst, 'Differential Fertility in the Netherlands.'
Population. vol. I (Special Memoir), April, 1935.

each. The following table shows the numbers of live births as they vary according to the religion of mothers:

Mother's religion	Families with no children per 100 families		Average number of live births per family	
	Urban	Rural	Urban	Rural
Protestant	14.1	10.3	3.5	4.0
Roman Catholic	13.1	9.3	4.0	5.7
Jewish	13.2	14.3	2.8	2.8
Other creeds	13.5	14.7	3.1	4.0
No creed	13.0	10.5	3.2	3.4
All groups	13.7	10.1	3.4	4.5

This pattern is familiar in that it reveals the lower number of live births per family among Jews irrespective of their residence in town or country; but unfortunately the Jewish sample of rural families is rather small, since it covers only 82 families in comparison with the 2,454 urban Jewish families. If, despite this shortcoming, we may venture to draw any conclusions from the sample, we may make the following point. While Jews follow the tendency prevailing in the wider populations towards a scaling down of family size, and even exceed in this the general populations among whom they live, it seems to matter little whether they live in the country or in the town. They are already urbanised to such an extent that their attitude towards life is not greatly influenced by that of non-urbanised neighbours. Erich Rosenthal has pointed out[1] that the marriage habits of Jews differed little from those of the general population of Berlin but greatly from those of the whole German people among whom they lived spread throughout the smaller towns and villages, although the majority resided in Berlin. However, if we keep to surer ground and examine only the urban sample in the Netherlands material, we still encounter the familiar fact that the Jewish birth-rate is lower than that of most other groups at a given time in any country under observation. The Dutch figures are valuable in that, like those for Canada and Germany, they are based on official information.

A survey made by Mr. M. Greenberg of 'The Reproduction Rate of the Families of the Jewish Students at the University of Maryland,'[2] to which we shall again refer, draws on material from

[1] 'Trends of the Jewish Population in Germany, 1910-1939,' *Jewish Social Studies*, 1944, vol. VI, part 3, pp. 233 *et seq.*
[2] *Jewish Social Studies*, July, 1948, vol. X, no. 3, pp. 223 *et seq.*

G

Indianapolis, giving the following picture of children born to 100 mothers of various religions in that city:

Jews ... 110   Protestants ... 147   Catholics ... 173

The Jewish sample consisted of 419 families. In a sample of Maryland Jews 84 per cent had at least one parent of foreign origin in 1936. The foreign-born population in the United States, Jewish as well as non-Jewish, is generally more fertile than the native-born. For this group the average number of children per family was:

Jews	4.1
Protestants	4.6
Catholics	5.5

During the decade 1921-1931 the birth-rate in England and Wales dropped from 22.8 per thousand to 15.6. There is no reason to suppose that the Jewish birth-rate did not fall at the same or a faster speed. From our investigation of the average size of the Jewish family, we can conclude that the Jewish birth-rate must have been falling during the last half century, that it must be rather low at the present time, and presumably somewhat lower than that of the general population of the country. The results obtained from our questionnaire A.J.S.-1 confirm these inferences. Thirty-six of the 55 provincial communities which returned the A.J.S.-1 forms responded to our inquiry into the number of local Jewish births during the five years 1945-1949. These communities cover between them a population which we estimate at 16,078. From these figures we can estimate the Jewish birth-rate at 11.6 per thousand. (See also Table VI, A.J.S.-1, p. 251.) This, of course, is a very low figure. If it is compared with an average birth-rate of 18.6 per thousand for the general population for the same years, we have a general confirmation of our earlier generalisation.

The estimated birth-rate of 11.6 seems to be confirmed by Mr. Olsover's survey of the Jews of Newcastle upon Tyne, cited above. His calculation of the birth-rate is based on the number of green ration books belonging to children from 0 to 5 years of age and handled by kasher butchers. He presumes the holders of these ration books to represent 80 per cent of the Jewish births in Newcastle during the years 1945-1950. In this way Olsover arrives at a birth-rate of 11.6 per thousand among Jews which he compares with a birth-rate of 16 per thousand for the population of the districts of Newcastle where most of the local Jews live. Reckoned on the basis of schoolchildren attending religious classes, the Jewish birth-rate is only 10.8 per thousand, but this way of estimating the birth-rate is obviously less reliable. It suffers from all the defects we discussed in dealing with the ' Yom Kippur ' method. One point, however, must be raised here, although it destroys the pleasant coincidence by which Olsover's estimate and our own both read 11.6. The holders of green ration books in 1950 are those of the total number of babies born in 1945-1950 who survived up to the latter date. They should be compared not with the number of births in the areas under consideration but with the number of children of the same age. And if this were done it remains doubtful whether this would give firm grounds for calculating the birth-rate. Possible differences between Jewish and non-Jewish death-rates would have to be taken into account. In any case, the rate of 11.6 per thousand, calculated from the green ration books, is not really congruent with our estimate for the country as a whole.

Our questionnaire A.J.S.-2, as far as it was collected in the provinces, gives 4,034 individuals and shows 294 children of the age-group 0-4 years living in the households surveyed. These again are the survivors of the babies born between 1945 and 1950. They represent an annual average of 58.8 children. The age-group therefore represents a rate of 14.6 per thousand. It is not necessary to jump to the conclusion that the earlier estimate of 11.6 per thousand must be too low. The children covered by A.J.S.-2 are not all the direct offspring of the householders enumerated ; some are grandchildren, nephews and nieces, offsprings of dissolved marriages, adopted children, and wards. However, there is also the possibility that not all births were covered by the figures in our questionnaire A.J.S.-1, and we are entitled to regard our estimate of the birth-rate at 11.6 per thousand as a moderate one. The facts that the Jewish birth-rate is lower and the size of the Jewish family smaller than those of the general population remain, nevertheless, true. The question arises whether any reasons can be suggested for these differences which accord with general theories of the birth-rate.

We must consider first the fact that Jews are an urbanised

people of whom at least six out of seven, in this country, live in towns with over 300,000 inhabitants. This can be used as an explanation only with great caution. Certainly, in general, the number of births and family size are greater in rural districts than in towns. However, the figures cited earlier for the Netherlands should make us wonder how decisive this factor is in this particular case. There is a general characteristic of rural populations which might not apply to Jews living in the countryside. Rural areas usually employ manual workers, often unskilled hands, in large numbers, while what remains of the Jewish working-class is predominantly resident just in the few big towns where the traditionally Jewish industries are located. Small wonder, then, that the Jewish birth-rate is low, since the majority of Jews nowadays belong to the class of non-manual workers, among whom birth control is much more frequent than it is lower in the social scale.[1] It is therefore natural that the average size of the Jewish family is between 3.0 and 3.4 as compared with that of the general population of 4.2. The picture may not even have been distorted too much by the omission of London in the estimate of 3.4 persons by family. The probability remains that the variation of the birth-rate with the size of the local population is almost negligible among Jews. The reasons for this phenomenon have already been gone into.

The Report of the Royal Commission on Population on Limitation of Family, 1949, was built upon the so-called ' K ' sample of 3,281 women, interviewed by hospital doctors, who were definitely not maternity cases. The total number of questionnaires filled in, however, was 10,297. We are obliged to Professor Glass[2] for information on the so-called ' M ' sample comprising the 5,082 maternity cases which were analysed in 1950 under his supervision at the London School of Economics. There is still the so-called ' remainder,' a group which has not been analysed. The ' K ' sample included 111 Jewesses and the ' M ' sample 76 ; the total of 187 Jewish women represents 2.2 per cent of the samples or more than twice the percentage we have estimated for the proportion of Jews in the total population of the country.

[1] See also *Report of the Royal Commission on Population, Family Limitation,* 1949.
[2] We are especially obliged to Professor Glass for his courtesy in obtaining for us the ' M ' sample figures ahead of the schedule of work.

It is significant that Jewish women represent a higher proportion of the non-maternity cases (3.4 per cent) among the hospital population surveyed than of the maternity cases (1.5 per cent). 64 per cent of the material was collected in London and Glasgow alone where nearly 68 of every 100 Jews reside. This fact explains the relatively high proportion of Jewish women in the sample. The Report (p. 81) also confirms that the decline of the Jewish birth-rate exceeds the fall of the general birth-rate. It shows that a higher proportion of Jewish women applied *birth control* among those married between 1920 and 1939 than was the case in any other religious group. Birth control was used by women of the ' K ' sample as follows :

Date of marriage	Percentage of Jewesses	Percentage of Roman Catholics	Percentage of others
1920-1929	83.0	35.5	62.0
1930-1939	67.0	46.0	66.3
Since 1940	46.0	39.0	58.0

The ' M ' sample analysis is at our disposal only for the period after 1930. It shows the following picture :

PERCENTAGE OF WOMEN USING BIRTH CONTROL (' M ' SAMPLE).

Date of marriage	Percentage of Jewesses	Percentage of Roman Catholics	Percentage of others
1930-1939	69.0	34.0	60.0
Since 1940	49.0	21.0	44.0

It is only in the ' K ' sample for the period after 1940 that the proportion of Jewish women using birth control is lower than that for other religious groups. It is just possible that this is a consequence of war-time conditions. The Jewish minority was affected by the general call-up at an earlier date and to a greater extent than the population as a whole, since fewer Jewish men were employed in the so-called ' reserved ' occupations, such as mining, agriculture, and the mercantile marine. Generally, the call-up in war-time leads to an increase in the number of marriages, many of which are anticipations of marriages which, under normal conditions, would have taken place later in life. During the war girls married younger and younger brides usually use birth control more sparingly. It remains to be seen in the future whether this accounts for the anomaly or whether the change will hold good in peace-time conditions. The birth-rate of the general population, in any case, has been falling again during the last few years, after having reached its peak under the influence of war and the immediate post-war demobilisation.

It is important to consider the class structure of the sample used by the Royal Commission. The sample is arranged in three social classes. The group of Class I comprises the classes I and II of the Census. At the same time the Commission transferred from the group of skilled workers to the professional group those engaged in commercial and clerical pursuits and shopkeepers and their assistants. Class III covers the Census classes IV and V and consists mainly of skilled manual workers. An abstract of the class structure of the 'M' and 'K' samples follows.

PERCENTAGE DISTRIBUTION BY SOCIAL CLASS WITHIN EACH RELIGIOUS GROUP (RELIGION OF WIFE).

'M' Sample

Social Class	R.C.	Jews	Others	None	Not stated	Total
I	10.1	35.5	15.3	14.4	34.8	15.2
II	43.3	23.7	46.1	42.8	40.6	45.3
III	46.5	40.8	38.6	42.8	24.6	39.5

This table shows that in the whole white collar group (Social Class I) the Jewish proportion is more than twice that of the total in the same category.

For the 'K' sample we quote below from table 61 of the Report.

Social Class	R.C.	Jews	Others	None	Not stated	Total
I	14.0	42.0	33.0	33.0	47.0	21.0
II	54.0	46.0	47.0	47.0	45.0	53.0
III	32.0	12.0	20.0	20.0	8.0	26.0

Here again the Jewish proportion exceeds in Class I that of the total by 100 per cent and underlines our statement that the Jewish population is a middle-class group and behaves as such in the matter of family size and birth-rate. It remains to be seen how far this class affiliation influences age at marriage, the number of marriages contracted, and all other marital questions, and whether the death-rate shows any features typical of a middle-class population.

It is obvious that *the age of women at marriage* greatly affects the fertility rate quite apart from birth control, since a woman who marries later in life has before her a shorter child-bearing period and is likely to have a lower capacity for healthy childbirth. It is therefore important to devote some attention to the age of Jewish women at marriage apart from the number of marriages contracted.

In connection with the increase of the age of women at marriage we must repeat our statement that in 1950 only one woman was married at the age of 19 among 1,667 families covered by our A.J.S.-2 sample, and this woman had no children. In earlier times, when the age of marriage was controlled by Jewish tradition, it was regarded as desirable that people marry early in life. Six mothers in our sample were nineteen years of age at the birth of their eldest child now living in the same household. They are over forty-five years old at the present time. Two of these six mothers had four children each. There was no household-family with more than four children in our sample. This seems to support our statement that the late age of Jewish women at marriage influences the birth-rate. The age at which the number of married women starts to exceed that of spinsters is between 25 and 29. For men the corresponding age is 30 to 34. Most mothers in our sample were between 25 and 29 at the birth of their first child. This fact bears out our estimate of the age at marriage, the majority of Jewish brides belonging to the same age-group. In 1929 Miron Kantorowitsch[1] reckoned the mean age of Jewish brides to be 25.76 and that of Jewish bridegrooms 29.24. (The corresponding ages for the general population were 26.56 and 29.08.) The increase in the age at marriage must have influenced considerably the decline of the Jewish birth-rate during the preceding thirty years. Of course, the higher age of men at marriage could be explained by the ascent of Jews to a higher social class, but this does not hold true for girls, who generally marry earlier the higher the social class to which they belong. In the case of women it is progressive assimilation that must be held to account for the increase in the age at marriage. The emancipation of women is utterly alien to Orthodox Jewish tradition. It was only reluctantly accepted. Assimilation and emancipation retard the age at which Jewish girls marry.[2] The trend in age at marriage among Jews and Jewesses

[1] 'Statistics of Jewish Marriage in England and Wales,' *Population*, November, 1936.
[2] We may support our remark on the discriminatory practices of the orthodox tradition by referring to a single example. It was only in 1954 that the United Synagogue, the largest association of synagogues in the country, granted a vote in their affairs to female members who paid full contributions.

seems to have been during the past half century continuously towards a later date. The conclusion we have drawn from the data provided by the A.J.S.-2 sample agrees with the results of Dr. Salaman's investigation.

Age at marriage is to some extent affected by marriages of necessity. This statement is supported by statistics of the number of months which elapse between the wedding day and the birth of the first child. Obviously not much information on this point can be expected in response to private inquiries. We may, therefore, insert some figures which refer to Amsterdam and which we take from an article on ' Population Phenomena in Amsterdam,' by J. H. van Zanden and T. van den Brink (*Population,* January, 1939). The table refers to pre-marital conception and sets forth facts which need no explanation.

RELIGION	PERCENTAGE OF FIRSTLINGS BORN		
	Within six months		After one year of
	1921-25	*1926-30*	*married life 1926-30*
Both parents Protestants	19.4	18.2	58.8
Both parents Catholics	14.9	14.4	52.7
Both parents Jews	16.1	15.9	62.5
Protestants and Catholics	33.5	31.5	47.1
The remainder	27.6	27.2	50.6

The two authors point out that ' it is noteworthy that the percentage of children born after one year in families where father and mother are of the same religion is the smallest for Roman Catholics, the greatest for the Jewish people.'

Marriage Rate

In 1934, which was the last year for which the Registrar-General made available the number of marriages solemnised by religious ceremonial, a total of 342,307 marriages took place in England and Wales. That is 17 per thousand of the population were married in that year. Of these marriages 2,233 were solemnised by a Jewish minister. If we compare the 4,466 persons so married with an estimated Jewish population for 1934 of 350,000 (based on Dr. Salaman's figure for 1914) we arrive at a rate of 13 per thousand, which seems improbable.

However, 28.4 per cent of the marriages recorded in 1934 were civil marriages, and if we were to assume that the total Jewish marriage rate was the same as that of the general population (*i.e.*, 17 per thousand) we should need to add a round figure of 700 Jewish civil marriages to those solemnised by Jewish rites. Mr. Olsover estimates the Jewish marriage rate in Newcastle to be 8.8 per thousand in comparison with a rate of 17.8 for the general population. Mr. Prais in a survey, part of which has been published in *The Jewish Monthly,* arrives at an estimate of 10.6 per thousand for Birmingham Jewry.[1] On the other hand, Kantorowitsch points out that more Jewish marriages are solemnised in London, Manchester, and Leeds taken together than could be expected from their aggregated Jewish population, and therefore presumes that Jews go to London and other large Jewish centres to be wed. We shall have, therefore, to retain the data derived from the Registrar-General's office as the basis for our conclusion and ignore local estimates.

The tables compiled by Kantorowitsch, in the article already cited, show that civil marriages during the years 1884 to 1934 increased from 26 per thousand to 28.4 per thousand. No comparable information, of course, exists for the Jews. It may, however, be possible to arrive at some indirect conclusions on the Jewish civil marriage rate. According to the Annual Report of Births, Marriages, and Deaths in England and Wales for the years 1904 and 1905, 'a considerable proportion of the civil marriages in Whitechapel took place among illiterates and nearly all the signatures by mark in London City, and a large proportion of those in Whitechapel and in Mile End Old Town, occurred in marriages of foreign Jews.' For England and Wales the proportion of civil marriages at that time was 17.9 in every hundred. There is no obvious reason why the proportion of Jewish civil marriages should have increased to a lesser extent than among the general population. Even if we assume that Jewish marital conditions were generally similar to those of the wider population the two groups, Jews and non-Jews, have quite different age structures ; and Jews, with their more rapidly decreasing birth-rate and their greater proportion of adults (partly the result of adult immigration), should be expected

[1] Mr. Prais compiled a Social Survey of Birmingham Jewry, part of which was published in *The Jewish Monthly,* of February, 1949. I am much indebted to Mr. Prais for his permission to cite the unpublished section of his survey.

to have not a lower but on the contrary a higher marriage rate than that of the general population. We must assume, therefore, that civil marriage was as common among Jews as in the general population, and, further, possibly more common. If religious considerations could not restrain Jews in 1904 from contracting civil marriages, they are much less likely to do so at the present time. Further, the increasing scale of intermarriage must play some part in the determination of the form of marriage. On the other hand, one consideration—lack of money—which may have led Jews in 1904 to dispense with a religious wedding is probably nowadays of smaller effectiveness. In 1904 the illiterates whom the Registrar-General's Report mentions were in the main destitute newcomers who could ill-afford the expenses of a ritual wedding and the well-nigh inevitable festivities which accompany it. At the present time paupers no longer form a significant element in the Jewish population. It may also be fairly assumed that no Jewish couple is likely now to be forced to forgo a ritual marriage for lack of resources, since financial help may be available in such cases. Nevertheless, we should not be justified in assuming that Jews make use of civil marriage to a smaller extent than members of other religious groups.

Of the 5,225 individuals included in the A.J.S.-2 sample, 2,789 or 53 per cent were married at the time of the inquiry, while 274 were either divorced or widowed. In other words, 58 per cent had been married at some time. If we compare the age groups 0-24, 25-54, and 55 and over for England and Wales, as they are given in the Statistical Review for the year 1949, with our A.J.S.-2 sample, males and females being taken separately, we arrive at the following statement:

	England and Wales MALES (Figures given in thousands to nearest thousand)				A.J.S.-2 MALES (Marital condition not entered: 22)			
Age	Total	Single	Married	Widowed Divorced	Total	Single	Married	Widowed Divorced
0-24	7,844	7,481	362	1	819	808	11	—
25-54	9,400	1,544	7,666	190	1,246	240	992	14
55 and over	3,995	344	2,992	659	425	30	348	47
Age unknown	—	—	—	—	97	30	61	6
Total	21,239	9,369	11,020	850	2,587	1,108	1,412	67

	PERCENTAGE				PERCENTAGE		
Age	Single	Married	Widowed Divorced		Single	Married	Widowed Divorced
0-24	95.9	4.6	—		98.6	1.4	—
25-54	16.4	81.5	2.0		19.3	79.6	1.1
55 and over	8.6	74.6	16.4		7.1	81.8	11.1
Total	44.1	51.8	4.0		42.8	54.6	2.6

England and Wales   A.J.S.-2

FEMALES   FEMALES

(Figures given in thousands to nearest thousand)   (Marital condition not entered: 27)

Age	Total	Single	Married	Widowed Divorced	Total	Single	Married	Widowed Divorced
0-24	7,571	6,795	772	4	801	745	55	1
25-54	9,737	1,661	7,613	463	1,219	187	1,001	31
55 and over	5,238	811	2,518	1,909	442	37	247	158
Age unknown	—	—	—	—	127	36	74	17
Total	22,546	9,267	10,903	2,376	2,589	1,005	1,377	207

	PERCENTAGE				PERCENTAGE		
Age	Single	Married	Widowed Divorced		Single	Married	Widowed Divorced
0-24	89.8	10.2	—		93.0	6.9	0.1
25-54	17.0	78.2	4.8		15.4	82.1	2.5
55 and over	15.5	48.1	36.4		8.4	55.9	35.7
Total	41.1	48.4	10.5		38.8	53.2	8.0

The first statement suggests that Jewish men marry later in life than their non-Jewish counterparts, but that fewer Jewish men in proportion remain bachelors, or widowed and divorced. The same holds true for Jewish women. They marry later in life than non-Jewish women, but more of them get married and fewer remain spinsters or widows and divorcées. This sample, if we may accept it, would again corroborate Dr. Salaman's statement concerning the age at marriage. It would not confirm his remark about a low figure for marriages. Obviously, it would bear out our point of view on the question of civil marriages. Since the marriage rate for the country as a whole was 17.9 in 1948, and since fewer people per thousand of the general population than among the Jews are married, the Jewish marriage rate must be higher than 17.9 and the difference between the marriage rate as computed on the basis of weddings solemnised by a minister of religion and the rate of more than 17.9 per thousand must represent civil marriages. However, some of these civil marriages will have taken place between Jews and Gentiles.

Intermarriage

The incidence of intermarriage cannot be established very easily from our sample. It is clear that Jews who are married to Christians and bring up their children as Christians are not likely to fill in a questionnaire circulated by Jewish organisations. To avoid some objections to the questionnaire, the inquiry into religion at birth was omitted from the form. We have felt that it is fair to assume that in cases where a man or woman entered himself or herself as married, but omitted information concerning his or her partner, the omitted partner was not Jewish. (The questionnaires returned from Hull have not been used for this aspect of our inquiry since lack of information on marriage partners may be the result of the fact that not all questionnaires were completed or filled in by the householders themselves.)

The reluctance to give information on mixed marriages may explain why only one man mentioned on the form that his wife and children were not Jewish. Another man stated that his wife was not Jewish before marriage. In all, 21 intermarriages were ascertained in the way described above. Fourteen Jewish men had married Christian women. Of these couples, five had brought up their children in the Jewish faith. Of seven Jewesses married to Christians, six brought up their children as Jewish. Ten of the mixed couples did not enter any children at all. This does not mean that these marriages produced no children, but it is safe to assume that, if there were children, they were not brought up as Jews.

Intermarriage, as a rule, once it has started, tends to become increasingly frequent. This is so as long as no artificial barrier is imposed, as, for instance, was the case in Nazi Germany. It is interesting to note that before the outbreak of the First World War there were in Berlin 45 mixed marriages to every 100 in which both partners were Jews. As early as 1905 the proportion had been 16 to 100.[1]

Interviews with ministers of religion and experienced representatives of Jewry in various parts of the country have shown that intermarriage at the present time has much increased. One informant, well acquainted with the Jews of London in his capacity as a communal social worker, has said: 'I cannot think of any family in which no intermarriage has taken place.'[2]

This problem of intermarriage, of great intrinsic interest, has attracted some attention. In two articles Dr. Elliot Slater has dealt with it at some length.[3] Dr. Slater bases his study of intermarriage on a sample of fifty soldier patients in a military emergency hospital in 1944-45. He tabulates information he received from his Jewish patients as follows:

Consorts of				Jewish	Non-Jewish
Fathers	...	...	...	49	1
Mothers	...	...	...	50	—
Patients	...	...	...	28	4
Brothers	...	...	...	52	12
Sisters	...	...	...	52	12
				231	29

The analysis of this table seems to indicate a rapid increase in intermarriage. While in the parent generation only one Jew has married outside the faith, in the present generation 28 of the 132 offspring of the original fifty couples have done so. Twenty-eight members of the present generation were not married at the time of the inquiry. Of the 16 male children (*i.e.*, the patients and their brothers) who had married outside the faith, 11 had children. Only 2 of the 11 families brought up their children as Jews. Of the 12 females who had married Gentiles, 4 brought up their children as Jews and 6 as Christians. We must, of course, remember that intermarriage is more frequent in some families than in others,

[1] Teilhaber, *Der Untergang der Deutschen Juden*, Munich, 1911.
[2] This is, of course, not the family consisting of father, mother, and children, but the wider family, including, for example, brothers and sisters of each parent and their offspring.
[3] 'A Note on Jewish-Christian Intermarriage,' *Eugenics Review*, vol. XXXIX, No. 1, April, 1947, and 'A Biological View on Antisemitism,' *Jewish Monthly*, November, 1949.

but it seems plausible that at the present time one in every eight marriages contracted by Jews is with a non-Jewish partner. This is the proportion arrived at by Dr. Slater for the year 1947 (after the elimination from his sample of one family with nine inter-marriages).

Of the fifty Jewish soldier patients, only seventeen rejected the idea of a mixed marriage outright. Ten had some hesitation, but did not raise insuperable objections. Twenty-three had no objections at all.

An imaginary experiment will show how intermarriage may affect the Jewish population if we use the conclusions drawn from Dr. Slater's figures. According to his investigation, one in every six marriages involving Jews is mixed.[1] If we take no account of the decreasing birth-rate and neglect the fact that the average number of children in a Jewish family is less than two, and if we disregard moreover the probability that the rate of intermarriage will increase during the next two generations, we may estimate the effect of intermarriage on the Jewish population after two generations. If we assume 60 couples in which there has been no intermarriage and which produce two children each who grow to maturity and in turn produce two children, the grandchild generation will number 240. If, however, ten of the 60 couples are mixed, and 75 per cent of their children are lost to Jewry, at a constant intermarriage rate of 17 per hundred marriages, after two generations only 183 children would be left to Jewry. In other words, there would be a loss of about 25 per cent. Since, however, the size of the Jewish family is less than four persons on the average, and the inter-marriage rate is steadily increasing, the cumulative effect of these two factors must necessarily result in a far greater loss. It is even possible that as much as half the Jewish population might have to be written off within two generations as a result of intermarriage alone.

Up to half a century ago intermarriage seems to have been more common in the higher social strata, but at the present time it appears more frequent at the lower class levels. The barriers to friendly intercourse between Jews and Gentiles at this end of the

[1] This figure covers the whole sample before eliminating the family mentioned above.

social scale seem to have been greatly reduced, and it is from Jews of lower socio-economic status that the drift from Jewry through intermarriage is possibly the strongest. In addition, intermarriage appears to have become especially frequent in the smaller towns and rural areas. Mixed marriages may well be the consequence of progressive anglicisation and the dispersion of the older centres of Jewry, but such a proposition, although in keeping with the logic of the situation, cannot be statistically validated.[1]

The low figure for intermarriage derived from the A.J.S.-2 sample does not contradict these statements. Contrary to Dr. Slater's findings, most of the mixed marriages which have led to the Christianising of their offspring have not been entered at all. In Dr. Slater's example marriages of this last kind are the majority of all mixed marriages, while 14 per cent of the mixed marriages were childless. In our sample 43 per cent of all the marriages taken to be mixed appear to be without children. The difference between these two percentages certainly suggests that, apart from the cases in which information was withheld altogether, many mixed marriages are given as childless when, in fact, there are children who are being reared as non-Jews.

The incidence of intermarriage in other countries can be documented from *Canada's Jews*,[2] from which we may take a table which is itself, with the exception of the Canadian figures, based on data given by Ruppin in *Jews in the Modern World* (1934).

For every 100 Jews entering marriage, mixed marriages were contracted as follows:

Country	Year	Jews	Jewesses
Germany	1930	26.60	17.60
Holland (Amsterdam)	1928-30	17.03	12.49
Hungary	1929	12.04	11.90
European Russia	1924-26	7.41	6.21
Canada	1931	2.74	1.63
Latvia	1930	1.96	1.96

It should be noted that, except in the case of Latvia, Jewish men marry out more frequently than Jewish women. This

[1] But see p. 153.
[2] Louis Rosenberg, *op. cit.*

95

material and the analysis of the A.J.S.-2 sample show the same bias. The fact that Amsterdam is mentioned separately in the table should not be taken to imply that the larger communities of Jews show an especially high rate of intermarriage. On the contrary, in small communities, where the range of choice of Jewish partners is restricted, the incidence of intermarriage cannot be expected to be smaller.

In his survey, ' Trends of the Jewish Population in Germany, 1910-39,'[1] Erich Rosenthal points out that the proportion of married men was somewhat larger, and the proportion of married women somewhat smaller in the Jewish than in the general population of Germany. This suggests, he concludes, ' (1) a higher percentage of widows in the Jewish group,' or ' (2) a higher proportion of Jewish husbands than Jewish wives in mixed marriages.' The latter conclusion is in line with our own.

Stanley R. Braw in his investigation of the Jewish community of Vicksburg, Mississippi, which forms about 1 per cent of the total population of some 30,000, records 38 marriages during the decade 1937-46, in which at least one partner was Jewish.[2] Three of these marriages involved new converts to Judaism, while eleven were mixed marriages in which each partner retained his or her own religion. Mr. Braw emphasises the difficulty that Jews have in finding suitable partners of their own religion in so small a community. Only 10 per cent of the members of the local community married within that community and twice as many Jewish men as Jewish women were partners in marriages out of Jewry. This appears to bear out our earlier remarks on the relationship between the size of the community and the intermarriage rate. Dr. Slater[3] cites a study by E. W. Burgess and P. Wallin, ' Homogamy in Social Characteristics ' (*American Journal of Sociology,* 1949, p. 109), in which the authors analysed 941 engaged U.S.A. couples among whom there were 177 Jews and 185 Jewesses. Only 17 per cent of these 362 Jewish people were engaged to coreligionists. This is an extraordinary case, which is scarcely comparable to anything in the Anglo-Jewish situation, but it may serve as a pointer to future events. Dr. Slater himself

[1] *Jewish Social Studies,* July, 1944, vol. VI, No. 3, pp. 233 *et seq.*
[2] ' Sampling Jewish Marriages,' *Jewish Social Studies,* 1948, vol. X, No. 1, pp. 71 *et seq.*
[3] ' A note on Jewish-Christian Intermarriage,' *op. cit.*

rightly comes to the conclusion that ' a corresponding rate of inter-marriage would lead to the practical disappearance of the Jews as an endogamous group within two generations.' However, even on the basis of present-day conditions, we must abandon notions of the Anglo-Jewish community as an inbreeding group, and recognise the significance of mixed marriages as a factor in the shaping of its future.

Age Structure

Another matter to be considered in this respect is the age structure of Anglo-Jewry. It is, of course, impossible to establish the facts of age distribution accurately. The following table compares the age structure of the Jewish population of Greater London, in 1929-33, as it appears in Kantorowitsch's estimates based on burial figures ; the distribution which we derive from the A.J.S.-2 sample for the country as a whole in 1950 ; and the age structure of the total population of England and Wales in 1948 (taken from *Whitaker's Almanack*, 1950).

Age Group	England and Wales 1948	A.J.S.-2 Sample 1950	Jewish Population London 1929-1933
0-4	8.3	8.1	4.7
5-14	13.0	12.3	13.9
15-24	13.7	12.2	17.7
25-34	15.1	13.6	17.2
35-44	15.8	19.5	14.2
45-54	12.9	16.6	15.0
55-64	10.1	9.9	10.6
65-74		6.4 ⎱ 8.0	5.1 ⎱ 6.3
75 and over	10.6	1.6 ⎰	1.2 ⎰

Of course, both sets of figures for Jewish populations are of doubtful value, but there may possibly be one point at which they have some significance. Kantorowitsch's sample for 1929-33 shows a remarkable swelling of the age group 15-34, while the 1950 sample shows a similar abnormality in the group 35-54. This would seem to agree with our earlier remarks on the falling birth-rate and its influence on the size and age structure of the Jewish population. Survivors of the higher birth-rate of earlier days distort the ideal age pyramid which would follow from a constant or increasing

H

birth-rate. These figures also suggest that the Jewish death-rate can be expected to become higher than that of the general population. However, one must not overlook the contribution which immigration (predominantly adult) has made to the distortion of the age structure.

Death-Rate

There are naturally many difficulties in the way of assessing the death-rate among Jews in this country. The reluctance of many Jewish burial societies to part with information is not the only obstacle. In the first place, even if the burial figures were available, there would remain the problem of the totals with which to compare them. For Jews who live in small communities may, when they die, be buried in the grounds of another community.

Thirty-five of the 55 communities which replied to questionnaire A.J.S.-1 entered figures for births and deaths which came to their notice for the five years 1945-49. Together these communities represent 15,928 individuals, or $3\frac{1}{2}$ per cent of our total population estimate. Thirteen of these 35 communities show death-rates which are higher than birth-rates. This may be due to the fact that non-residents were buried in the local Jewish cemetery and included in the death figures. Alternatively, this state of affairs might be explained by the fact that the records of death are more accurate than those of births, or by the residence of an unusually high proportion of elderly people in the locality concerned. It may, of course, be that all these three factors have worked together.

On the other hand, not all Jews are buried in Jewish cemeteries. Some are cremated. Birmingham is the only place for which we have information on this last matter. The Birmingham community recorded 359 burials and 24 cremations for the five years under review. If we compute the death-rate among Jews in Birmingham on the basis of the burial figures alone (taking the total population to be 5,500) we arrive at the rate of 13.0 per thousand. If we include the figure for cremations, this rate increases to 13.9 per thousand. Lack of information concerning cremations, therefore, may throw out estimates of the death-rate quite seriously. Of course, one may not assume that the ratio of cremations to ritual burials will be lower in bigger centres such as London. On the contrary, we may take it that proportionally more Jews are cremated in London than in the provinces and 65 per cent of the Jews of the country live in London To stress the vagueness of the information available, we may add here the results obtained by Mr. Prais in his survey of Birmingham Jewry.[1] He reckons a death-rate of 11.7 per thousand, taking the population at 6,300. If we accept his statement that for every 70 Jews buried, three are cremated, the death-rate increases to 12.2. This is higher than the death-rate of 11.6 computed by Mr. Olsover for Newcastle upon Tyne. Without the cremations Mr. Prais's estimate is almost the same as Mr. Olsover's. These death-rates compare with a birth-rate of 11.6 per thousand given by Mr. Olsover and 11.3 per thousand by Mr. Prais. In this way even the lower death-rate of 11.7 for Birmingham still exceeds birth-rates, supporting the estimates of the 13 communities mentioned above which returned death-rates higher than birth-rates. The details are set out as follows:

| | Average 1945-1949 number of | | Total Population as stated |
	Births	Deaths	in Questionnaire
Aberavon	0.2	0.4	44
Birmingham (including cremations)	51.6	76.6	5,500
Bristol	2.0	3.2	410
Cambridge	0.8	1.6	200
Chester	0.6	0.8	30
Derby	1.0	2.4	205
Eastbourne	0.6	1.0	60
Harrogate	3.6	4.8	385
Hull	15.0	25.0	2,000
Plymouth	4.6	7.4	350
Pontypridd	0.2	2.0	110
West Hartlepool	0.6	0.8	80
Whitley Bay	2.0	3.0	175

These figures show considerably higher proportions of deaths than births, especially in Aberavon, Birmingham, Cambridge, Derby, Hull, and Plymouth, and therefore support our previous conclusion. It is not difficult to see that the considerable decline in the birth-rate during the last three decades, and the decreasing average size of the family, must lead to a point where the number of elderly people by far exceeds that of the lower and middle age-

[1] S. J. Prais, *Social Survey of Birmingham Jewry* (unpublished).

groups. The low birth-rate of today cannot make up for the high death-rate brought about by the peculiar weighting in the age structure.

There was a time, during the last decade of the nineteenth century and the first decade of the twentieth, when the Jewish death-rate was definitely lower than that of the general population. In spite of the overcrowding and the bad living conditions in which the majority of the Jews in the East End of London and other poor districts existed, at the beginning of the century the Jewish infant mortality rate was surprisingly low. There may have been several reasons for this state of affairs, most of them bound up with the traditionally high standards of child care among Jews. Presumably, since this time, the difference between the mortality rates of the Jewish and the general population has been severely reduced, if not eliminated. We may expect, therefore, that the Jewish population will not only decrease absolutely, but will decrease at a faster rate than the total population of the country.

The death-rate calculated on the basis of the information provided by 41 communities replying to Questionnaire A.J.S.-1 (including the 13 communities already referred to) is 13.2 per thousand, a figure which may be compared with the average death-rate for the general population during the years 1945-49 of 12.0 per thousand.[1] The birth-rate as established from the information given by 36 communities is 11.6 per thousand, compared with 18.6 per thousand for the general population for the years 1945-48. The death-rate of 13.2 per thousand should be compared with the rates estimated by Mr. Olsover for Newcastle (11.6 per thousand) and Mr. Prais for Birmingham (11.7 per thousand). It is difficult to judge whether these estimates are nearer the mark than those derived from the analysis of our questionnaire. There is, of course, the probability that their results are more reliable, but even their figures still leave the balance in favour of the death-rate.

The figures provided by various burial societies do not furnish any basis for a calculation of the death-rate, since we are generally not in a position to relate burial figures to relevant populations. In one case, however, we are able to remedy this deficiency. The United Synagogue has enabled us to establish figures for burials

[1] See also Table VIII, A.J.S.-1, Appendix, p. 252.

100

of its members and dependants of its members during a period of four years, 1946-49, when the average membership during those years was approximately 28,000, of whom the male members are assumed by the organisation to have on the average two dependants and the females none. The proportion of males and fully paying females in the membership is estimated to be one female to seven males. This means that since in the four years 717 members and dependants were buried each year on the average, and the membership consisted of 24,446 males with two dependants each (or 73,338) and 3,554 females, the total with which the 717 burials should be compared is 76,892. This produces a death-rate of 9.3 per thousand. This death-rate would allow a birth-rate excess of 2.3 per thousand and, realising that this is the only authoritative information we have obtained on the death-rate, we might be somewhat more optimistic concerning the numerical future of Anglo-Jewry. Of course, the membership of the United Synagogue is not fully representative of Anglo-Jewry as a whole. It may be assumed that the members of the United Synagogue belong mainly to the better-off elements of the middle-class and have a disproportionate element of long-established Jews.

Even if we were to accept this information as completely reliable we should still have to realise that there is a possibility that the birth-rate of the future may not be kept up to the level of the period 1945-49 which was inflated by post-war influences. It should be noted also that the death-rate of 9.3 per thousand is lower than that of the general population for the years 1945-48 which was 11.9 per thousand. Therefore, even if we accept this Jewish death-rate, we have no reason for undue optimism.

As for the Federation of Synagogues, we have the information that their total membership is 14,600. The number of burials to be correlated with this figure (plus dependants) is the average of 510 per annum for the five years 1946-50. The number of dependants per member is probably greater and the proportion of female members perhaps lower than in the membership of the United Synagogue, since we may assume that the membership of the Federation belongs to a lower economic class and maintains a more traditionally restrictive attitude towards the participation of women in communal affairs. If, however, for the sake of argument, we make the same assumptions in the case of Federation membership as were made earlier for the membership of the United Synagogue, we should arrive at the following results. Male members with their dependants would number 37,548 and female members 2,086 making a total of 39,634. These figures yield a death-rate of 12.9 per thousand. This figure comes very much nearer to the death-rate of 13.2 calculated from the information received from the provincial communities. It also approaches the death-rate of the general population of 11.9 for the years 1945-48. However, it is probable that even this death-rate is too low an estimate, since in the United Synagogue and the Federation of Synagogues, in addition to fully paying female members, there are a number of women who do not fully pay, which fact must reduce the number of members with two dependants each and increase the number of members without dependants, and so considerably decrease the total figure which has to be compared with the incidence of death. There is one further striking difference in the Jewish burial records from the death figures for the population as a whole. During the last hundred years the male death ratio of the general population has been steadily increasing and so consequently the proportion of females in the population, but this high death-rate of males is accounted for by the greater number of boys than girls at birth. The deficiency of males in the age-groups from 35 years upwards is balanced by the higher birth-rate of males. The excess of males over females in the age-groups 0-34 decreases rapidly in the higher age-groups as the higher male mortality rate turns the balance in the favour of females. From age-group 35 onwards there are more women than men. In the United Kingdom in the years 1936 to 1940, there were for every hundred female deaths the following male deaths:

Age Group	No. of Male Deaths
35-44	129
45-54	147
55-64	152
65-74	136
75-84	130
85 and over	113

For all age-groups, male deaths were in the ratio of 126 to 100 female deaths.

Comparative burial figures for males and females in various Jewish communities are set out in the following table:

FIVE YEARS' TOTAL OF BURIALS

	Males	Females	Males per 100 Females
United Synagogue	3,796	3,286	115
Federation of Synagogues	1,885	1,868	101
Belfast	66	31	213
Bournemouth	58	31	187
Bradford	21	16	131
Bristol	9	11	82
Dundee	3	3	100
Edinburgh	63	50	126
Glasgow	35	17	206
Grimsby	20	8	250
Manchester Communal Burial Board	133	111	120
Manchester Central Synagogue	244	251	97
Manchester Jewish Burial Society	48	43	112
Manchester Rainsough Hebrew Joint Burial Society	354	315	112
Newport	8	9	89
Norwich	6	4	150
Ramsgate	10	13	77
Stockport	6	9	67
Swansea	20	18	111
Total	6,785	6,094	111

Five of the 19 burial grounds report an excess of female burials over males, but of these five only the Manchester Central Burial Board gives a sample large enough to be regarded as representative. Eliminating these five burial grounds we arrive at the following statement:

	Males	Females	Males per 100 Females
Grimsby	20	8	250
Belfast	66	31	213
Glasgow	35	17	206
Bournemouth	58	31	187
Norwich	6	4	150
Bradford	21	16	131
Edinburgh	63	50	126
Manchester Communal Burial Ground	133	111	120

	Males	Females	Males per 100 Females
United Synagogue	3,796	3,286	115
Manchester Jewish Burial Society	48	43	112
Rainsough Hebrew Joint Burial Board	354	315	112
Swansea	20	18	111
Federation of Synagogues	1,885	1,868	101
Dundee	3	3	100
Total	6,508	5,801	112

It is difficult to explain why the Jewish female death-rate in comparison with the male death-rate is so much higher than in the general population. In his survey of Newcastle, Mr. Olsover states that the number of men who died was exactly twice the number of women. The same is true of Belfast, where the ratio was 213 to 100, and of Glasgow, which shows a ratio of 206 to 100 : but these figures are too small to be significant. The larger burial records, especially those of the London burial societies, show a much lower male ratio (101 to 100 and 115 to 100) than that of the general population of the United Kingdom (126 to 100).

One possible clue to the reason for lower Jewish male mortality is the fact that London shows the greatest deviation from the national norm, and, further, that within London the records of the Federation of Synagogues show this deviation more strongly than those of the United Synagogue. Between 1933 and 1939 London absorbed a greater proportion of the Jewish immigration than other parts of the country. Twenty thousand of the 30,000 people naturalised between 1938 and 1948 lived in London. The Report of the Jewish Refugee Committee states that of every 100 people to arrive in the country, 55 were females and 32 males, the remaining 13 being children evenly distributed in sex. This means that for every 100 adult males arriving in the country there were 172 adult females, if we disregard the children. If we include the children, the ratio still remains 160 females to 100 males. (The surplus of female arrivals was caused by the fact that women were in a better position to obtain entry visas on the basis of domestic permits.)

The still greater discrepancy shown in the male death ratio in the records of the Federation of Synagogues may be due to the fact that its burial society runs a scheme for small contributors which may have been an attraction to a disproportionate number of refugees and therefore to a disproportionate number of females. However, there is another possible reason for the anomaly.

The constant excess of the number of male deaths over female deaths is only possible because more boys are born than girls. As soon as the total number of births decreases, we may expect a reduced excess of the male sex in the lower age-groups. The death-rates for the two sexes below the age of 34 must in this way more and more approach one another. The higher age-groups, however, remain as they were during the phases of greater fertility of which they are the survivors. These facts may account for the higher female death ratio among Jews. Because of the more rapid fall of the Jewish birth-rate[1] in comparison with the general birth-rate there is little or no preponderance of the male sex in the lower age-groups, and consequently the ratio of male deaths is lower also in those age-groups. This fact makes the Jewish female death-rate higher in comparison with the Jewish male death-rate than the ratio of the comparable death-rates in the general population. The higher female death figures are increased by the disproportionate influx of female refugees, but more important still is the decreasing number of births. Here again a fact which emerges from information obtained from burial records supports conclusions we have already drawn from other material. The structure of the Jewish population reflects the falling birth-rate, which is at present even lower than that of the general population.

Reproduction Rate

In the long run, the reproduction rate[2] is decisive for the maintenance of a population. This means that the population can remain constant only as long as for every married female in the child-bearing age of one generation another female is produced and gets

[1] The higher male mortality ratios reported for Belfast and Glasgow agree with the greater average size of the family recorded there. Small as these samples are, they suggest a consistent demographic pattern.

[2] For technical reasons, it might be preferable to use the term *replacement rate* instead of *reproduction rate* in this context ; but since the sources which we use here employ the latter term, it has seemed convenient to retain it.

married in the next generation. Clearly, even if the average family consists of four persons this condition is not necessarily fulfilled. Not all children survive until a marriageable age ; not all people get married when they reach that age ; not all married couples produce children. It may be assumed, therefore, that three children per family is the minimum number needed to keep the population stationary. Here again we may be permitted to draw some inferences from Jewish communities abroad.

We refer again to Mr. Greenberg's study of the families of Jewish students at the University of Maryland.[1] Of the 161 students who furnished information, all but three came from urban families. Most families were considered complete. There were no mothers under 35, and only ten per cent between 35 and 38 years of age. The fathers and mothers of the 161 students had produced 424 children, of whom 17 had died. These 424 children represented an average of 2.6 per family or 2.5 survivors under the age of 20. Mr. Greenberg reckons that ten per cent will remain single, that 15 per cent will remain childless, and that some, of course, will die before the age of marriage. In this way he calculates the reproduction rate to be 87 per cent.

In Chicago in 1930 the deficit in the reproduction rate of Jews was one-third. Jewish mothers (completed families) of Buffalo, New London, Norwich, and Pasgaio had 2.2 to 2.6 children (average of 2.4) with a reproduction rate of 80 per cent.

In nine other American cities, including Chicago, with a Jewish population of half a million, the reproduction rate was 59 per cent in the 1940s. The situation in Canada, as seen in the 1941 Census, was similar. Mr. Mortimer Spiegelman has made an exhaustive study of " Reproductivity of Jews in Canada, 1940 to 1942," published in *Population Studies,* December, 1950.

He reckons that the net reproduction rate for Jewish women (on the basis of their fertility in comparison with their mortality) was 0.65 in 1941 to 1942, and that of the entire female population 1.27. He estimates the gross reproduction rate at 0.68 for Jewish females and 1.42 for all Canadian females. He stresses the factors which influence the birth-rate in any community to be ' broadly speaking, without losing sight of their interdependence . . . biologi-

[1] See Note 2, p. 81.

cal, socio-economic, and psychological in nature.' Among the biological factors he emphasises the importance of the proportion of people at the reproductive ages, the proportion of these men and women who are married, and the sex ratio in this age-group. There are proportionally more women in the age-group above the child-bearing age among Jews than in the general population. This is partly due to the fact that many are foreign-born and have arrived in Canada as adults, have married later in life, and are concentrated in the later reproductive and higher age-groups. Although the sex ratio among Jews is more balanced than that of the total population of Canada, and 99 per cent of all Jewish women over the age of 64 have been married at some time in their life (in comparison with 89 per cent in the general population), the Jewish birth-rate is smaller.

The socio-economic reasons for this state of affairs are that Jews are, to a great extent, residents in towns of over 30,000 inhabitants ; that they undergo longer schooling, which means a later start in earning a living and setting up in married life ; and that they are largely engaged in occupations which have the smallest family size. There was, Spiegelman states, ' no material to ascertain whether Jews in any occupation have smaller families than their neighbours.'

Since we must treat the capacity of any population to reproduce itself biologically as of chief importance in the prediction of future trends, we shall now turn to a calculation of the reproduction rate of Anglo-Jewry on the basis of Greenberg's methods.

Information obtained from answers to our questionnaire A.J.S.-1 gives us the basis for estimating the average size of the Jewish family in this country at 3.4 persons. This means 1.4 children per family instead of the 3 required to keep the size of the population stationary. From this figure we arrive at a reproduction rate of 46 per cent ; in other words, there is a deficit of 54 per cent. Our questionnaire A.J.S.-2 in the information it provides on married females of this generation, i.e., under 45 years of age, gives an even lower reproduction rate. Since the number of children in this sample covers mainly those who live with their parents in the same house-holds, and some of the families analysed are obviously not yet completed, we shall here concentrate on the information collected from the A.J.S.-1 sample. A deficit of 54 per cent, if maintained constantly for some generations, would inevitably lead to the obliteration of Anglo-Jewry, the age structure of which holds out little prospect of a change in the direction of increased fertility. The numerically stronger age-groups are those which are past the child-bearing age. The younger generations have for more than half a century failed to show any desire to increase the size of their families beyond that of the preceding generation. Nor must we underrate the importance of a steadily increasing intermarriage rate. We have no material on the extent to which conversion has influenced the numerical strength of the community, but it must be considered as one further possible factor diminishing the Jewish population of this country.

Unless the trend prevailing today in the Jewish birth-rate undergoes a profound change, or a more fertile Jewish stock is added to the community by immigration from outside, the future of Anglo-Jewry is very seriously threatened.

Social and Economic Data

The final sections of this study touch upon certain religious, cultural, and economic aspects of Anglo-Jewry. The first question that springs to mind is the extent to which the foreign element in the community can be said to be of importance. This is by no means a simple problem. In the first place, it must be remembered that foreignness in Anglo-Jewry may have several sources, and they are not easily disentangled. Another difficulty arises in the definition of 'foreign' itself. At what point can assimilation be said to remove immigrants from the status of foreigner ? It is clear that assimilation is not a uniform process in which all individuals move at a steady rate. Some immigrants may pass on the habits and traditions of the land of their birth to their English-born offspring ; others may seek to strip themselves of their foreignness as soon as they arrive on English soil. An important factor in the maintenance of foreign ways is a steady stream of immigrants from one source over a considerable span of time. Similarly, the motivation of migration must influence the extent to which newcomers assimilate. Those who arrive without intending to make the new country a permanent home will be less likely to abandon old ways of thinking and behaving. Furthermore, the external resistances to the integration of the minority group into the wider community may vary over time and make the process of assimilation uneven.

When, in what follows, we refer to 'foreign' influences and 'foreign' elements we shall on the whole be speaking of first-generation immigrants (*i.e.*, foreign-born Jews). It is only with such a definition that we can here take account of foreignness at various periods of Anglo-Jewish history and place it on a reasonable numerical basis.

In 1911 the foreign section of the community was large enough to exercise an important influence on Jewish affairs. We have already referred to the issue of 30,000 census schedules printed in Yiddish in that year, and to the implication that these would seem to have for the unassimilated nature of a large section of the community.[1] Even if these 30,000 householders were not all newcomers, they and their families represented about half the Jewish population, a division of Anglo-Jewry distant in culture from the old-established core of Jewry in Britain. This large unassimilated block differed in language, in social and economic status, and in religious tradition. In that it originated from the Eastern European ghetto world, it was in itself a fairly homogeneous group. Its members spoke Yiddish, practised Ashkenazi Judaism, and economically fell into the class of unskilled and semi-skilled workers (whatever their occupations might have been before emigration). As they had done in ghetto conditions, so here in Britain they brought up large families. Obviously, during the past 40 years their situation has changed drastically. The generation of their children has participated widely in the general English environment, although most of them have grown up in more or less orthodox homes and received some sort of Jewish education. English has become their only mother tongue. They have moved up in the social scale. The lack of working-class consciousness among Jews[2] has been one of the factors making for this social

[1] See p. 63 above.
[2] It is this lack of working-class consciousness which made the Jewish trade union movement unsuccessful. As every Jewish labourer desired to

ascent, but the process of assimilation was greatly helped by the fact that this particular form of immigration came to an end with the outbreak of the First World War.

The 60,000 newcomers who settled in this country between 1933 and 1939 were of a quite different category from the pre-1914 arrivals. They were Central Europeans who did not originate from an exclusively Jewish environment. In religious observance and outlook they were by no means homogeneous ; generally speaking, they were far from orthodox. The majority of them had already gone through a process of assimilation and had only loose ties with traditional Judaism. As a result, their birth-rate was small, their fertility low, and the average size of their families small ; so that in these demographic ways they resembled the assimilated Jews of Britain. Their language was not a specifically Jewish language. In their native country they had been members of the middle and upper middle classes, a high proportion of them being members of the professions. In their new setting they formed a small minority ; for there was only one of them for every seven already established British Jews. These were some of the factors that led to their quick absorption into English life and their assimilation at a much faster rate than that of earlier arrivals.

Assimilation is not, of course, easy to measure. The only aspect of it on which we are able to produce numerical data is that of nationality. Questionnaire A.J.S.-2 deals with nationality at birth and current nationality.[1] Our sample covers 5,225 Jewish individuals, of whom 192, or less than 4 per cent, were not British at the time of our inquiry. This proportion is so small that it cannot stand comparison with the group of 30,000 householders who received Yiddish census schedules in 1911. Of the 192 foreign Jews in the sample, 109 were females, some of whom had retained their original nationality after marriage to British Jews. Of the 83 males, only 49 were in the age-group 20 to 40 years. Eight hundred and one individuals in the sample were of foreign birth, which

become—or, failing this, to see his offspring become—a master of his craft, his interests were from the beginning divided between the sides of employees and employers. Owing to this attitude only one Jewish trade union, affiliated to the Trades Union Congress, has survived, i.e., the London Jewish Bakers' Union with a membership of 100.

[1] See Appendix, A.J.S.-2, Table IX, p. 252.

again gives a ratio of one in seven. However, the coincidence of this ratio with the ratio of new immigrants during the years 1933 to 1939 is misleading, since most of the foreign-born Jews in our sample were of Eastern European origin. The age-groups to which the foreign-born Jews belong confirms the belief that their influence on Anglo-Jewish life cannot last for long. As far as we can tell from vital statistics this foreign element is now of no demographic significance.[1]

Synagogue Membership

'A Study of Churchgoers' carried out by Mass Observation for, and published by, *The British Weekly*, in the issues of January 6th, 13th, 20th, and 27th, and February 3rd and 10th, 1949, deals with religious attendance. In the issue of January 20th it states that '. . . in the last year and a half polls [*i.e.*, public opinion polls] published in the *Daily Graphic, News Review, News Chronicle*, and *Daily Express*. . . . ' had all given 'figures for the percentage who go regularly to church in this country and in all the cases the figure has been in the region of 15 to 20 per cent.' In the January 6th issue we find that Mr. Seebohm Rowntree stated in an article published by the *Observer* in July, 1948, that 'even between 1935 and 1947 percentages represented by a census of persons over 16 attending the churches of York had fallen from 17.7 to not significantly over 10 per cent.'[2] For this survey we can neglect the exact proportion and confine ourselves to the statement that active interest in religion exists among only a small minority in this country. If assimilation is as complete among Jews in this

---

[1] The survey of the families of Jewish students at the University of Maryland gives 68 children per hundred foreign-born mothers and 64 children per hundred native-born mothers. An excellent survey by Grethe Hartmann and Fini Schlesinger *Physical and Mental Stress and Consequential Development of Arteriosclerosis*, Copenhagen, 1952 (p. 45), which deals with the Jewish population in Denmark, states that in 1921 among Russian Jews there were 3.04 children at home per marriage, while the corresponding figure for established Danish Jewish families was 1.59. Such obvious consequences in biological trends of a foreign tradition can no longer be assessed for Anglo-Jewry.

[2] When introducing a Sunday Observance Bill in the House of Commons on January 30th, 1952, Mr. John Parker, M.P., stated that of all countries in Northern and Western Europe, leaving out Scotland and Wales, church attendance was lowest in England ; in London under 10 per cent of the population attended a service on any Sunday.

country as one is inclined to believe, then religious attitudes and practices must have changed in this minority group during the past half century as they have changed in the general population. However, the extent to which religion has lost its grip on Anglo-Jewry is extremely difficult to assess.

Even in countries where religion is inquired into in the census, the information so obtained does not give a true index of the strength of religious activity. It is important where Jews are concerned to look into the question of synagogue organisation, for it is about the synagogue that Jewish religious life turns. The Rev. Dr. A. Cohen, President of the Board of Deputies, estimates synagogue membership in this country at around 50,000.[1] We may assume that two-thirds of the total Anglo-Jewish population of 450,000 (*i.e.,* those over 25 years old) are potential synagogue members. We must presume, however, that the ratio of female to male membership is only about 1 : 7. If for the sake of argument we accept Dr. Cohen's figure and assume that there are about 7,000 female members and moreover that the two sexes are evenly distributed within the Jewish population, we can compare 43,000 male synagogue members with 150,000 males of the age-group from which membership is recruited. In other words, little more than one quarter of Jewish men are members of synagogues.

In an address to the Jewish Historical Society of England, Dr. V. D. Lipman stated that in 1857, when the Jews in Great Britain numbered 35,000 there were 6,000 synagogue seatholders.[2] If we may take it that in 1857 only men were members, and that the age and sex structures were the same as they are today, then at that time synagogue members represented more than fifty per cent of the male adult population. Furthermore, we need to remember that some potential members at that time were prevented from holding seats by virtue of their poverty, and that indirect membership was also greater at that time because of the larger size of families. If we look at our numerical material from another angle, we can see

[1] *The Jewish Chronicle,* 28.4.50. But see page 230 below for a higher estimate for the year 1954. Dr. Cohen's figure may refer to fully paid membership, which is known to be less than total membership. Alternatively the figure of 80,000 on p. 230 may include holders of temporary tickets for High Holy-days.

[2] *The Jewish Chronicle,* 21.7.50.

that while the Jewish population had increased about thirteenfold, synagogue membership has multiplied only eightfold. If we assume that the membership figure for 1857 contains no females, the increase has been only sevenfold.

We must also take into account some evident duplication of synagogue membership at the present time. It is known, for example, that people who have moved away from the East End of London, while becoming members of synagogues in their new neighbourhood, still retain their old membership in an East End synagogue for sentimental reasons. As we cannot quantify this duplication, it enters as a factor of unknown size to inflate present-day synagogue membership.[1]

An article in *The Jewish Chronicle* (6.10.50) entitled ' Holy-Day Appeals in Synagogues ' tells of a Day of Atonement sermon in which the complaint was made that members attend synagogue only on New Year and the Day of Atonement ; that it is difficult to assemble a *minyan* on the Sabbath and at festivals, absence being due to the fact that members work on these days. It is worth stressing that these remarks refer to synagogue members, that is to say, to that quarter of the community which is still formally linked to the religious centres of Jewish communal life. Many such complaints are heard, especially in the East End of London where one would have thought that Jewish tradition was likely to be most strongly maintained.

Dietary Laws

The information we have been able to bring together on the observance of dietary laws serves as a further indication of the decline in the strength of religious tradition. In Greater London, with a Jewish population of between 280,000 and 290,000, only 161,000 individuals were registered with kasher butchers in 1950.[2] This figure

[1] Trends and developments within the global synagogue membership are omitted here, since the religious and other organisations of the community are dealt with elsewhere in this book.

[2] It is interesting to note that at a meeting of the Jewish Historical Society on May 18th, 1953, the Chief Rabbi gave 190,000 as the figure for kasher meat registration in this country. In a Jewish population of 450,000 this figure would give a percentage of Jews registered for kasher meat somewhat lower than arrived at on the basis of the data in the text.

I

was cited by the *Evening Standard* (in ' The Londoner's Diary ') of May 19th, 1950. In considering its significance we must realise, in the first place, that the total population figure includes persons (such as children in institutions and those serving with the forces) who cannot be individually registered at butchers. And, of course, there are other reservations to be made.

In an interview with Mr. Brenner, the Secretary of the Board for Shechita, which is responsible for the supervision of ritual slaughtering and the distribution of kasher meat, the following important points were made:

(1) Some non-Jews were in fact registered with kasher butchers. Their number is not known.

(2) In 1950, in the London area there were 300 kasher butchers and 75 kasher poulterers. Of these, 30 per cent were in the East End and 60 per cent in North London (half of whom were in the Stamford Hill area), while the remaining 10 per cent were in Woolwich, Richmond, Ilford, and the West End. The distribution of kasher butchers does not follow closely the distribution of the Jewish population of London, since there is a tendency for people who move from one district to another to continue to shop in the same place.

Such considerations should make us wary of estimating local Jewish communities on the basis of numbers registered with kasher butchers. Mr. Olsover, however, seems to have used this method with success in checking his estimates of the Jewish population of Newcastle. He assumes that 20 per cent of Newcastle Jewry were not registered with kasher butchers. The much larger proportion of London Jews similarly unaccounted for is not a clear index of the extent to which observance of the dietary laws has declined locally. Quite apart from the registration of non-Jews and the registration of Jews outside their locality, which may in some degree cancel one another out, there is a further fact which reduces the significance of such registrations. It is a well-known characteristic of Jews on the fringe of orthodoxy that, while they keep kasher kitchens at home, they often take food indifferently at both Jewish and non-Jewish restaurants. It follows that the figure of 161,000 is likely to be greater than the true figure which expresses the present-day scale of acceptance of orthodox dietary laws among London Jews. To say that half of the Jews of Britain abided strictly by these laws would be an exaggeration.

Other Religious Factors

Other facts pointing to the attenuation of tradition may be very summarily mentioned here, since they have been discussed more fully in an earlier context. They are: the marriages not conducted by religious rites; the incidence of intermarriage; burials in non-Jewish cemeteries and the cremations; the retardation of the age of marriage; the declining birth-rate. The same general trend in the secularisation of Jewish social behaviour is reflected in Mr. Baron's survey of Jewish students in Britain, from which we take the following table[1]:

SUMMARY OF RELIGIOUS TRENDS (PERCENTAGES)

	Very Orthodox and Orthodox	Moderately Orthodox and Moderate	Reform and Liberal	Others	Total
PARENTS (*Religious Outlook*)					
Fathers	20	52	12	16	100%
Mothers	19	57	11	13	100%
STUDENTS (*Religious Views*)					
Men	12	39	13	36	100%
Women	13	39	13	35	100%
STUDENTS (*Religious Observance*)					
Men	11	39	8	42	100%
Women	12	40	11	37	100%

" Others " in this table presumably indicates religious indifference, which is apparently twice as common in the generation of the students as in that of their parents. Two in every five of the students who answered the questionnaire were indifferent to religion, and yet the sample of students must be assumed to be

[1] Raymond V. Baron, 'Jewish Students—A Survey,' *The Jewish Chronicle*, 23.2.51.

115

biased in favour of observing Jews, since most of the forms were filled in by members of the Inter-University Federation of Jewish Students (some of whose affiliated societies provide kasher food for their members), and the respondents may be taken to have had an interest in Judaism or Jewish affairs. So that, while this information demonstrates the trend away from tradition, it probably exaggerates the rôle of orthodoxy and near-orthodoxy. These figures say something about the situation among young people beginning their independent adult lives. We must now examine the place of religion in the lives of children.

Religious Education

It is a notable feature of the educational system of the country that ample opportunity is given to parents to have their children practise their religion and receive the necessary religious instruction. At the request of parents children can be withdrawn from general prayers and from religious tuition where this is included in the curriculum. Children can be taken from school early enough on Friday afternoons to allow them to attend to their religious duties and they can be withdrawn on Holy Days. Where there is a sizeable Jewish school population, special withdrawal classes are arranged.

The Jewish community itself organises specifically Jewish education. There are full-time Jewish schools enjoying State recognition and there are a number of nursery schools and kindergartens. Nearly every synagogue offers religious classes for children where instruction, if so desired, is free. At lay schools Jewish religious instruction is often provided where withdrawal classes are organised. What is the result of these attempts to smooth the path for Jewish parents?

We know from correspondence in the press that Jewish parents are not always very assiduous in claiming exemption for their children from general religious instruction. In Ilford, for example, only one of sixty Jewish pupils was withdrawn from such tuition at a certain school.[1]

In our Questionnaire A.J.S.-1 we have collected data on the

---

[1] See 'The Conscience Clause,' *The Jewish Chronicle,* 9.6.50.

religious education of children. A table in the Appendix[1] shows that approximately 7 per cent of the provincial Jewish population (in the areas which replied to the relevant section of the questionnaire) are enrolled for some sort of Jewish instruction. If we compare this figure with the proportion that the age group 5-15 years forms in the general population, we arrive at the conclusion that only half of all Jewish schoolchildren receive religious education.[2] But this, of course, is a gross over-simplification. There is every reason to believe that even if this age group is as large in the Jewish population as in the general—which, in the light of our earlier discussion on the birth-rate, we may well doubt—few Jewish children attend religious classes for as long as ten years.

From many statements in *The Jewish Chronicle,* from interviews, and from the reports of communal education bodies it is clear that most children stop attending classes at the age of thirteen (which for boys is the age of *barmitzvah,* the rite by which they attain ritual maturity). The figures shown in Table XV[3] supplied by the London Board of Jewish Religious Education[4] indicate quite clearly that 87 per cent of boys and 84 per cent of girls receiving religious instruction under the Board's auspices are under thirteen. If the figures for withdrawal classes—where the influence of non-Jewish education authorities can be expected to be felt—are left out, the percentages shoot up to 96 per cent and 95 per cent respectively. Similarly, while on the face of it 38 per cent of all children receiving religious instruction are girls, a consideration of the figures exclusive of withdrawal classes brings the percentage down to 35—an eloquent testimony of the greater importance attached by Jewish parents to religious instruction for boys. Moreover, only a minority of children begin their religious education at the age of five. Rarely are they sent to classes under the age of seven, and it is common for them not to start until they are

1 See Appendix, Table X, A.J.S.-1, p. 253.
2 But in the *Inspector's Report* for the year ending October, 1953, Mr. Harold Levy, Inspector of the Central Council for Jewish Religious Education, estimates that outside Greater London there are 12,500 Jewish children, of whom about 7,500—60 per cent—receive religious instruction.
3 See Appendix, Table XV, p. 258.
4 *Fourth Report: May,* 1952-*December,* 1953, London Board of Jewish Religious Education, pp. 24-30.

ten, eleven, and even twelve years of age. A very general apathy on the part of Jewish parents in the matter of providing religious tuition for their children is often reflected in the strenuous efforts made by Jewish educational bodies to attract children by a variety of inducements. Such efforts, however, do not overcome widespread indifference, and in the East End of London, for example, only about half of the ascertained number of Jewish schoolchildren are enrolled in religious classes. Average attendance at synagogue classes and Talmud Torahs held under the auspices of the London Board of Jewish Religious Education is on Sundays 70 per cent of the total number of pupils enrolled and on weekdays 49 per cent.[1]

If we bear in mind the reservations that need to be made in interpreting the data on enrolment at Jewish religious classes, the existing situation may be compared with that a generation ago. *The Jewish Year Book,* 1924, gives a detailed list of such classes and their pupils. In Greater London pupils totalled some 19,000, while the Jewish population of the area was estimated at 175,000. If, on the analogy of the general population, we took Jewish schoolchildren to be one-seventh of the Jewish population, we should estimate the Jewish population of Greater London in 1924 to have been 135,000. The difference between the two estimates is explained by the different age structure of the Jewish population and by the uneven and incomplete attendance of Jewish children at classes. However, the figure for pupils in 1924 may be compared with some profit with the corresponding figure for 1953. Although some of the figures shown in Table XVII[2] are only rough estimates, they give food for thought.

According to this table we may estimate the number of children enrolled for organised religious instruction in 1953 at no more than 18,650—a figure which may well be an overestimate, since many children attending synagogue and Talmud Torah classes undoubtedly already appear in the figure for withdrawal classes. Even so, the figure of 18,650 is a little less than that of 19,000 in 1924. Yet during the same period the Jewish population of Greater London increased by about 110,000, and we seem therefore to have further proof of the decline in Jewish religious tradition.

[1] See Appendix, Table XVI, p. 258.
[2] See Appendix, Table XVII, p. 259.

Youth Organisations

However, the training of children in things Jewish is not covered by an examination of religious classes. Another important focus of Jewish activities for children is the Jewish youth movement. Youth organisations are perhaps also more significant than religious classes in that to a large extent they are under the control of the young people themselves and represent more closely their own interests. On May 2nd, 1952, the *Jewish Observer* published an article entitled 'An Inquiry into Anglo-Jewish Youth,' which divides Jewish youngsters into three sections. An overwhelmingly large proportion of the junior community is said to be still affiliated to synagogues (mainly orthodox) by virtue of their parents' membership, while they themselves 'display very little interest in Jewish culture and religious practices, although they may belong to Jewish social clubs and attend dances of a predominantly Jewish character.' A second group, said to be larger in numbers than is commonly realised, has broken away completely from Judaism, some of the youngsters having 'deliberately renounced or concealed their Jewish identity.' Finally, there is a group of young people 'attached actively to Judaism' which adheres to religious practices and which is active in Zionism.

The Association for Jewish Youth, with 13,000 members, and the Union of Maccabi Associations, with 5,000, are the biggest youth organisations. Generally speaking, they concentrate on social and sports activities and provide such amenities as playing fields, camping sites, and youth centres. It appears that there is little demand in these circles for specifically Jewish activities. The survey points to a trend towards Reform Judaism in the active Jewish group, although on the whole religion seems not to be an attraction to Jewish youngsters. 'About fifty per cent of all Jewish children,' it is estimated, 'have had no religious or Hebrew education whatsoever,' and more revealing still: 'Interest in Israel . . . has been declining since the Jewish State has begun to lose the attraction of romance and novelty.' There is, of course, a Zionist Youth Movement, but 'it would be misleading to assume from the strength of these Zionist Youth Movements' (with a combined membership of 6,500) 'that a majority of their members will eventually settle in Israel.' Only a tiny number is expected to do so.

119

The article arrives at a few final conclusions of general interest. 'The overwhelming majority' of Anglo-Jewish youth is 'rapidly losing distinctive Jewish characteristics.' Again: ' . . . there is no doubt that, seen from the perspective of its youth, the Jewish community is declining,' and ' . . . the time may not be distant when the majority of Jews now growing to adulthood will assume almost automatically that their future is no different from that of the non-Jewish population.' Since most of the writer's informants were organisers and members of Jewish youth clubs, we may assume that the trends which he describes are perhaps even more generally true of Jewish youth as a whole. As for the general significance of youth organisations, we must also note that, although about fifty to fifty-five per cent of Jewish young people have at some time in their life been members of one youth organisation or another, they drop out sooner or later to give the organisation the well-known pyramidal age structure in its membership. Whatever the merits of youth organisations, their hold over Jewish youth cannot be said to be very secure.

We have yet to consider a few further matters concerning adult attitudes towards Jewish affairs. One of these is connected with Jewish youth. There is a shortage of teachers and leaders in the youth movements, and while the Association for Jewish Youth trains youth leaders, this shortage seems to be permanent. Of course, one needs to add that salaries paid by the community do not compete with those of alternative occupations.

A similar situation prevails in respect of Jewish teachers. The Board of Jewish Religious Education runs three different courses, one of which is full-time, to train badly needed personnel. The wide scatter of Jews in the country calls for a greater number of such people than the relatively small demand for religious education might suggest.

Shortage of Ministers

Perhaps more surprising still is the shortage of ministers. Before the Second World War ministers were called from abroad to serve the Anglo-Jewish community. These foreigners received less pay than men trained by Jews' College, in London, and they were prepared to take up positions in smallish congregations which could not afford the full-time services of a Jews' College graduate. But recruitment from overseas has now stopped. In an interview in 1951, Mr. Stephany, Secretary of Jews' College, stated that in one respect the situation has improved. More British-born Jews are now trained at the College, and there is no difficulty in placing those who complete their training. The main problem is to attract the right people to the profession in sufficient numbers. Part of the difficulty at the present time in recruiting suitable candidates lies in the shortage of money for providing scholarships for the College ; but years ago, when the College was able to grant a number of full scholarships and candidates were more numerous, graduates did not always take up the career for which they had been trained. As a career, perhaps, the ministry does not carry with it the prestige in Anglo-Jewry that its counterpart enjoys in other faiths. The recruitment of ministers has now become so difficult that some congregations have been left without ministerial attention for many years. Even the number of *shochetim* (ritual slaughterers), if we may judge from remarks in the Jewish press, is insufficient to meet the need of even that half of Anglo-Jewry which still requires their services.

Zionism

All these facts—the shortage of leaders and the decline of Jewish education—indicate the attenuation of Judaism in Britain. Bertrand Russell has said that nationalism ' has transferred to the State many emotions which formerly found their outlet in religion. The diminution in the strength of religion is partly the cause and partly the effect of nationalism. . . .'[1] From this point of view it would be interesting to examine the position which Zionism, in the sense of an attachment to the idea of the Jewish State which outweighs other spiritual and idealistic considerations, occupies in Anglo-Jewry today. We shall here not be dealing with the history of organised Zionism. Within Zionism itself, of course, there is a cleavage between those who regard religious Judaism as an integral part of the movement and those who see their aims in purely political terms. In this survey, which is concerned with present-day trends within a relatively small minority, we can limit our observations to the inquiry into the extent to which Jewish

[1] Bertrand Russell, *Power, A New Social Analysis,* London, 1948, p. 176.

nationalism today may have replaced religion as a factor in the survival of the minority as such.

It would be a mistake to base an appreciation of the importance of Zionism in Britain on the much publicised collections of funds for Israel. It is clear that much of the money contributed by Jews in this country has little to do with Zionism as a positive affirmation of a given individual's political outlook and much to do with the giving of charity to Jews in less fortunate circumstances.[1] Moreover, the proportion of Jews who make contributions to Zionist funds is smaller than might be imagined. In the London area, for example, the Jewish National Fund distributes 28,340 collecting-boxes. Greater London's Jewish population is estimated at 280,000.[2] If the average Jewish family is taken to consist of 3.4 persons (see p. 69) the number of Jewish households in London would be around 82,000. Allowing for the presence of a certain number of collecting-boxes in synagogues, clubs, business premises, etc., it would be reasonable to say that no more than thirty per cent of London Jewry make regular contributions to the Joint Palestine Appeal.

The composition of the Synagogue Council of the Zionist Federation of Great Britain may afford us a better insight into Zionist activities in the country. Membership of the Council is by synagogues and not by individuals. Most of the constituent synagogues of the Federation of Synagogues are affiliated to the Council. Members of these synagogues are predominantly orthodox and immigrants of various immigration waves, and their Zionist sympathies may well have been formed outside this country. The synagogues affiliated to the United Synagogue, whose members are also orthodox, but consist rather of longer-established Jews, are on the whole not affiliated to the Council. One explanation offered for this is that the constitution of the United Synagogue excludes politics, and therefore Zionism, from its activities. Such an attitude of avoidance of organised Zionism among most of the hard core of religious Anglo-Jewry makes the chances seem very slender that Zionism should ever become a substitute for religion in this country.

Still more light is thrown on the significance of Zionism by the

[1] For an appraisal of the social significance of pro-Zionist well-wishers see p. 237.
[2] *The Jewish Year Book*, 1954.

working of the institution of *shekalim*. *Shekel* ownership, which is acquired by paying the sum of two shillings, is the qualification for casting a vote in the election of delegates to the Zionist Congress, the supreme governing body of the World Zionist Organisation. There were in 1946 46,000 *shekel* holders in the country, but in 1950 this figure had declined by 10,000. On the other hand, the actual number of voters, 11,000, was the same in both years. It is possible to infer from this that, while popular enthusiasm for the cause may have declined since the establishment of the State of Israel, a hard core of Zionists has persisted unchanged. In one important respect the creation of the State of Israel has proved to have a positive influence on Anglo-Jewry's Zionism ; for the anti-Zionist movement has ceased to exist in an organised form. Perhaps the misgivings lest Jews in the Diaspora be torn between two loyalties has, since the realisation of Zionist hopes, proved to be unrealistic. Certainly, the low figures for British Jews emigrating to Israel[1] may have stilled anxiety that the Jewish State would be a drain on the population of Anglo-Jewry.

None of this is to be taken to mean that there does not exist very generally among Jews in this country a sense of pride in and an emotional attachment to the new State. This is perhaps most marked among the young people, and yet Zionist circles estimate that only eight per cent of Jewish youth in the country is organised by the movement and that even this cadre holds only a very small number of prospective settlers. There is, of course, no want of effort on the part of the Zionists to attract young people to Israel. There are a number of schemes for encouraging visitors and settlers to Israel. There are organisations to train youngsters in this country on model farms for work on the land, and other bodies seek to attract professional and technical workers and to arouse the interest of students and graduates in the new State as a new home. A few figures to illustrate the results of this effort may be of interest. A relatively new organisation, the Professional and Technical Workers' Aliyah (better known as PATWA), seeks to find vacancies in Israel for a special class of badly needed workers. With their assistance, fifty-three individuals left this country for Israel between May 1st and December 5th, 1950. These included twenty-six

[1] See p. 58f.

123

engineers, seven teachers, four doctors, two economists, two scientists, three secretaries, two nurses, two social welfare workers, a chemist, a pharmacist, an optician, a fashion-design teacher, and a French translator.

The *Hechalutz B'Anglia,* the organisation of Jewish pioneers for Israel, also known as *Bachad,* was formed in 1938 and at the moment (1952) cares for 157 prospective emigrants. From January, 1944, to December, 1950, the organisation sent 1,240 young people to Israel more or less evenly divided between the sexes.[1] No accurate figures are available for the number of foreigners in this figure, but it has been estimated that, among those who left in 1944-46 and 1946-47, approximately 75 per cent and 50 per cent respectively were ' non-English.' The gradual decline in numbers sent annually to Israel is therefore probably due to a large extent to the lack of foreign trainees.

The by now much quoted survey by the Inter-University Federation of Jewish Students states that settling in Israel was mentioned in replies as a possibility by 32.4 per cent, as a probability by 12.7 per cent, and as an intention by 12 per cent. One should point out, of course, that the Federation's inquiry is biased towards the more orthodox and more Jewish-minded section of the total Jewish student body.

It seems clear enough, then, that while militant organised Zionism attracts a comparatively small minority of Jews in this country, it does not operate as a focus of Jewish loyalty in the same way as religion in earlier generations.[2]

Occupational Structure

Our Questionnaire A.J.S.-2 inquired into gainful occupations. Unfortunately, we have reason to believe that the biases in the sample are likely to distort the meaning of the answers to this question even more than in the case of the data on vital statistics. Because of gross distortion brought about by the way in which forms were distributed through two particular channels,[3] we confine

[1] The distribution of this figure over the seven years is not known, but in 1949, 1950, and 1951 the annual figures were 123, 91, and 50 respectively.
[2] See p. 237.
[3] The forms distributed through the staff of *The Jewish Chronicle* over-represented the occupations which one would expect to find among the

the following analysis to the forms which were returned by the Representative Councils of Hull and Sheffield, and by the various branches of the Association of Jewish Ex-Service Men and Women. Our reduced sample consists of 4,949 individuals. From this number we remove all those under fifteen years of age since they have no bearing on the question of gainful occupation. This leaves a sample of 3,977, of whom 1,992 are males and 1,985 females. 1,244 males were occupied in trades and 342 in professions ; which gives a figure of 1,586 gainfully occupied males in a total male sample of 1,992, or 80 per cent. This compares with an analogous figure of 86 per cent for the general population. Among 1,985 females over the age of fifteen in our sample, 181 were engaged in trades and 46 in professions ; which gives a percentage of eleven. This percentage compares with 34 per cent in the general population.

The following table tentatively compares an analysis of our sample with figures taken from the one per cent sample of the 1951 census of the United Kingdom :

OCCUPIED IN ALL INDUSTRIES (Persons over 15 years old)

	A.J.S.-2 Sample			One per cent Sample Census, 1951		
	Males	Females	Total	Males	Females	Total
Over 15 years	1,992	1,985	3,977	17,817	20,037	37,854
Occupied ...	1,586	227	1,813	15,336	6,797	22,133
Occupied in %	80	11	46	86	34	58

The comparability of these two sets of figures is, of course, questionable, but differences in the proportions of gainfully occupied men and gainfully occupied women between the two samples are large enough perhaps to represent some significant economic difference. It appears that by far the main burden of bread-winning rests on the shoulders of Jewish men, and that Jewish women still have not moved out of Jewish tradition to the extent of earning their own living on an appreciable scale. The concentration of women in the home, which can be supported from general knowledge and observation, has a bearing on other than purely economic matters. The fact that most Jewish mothers remain

distributors ; *viz.*, journalism and editorial and clerical work. Similarly, the forms distributed among Londoners by the Jewish Hospital seem to exaggerate the number of people engaged in occupations associated with the running of a hospital.

at home and do not go out to work may possibly be one of the factors in the production of a low infantile mortality rate among Jews. It may also be to some extent responsible for the low rate of Jewish juvenile delinquency. It is also possible that the solidarity of home life, which the domesticity of women would suggest, may be one of the reasons for the late marriage of Jewish men and women, since for young Jewish men and women marriage is not the only means of enjoying the amenities of a closely knit home life.

Interviews with both Jews and non-Jews in the East End of London confirm that Jewish women are normally expected to confine themselves to household duties, and it is said, moreover, that Jewish working-class men tend to deprive themselves of luxuries rather than allow their wives to share the wage-earning burden. Only 57 of 227 gainfully occupied females in our sample, that is, about a quarter, were married at the time of the inquiry. In the general population almost one-third of the gainfully employed women are married.[1] The majority of gainfully occupied married women in our sample had neither infants nor children of school age living with them in the same household. Some of those with children under fifteen years of age living with them were schoolteachers whose off-duty hours and holidays probably corresponded with the time their children were at home.

Of the gainfully employed Jewish males in our sample, the greater number returned themselves as being engaged in commerce and industry on their own account. Nine hundred and twenty-one of the 1,244 men in trades, or about three in every four, worked on their own account. In the professions, half were employed and half were independent. In the general population, three in every fifty men in the trades and professions work on their own account.[2] Twenty-two per cent of all gainfully occupied males in our sample

[1] *Gainfully Occupied Females*
    (A.J.S.-2 Sample)

		One per cent Sample Census 1951
All females occupied	227	6,797.1
Married	57	2,044.0
In percentage	25	30

[2] *Males Occupied*
    (A.J.S.-2 Sample)

		One per cent Sample Census 1951
All males occupied	1,586	15,366.1
On own account	1,092	877.4
In percentage	69	6

were engaged in professional pursuits, as against five per cent in the general population. We may check these results against findings arrived at in other ways.

In 1945 the Trades Advisory Council published a pamphlet, *The Jews in Work and Trade,* by Dr. N. Barou,[1] which gave a percentage of fifteen as the proportion of all gainfully employed Jews carrying on business on their own account. Further: '. . . the participation of Jews in the professions is a limited one.' Even if we include the females in our sample we cannot approach Dr. Barou's results. Of these females, 65 were engaged in trades on their own account and 116 employed in trades and services ; two females in every three gainfully occupied being employees. Among females engaged in the professions, 10 of the 46, or less than one in every five, worked independently. If we take the figures for both sexes together, for both trades and professions, approximately two in every three persons gainfully occupied worked on their own account.

Dr. Barou emphasises the fact that the investigation on which his report is based was carried out during the third and fourth years of the war, '. . . which has had a great influence on Jewish occupational distribution. . . .' Elsewhere in his survey the author states that it was estimated that in the clothing trade alone (in which he includes furriers, dry cleaners, repairers, etc.) more than one-third of the Jewish firms had gone out of business since the outbreak of the war. A considerable proportion of the 500 furniture firms which had been 'concentrated' were Jewish. It is possible that many of these traders may have since reopened their businesses, and it is likely that a number of young Jews have set up independent businesses after demobilisation. This last supposition is supported by the experience of the Boys' Department of the Board of Guardians. In an interview it was stated that boys to be apprenticed preferred trades in which business can be started with relatively small assets. At present, therefore, hairdressing is one of the trades which exercises a great attraction. It may also be of interest that Jews are represented in a remarkable proportion among taxi drivers. The officer interviewed also stated that there is a 'craze' for accountancy among youngsters who approach the

[1] A third edition was published in 1948.

Department for advice and assistance. One must note that apprentices to this profession are paid by their employers.

Dealing with the food trade, Dr. Barou points out that many businesses are too small to be traced in telephone directories and so escape the investigator's attention. It is not, however, only in the food trade that businesses exist which are not entered in telephone directories. In Hull, for instance, in our total male sample population of 659 there were 89 tailors and clothing traders.[1] The differences in the conclusions between Dr. Barou's work and those drawn from our sample are to some extent the result of a difference in method. Dr. Barou counts firms, and we count individuals.

The Trades Advisory Council survey states that Jews participate in only a limited number of the trades of this country. Of the 1,040 trades listed in Manchester directories, Jews were connected with only 250 (or 24 per cent); of 1,650 trades in Glasgow directories, Jews participate in 128 (or 8 per cent); and of 1,200 trades mentioned in Liverpool directories, Jews participate in 155 (or about 13 per cent). There is, of course, nothing strange in these figures. Jews are normally presumed to concentrate on the manufacture and distribution of consumer goods. Their numerical strength in the clothing, fashion, footwear, and furniture and allied trades is great in all countries to which there was considerable immigration from Russia between 1881 and 1914. These immigrants, and to a greater extent their offspring, are known to have swollen the number of small business owners in these trades. On the other hand, of course, in the same field of activity some Jews have created great organisations catering for mass consumption. It is beyond the scope of this essay to embark on a history of Jewish industrial enterprises, but it would be misleading to mention the figures for small Jewish traders without a reference to the giant enterprises which have grown from small beginnings. When we mention in what follows the names of a few businesses, our purpose is to remind the readers of merely a few firms whose activities are common knowledge. We refer to them only to demonstrate certain features which are typical results of the activities developed by Jews in their long history of migration,

[1] It is more than improbable that of the total Jewish population of 2,000 there are 89 entered in the local classified telephone directory as tailors, etc.

or to show that Jewish labour, capital, and organisation are at least as important in the growth of some trades as the great proportion of business firms working on their own account. Dr. Barou states that over one-quarter of the firms engaged in the textile, drapery, and fashion trades in London, Manchester, Leeds, Glasgow, Cardiff, and Newcastle upon Tyne were Jewish at the time of his survey. These cities then covered over 80 per cent of the Jewish population of the country. It is important to realise that one large organisation, such as Marks and Spencer, is likely to make the Jewish share of the business done in these trades larger than the proportion of Jewish firms in the total number of firms. Similarly, Jewish participation in the catering industry is largely weighted by the existence of J. Lyons, in the clothing trade by the existence of Montague Burton, and so on.

While the Jewish rôle in the trades concerned with consumer goods is well known, they have also played some part in such industries as the production of high-precision instruments, chemicals, plastics, leather tanning, and various branches of engineering. In our small sample, moreover, we find railwaymen and stevedores, laundry workers and men in the Merchant Navy, and many others whose occupations indicate that assimilation moves forward in the economic field as in others. The diversification of Jewish economic activities is, of course, of some importance to the community as a whole in that depression in one trade need not necessarily affect the economic basis of the whole group.

Two further causes of the differences between Dr. Barou's conclusions and our own need to be mentioned. In the first place, there is a tendency for people to upgrade themselves occupationally when they fill in questionnaires, and this tendency may very well have over-emphasised the independent workers in our sample, since there is an ambition among Jews to be independent in business. More important is the factor indicated in the following quotation from Dr. Barou : ' The proportion of Jewish traders and professional men is higher in smaller Jewish communities than in the larger ones, where the predominant majority of Jews are employed as wage and salary earners.' Clearly, our sample, by dealing with smaller centres of Jewish population and neglecting the large centres, biases our results in this direction. However, one useful

129

K

result which we have arrived at appears, despite the distortions of the sample, to be the proportion of males and females gainfully employed.

Dr. Barou, citing the 1901 Census, shows that among Russians and Poles in London (most of whom were probably Jewish), 91 per cent of the men and 23 per cent of the women over ten years of age earned their living. These proportions are somewhat at variance with those established in our sample but compatible with our results if we may assume that with improving economic conditions more Jewish men and less Jewish women will be in employment, and both sexes will start making a living at a higher age.

The high proportion of professional people in our sample is also less strange than might appear at first sight. Dr. Barou points out that it was not until the latter half of the nineteenth century that the professions were fully opened to Jews. This fact he assumes to account for limited Jewish participation in the professions in modern times. What seems to emerge from the data provided by our sample is that a new group of professional men exists nowadays among Jews in this country which has a lower economic standard than the members of old-established professional families. This point may be illustrated by some figures. Of four artists in our sample of men, only one was employed, and he was foreign-born. Of fifteen estate agents, three were employees, and of these two were foreign-born ; the twelve self-employed men were all British-born. Of seventy-two medical men, nineteen were employed, and six of these were foreign-born. Of nineteen dentists, three were employees, of whom two were foreign-born. These figures, which could be greatly extended, prove that the newcomers have formed a sub-group among Jewish professional men, whose members do not enjoy the independence which Jews normally treasure so highly. These men do not have the same standard of security as their more fortunate fellow-Jewish professionals, who are the offspring of families settled in this country, nor presumably do they have the same social standing in the Jewish community.

Foreign-born Jews and Jewesses form 9 per cent of the people in our sample who return themselves as belonging to the professions. This group may increase still further when the children of those refugee professionals who were forced to take up new careers in this country grow up. Dr. Rosenstock, Secretary of the Association of Jewish Refugees, said in an interview: ' The children of professional men who had to take up other work when they arrived here are making their way back into the professions by means of scholarships.' This new Jewish element in the professions comes from countries where Jews have been in professional callings for generations. Our figures on this subject are perhaps particularly striking in that we scarcely touch the districts which felt the main impact of the post-Hitlerian immigration wave. Even if our sample is rejected as unrepresentative, we could support our general conclusions from material drawn from another source.

In 1947 Dr. Redcliffe N. Salaman published a paper entitled ' Jews in the Royal Society, a Problem of Ecology.'[1] He takes election to the Society as a ' reliable yardstick by which to gauge the volume of output of scientists of high rank . . . ' (because Fellowships in the Society since 1847 have been given to a strictly limited number of individuals solely on the basis of their scientific output, without political, religious, or any other form of discrimination). ' Today,' Dr. Salaman writes, ' the number of Fellows of full Jewish parentage is more than five times that which their proportion to the general population would justify, whilst in respect of the foreign Fellows the percentage is very much higher, having reached twenty-five per cent in 1939.' Between 1848 and 1900 ' only seven Jews were elected to the ordinary Fellowships, as against 869 non-Jews, i.e., 0.8 per cent of the whole, a proportion not much above that to be expected on the basis of the relative size of the two communities.'

Dr. Salaman then speaks of the flow of population from Russia and Poland between 1881 and 1905, and its expansion of the Jewish community in Great Britain. ' The newcomers were extremely poor and unused to Western learning and ways of life.' But the second generation that followed this movement assimilated itself to the modern world and its learning, and Jewish membership of the Royal Society has reflected the process of assimilation. While throughout the present century Jews have remained under one per cent of the total population of Great Britain, in 1901 Jews formed

[1] *Notes and Records of the Royal Society*, Vol. XVII, No. 1, pp. 61 *et seq.*

One per cent, in 1920, 2 per cent, in 1940, 3.7 per cent, and in 1948, 5 per cent of the Fellows.

It seems clear that immigration between 1933 and 1939 is to a large extent responsible for the increase in the proportion of Jews in the Royal Society during the last decade.

This investigation seems to support our earlier conclusion, for a relatively strong numerical representation of Jews among top-ranking scientists could hardly be achieved without a broad mass of intellectuals from which the cream could be taken. The figure of 3,000 Jewish University students which Mr. Raymond V. Baron gives in his survey[1] compares with 85,421 full-time students in this country which is given in *Return from Universities and University Colleges in Receipt of Treasury Grants, 1949-50*. This means that while there is less than one Jew in every hundred persons in this country, there is one Jewish student in every twenty-eight University students. This disproportion suggests a disproportion in Jewish entry to the professions.

In a similar way Jewish children are generally estimated to receive secondary education to a greater extent than those of the general population. In England and Wales as a whole, sixteen per cent of all children attending school are educated at grammar schools. In Manchester, the only area for which we have full information, 24 per cent of all Jewish schoolchildren attended Manchester grammar schools in 1950.

Conclusion

In the foregoing we have examined various demographic data. The inferences to be drawn from them—as has been repeatedly stressed—must be viewed with great reservation owing to the uncertainty of the basic facts. As far as can be seen, however, the Jewish birth-rate, the average size of the Jewish family, and the Jewish reproduction rate all seem to be lower than those of the population as a whole. Although it is already known that the age structure of the general population leans towards an increasing proportion of older people, this is even more true of the Jewish community. To this must be attributed the fact that the male

[1] See footnote on p. 65.

mortality rate among Jews, in relation to every hundred female deaths, seems on the other hand to be lower.

It is no longer possible to accept the principle that Jews will overwhelmingly marry within their own community. Anglo-Jewry is therefore biologically on the decline.

The religious ties which in the past held the group together have now very much weakened, while their place has not been taken by any alternative binding influence. Anglo-Jewry has more and more become a middle-class group, culturally assimilated to the nation, but the assimilation has not been so complete as to remove from the Jewish community certain characteristics: in family organisation, in the emphasis on education, and in occupational structure.

As long as the trends in the vital statistics of the general population remain unchanged, the attitude of the majority group towards the Jewish minority is the same as at present, no other influences from outside make themselves felt, and, above all, the trends within the Jewish community are stable, the processes of absorption and assimilation are likely to continue unabated. The proportion of Jews in the general population will presumably fall steadily while those Jews who remain will be more and more integrated into the majority group. Thus, after the passage of some time, little may be left that is distinctively Jewish in this country.

PART THREE

The Outlines of Jewish Society in London

HOWARD M. BROTZ, M.A., Ph.D.

The Outlines of Jewish Society in London

Introduction

THE investigation on which this essay is based[1] was carried out in the years 1949 and 1950, and was primarily an attempt to analyse the ways in which Jews in this country rank one another socially, although, necessarily, the more general question of the nature of Anglo-Jewish society came within my purview. It is a canon of modern field-work which is aimed at more than a superficial appraisal of social life that the investigator base his generalisations on data gathered in the course of prolonged and intimate contact with the people whose society is being studied. My own field-work was concentrated on a North-West London suburb where, by means of a sample constructed from the rolls of a particular synagogue, I gathered a systematic body of information by intensive interviewing. However, interviewing was only one source of data, for by participating in many varieties of Jewish social life in London—not only in my chosen suburb—I was able to gain some insight into the workings of metropolitan Jewish life. My investigation naturally included an analysis of many kinds of published material, both academic and journalistic.

In this essay I have made illustrative use of some of the interview material collected in the course of my field-work. In most cases I have given the coded initials of my informants. I have done this simply to facilitate comparison with the material contained in the thesis which I have already cited. Of course, the statements by informants which I quote merely represent their own interpretation of the society in which they live.

[1] Howard M. Brotz, *An Analysis of Social Stratification within Jewish Society in London,* unpublished Ph.D. thesis, University of London (London School of Economics), 1951.

Areas of Settlement

The original community of the Resettlement was located in the eastern fringes of the City of London. As its ranks were swollen by immigration from the Continent, the community overflowed into the adjacent parts of East London. This was the ghetto—a voluntary one to be sure—which remained the base of Jewish social life in London until the most recent times. Like the Near West Side of Chicago and the Lower East Side of New York, Whitechapel is ceasing to be the centre of the urban Jewish population as its residents move up in the world and migrate to other areas.[1] It is also losing those communal institutions, the headquarters of one group or another, which have remained behind in the exodus of residents, but which also are merely marking time. Even by the early years of the nineteenth century, however, the wealthier members of the community had begun to move out of the City and its eastern environs to North London ; a subsidiary settlement of Jews of higher social and economic standing has long been in existence there.[2]

With the outbreak of intense anti-Jewish violence in Russia in the 1880s there began a mass exodus of Jews from what was the most densely populated Jewish region in Europe. These emigrants largely had the United States as their destination ; English ports were but ports of transhipment where they changed from the Baltic to the transatlantic steamers.[3] A number who arrived in England with no further funds made for the Whitechapel area as a zone of first settlement where they could obtain advice, lodging, and employment. In part, Whitechapel performed the function of a staging area in the vast dispersion of East European Jewry through-out the English-speaking world : to other parts of London, the provinces, the Dominions, and the United States. This dispersion was encouraged by the established Anglo-Jewish leadership, which

[1] Cf. Louis Wirth, *The Ghetto,* Chicago, 1929, for a description of the residential shifts among the Jews of Chicago. Other immigrant groups are discussed in E. W. Burgess (ed.), *The Urban Community,* Chicago, 1927.
[2] Elkan Adler, *A History of the Jews in London,* London, 1930, p. 194. V. also the plight of a lonely Jew in Hampstead in 1820 in Cecil Roth (ed.), *Anglo-Jewish Letters,* London, 1938, p. 247.
[3] Many, in fact, in this transhipment scarcely set foot on English soil, changing ships in port.

138

was concerned about the effects of a concentration in the ghetto.[1]
A committee had been established in the '80s, for example, to give
financial assistance to immigrants wishing to go on to America.[2]

The expansion of London Jewry that resulted from the East
European immigration is indicated in the following table:

INCREASE OF JEWISH POPULATION[3]

Date			Estimated Jewish Population in London
1800	...	...	20,000
1883	...	...	47,000
1902	...	...	150,000
1950	...	...	250,000

At the peak of the influx East London contained most of the
foreign-born Jews in London (and 90 per cent of the metropolitan
Jewish population[4]) who imported whatever they could of their
East European culture: their Yiddish language, their respect for
the Law, and their deeply traditionalist religious practices,[5] and
their accustomed modes of organisation in groups. In neighbour-
hoods which quickly became completely Jewish a multiplicity of
small synagogues (*shtiebl*) organised by men from the same
small town (*shtetl*) sprang up. At first these hardly came into
contact with the established Anglo-Jewish leadership. Relatively
indifferent to the prestige value of membership in the larger synagogues, and even critical of their Orthodoxy, the immigrants
preferred to worship in their own ill-lit and ill-ventilated basements.[6]

[1] Henrietta Adler, 'Jewish Life and Labour in East London,' in *New
Survey of London Life and Labour*, London, 1934, vol. VI, p. 271.
[2] I note briefly that the migration was by no means completely in a
one-way direction or continuous. There are cases, *e.g.*, of those who,
dissatisfied, unsuccessful, or homesick, returned to Eastern Europe and then
re-emigrated. It may also be suggested that the more desirable and attractive
a locality appears the more likely is emigration to this new place to involve
entire families. It is my impression that the migration between England
and America has consisted more of single individuals (offshoots of a family
settled in England) than did the migration from Eastern Europe to either
England or America.
[3] Source: Cecil Roth, *A History of the Jews in England*, 2nd edn.,
London, 1949, pp. 239, 265, 267. For another estimate of the present-day
Jewish population of London see p. 74 above.
[4] Adler, *op. cit.*, p. 291.
[5] Many of these were but local usages.
[6] Beatrice Potter, 'The Jewish Community (East London),' in Charles
Booth (ed.), *Life and Labour of the People*, 1892, vol. III, pp. 171-2.

Here they had autonomy, more of a feeling of acceptance, and the leadership of men esteemed in the *haim* (Eastern Europe; literally, ' homeland ').[1] Similarly, a network of friendly societies mushroomed in growth. There was a highly developed Yiddish cultural life, including the theatre and a vernacular press.

With prolonged residence wider standards of social aspiration began to penetrate their little worlds. This was heightened by the birth of a new generation who very rapidly became secularised.[2] Less attached to local institutions which they had not founded, they would as they grew older press their parents to move. With the expansion of the economy during the First World War, Jews, as they became more prosperous, began to move out of the Whitechapel ghetto, following a route already laid down by their predecessors. They moved north: to Hackney and Dalston, where the fares to the East End workshops were low, and following this, to Stamford Hill and Stoke Newington. The third move out of the East End has characteristically been not to the older section of Hampstead which was in the path followed by the previous generation, but to the newer and, on the whole, more modest suburban areas in North-West London. This move was facilitated by the extension of the Northern Line Underground. Beginning in Golders Green, Jews have spread into the surrounding areas of Finchley, Hendon, and beyond.[3] Though districts within the whole of the North-West London area vary in prestige value, the fourth distinctive move is the return to a flat in Central London, to St. John's Wood (where the synagogue has a waiting list), or to Mayfair.

During the Second World War the depression of rents and the price of property made it possible for many to move directly from East to North-West London, short-circuiting the North London stage of the migration.[4]

1 Under the leadership of the first Lord Swaythling, many of these small synagogues became federated. (cf. p. 28.)

2 C. Russell and H. S. Lewis, *The Jew in London*, London, 1900, p. 24.

3 The simplest index which I have used for the emergence of a *new* Jewish concentration is the establishment of a synagogue and its membership figures. Statistics on this are presented in Brotz, *op. cit.*, p. 95.

4 Since 1930 there has developed an avenue of exit eastwards from Whitechapel to Ilford and Woodford, with the growth there of suburban housing estates similar to those in the North-West area. The Eastern

The following table may serve to convey a rough impression of the population changes within London:

ESTIMATED RESIDENT POPULATION IN LONDON BOROUGHS[1]

Borough	1938	1942	1948
Bethnal Green	92,910	47,410	60,580
Finchley	65,140	59,990	70,960
Hackney	205,200	131,200	172,900
Hendon	145,100	132,200	156,400
Stepney	200,500	71,980	99,470
Stoke Newington	50,480	33,440	45,370

The above is a table of estimated population in six London boroughs which have large concentrations of Jews. Though the population of all the boroughs declined during the war, it has increased in 1948 beyond the 1938 figures only in Finchley and Hendon (North-West suburban). Consider particularly the impressive loss of population in Stepney.

Whereas in 1889, 90 per cent of the metropolitan Jewish population was concentrated in East London, it accounted for only 60 per cent of this population in 1929.[2] There are other indices of the continued disappearance of the East London ghetto as the centre of Jewish life in London which were already evident at the time of the New London Survey (1929). In 1889 the Jews' Free School was full (3,500 pupils). In 1929 there were only 1,737 pupils.[3] Today it is closed. The building was bombed during the war while the school population had been evacuated and it was decided not to reopen it. In 1929 seven of the elementary schools in the Jewish area of London had been put to other uses,[4] and today there are only two L.C.C. Jewish schools left in London, the Solomon Wolfson School, in Bayswater, and Stepney Jewish School.

The ghetto in East London has not yet ' vanished,' though there are few, if any, goods and services to be found there which cannot be obtained elsewhere.[5] It is in the last stage of decline and, to a suburban zone, however, with its ' E.' postal district numbers ranks somewhat below the Western one in prestige value.

[1] Source: *The Registrar-General's Statistical Review of England and Wales for 1938, 1942, 1948. Part II, Civil Tables, Table E.*
[2] Adler, *op. cit.*, p. 271.   [3] *Ibid.*, p. 270.   [4] *Loc. cit.*
[5] Marketing for food, particularly before Holy-days, may be somewhat more convenient in the East End, as a greater variety of goods is available in a smaller space. The street market in Middlesex Street, ' Petticoat Lane,' is one of the sights of London on Sundays; but on Thursdays, when Orthodox Jews shop for the Sabbath, it goes back to being a Jewish affair.

great degree, run by remote control. Though Jews' College and the offices of the main Anglo-Jewish organisations, such as the Board of Deputies, the Anglo-Jewish Association, and the United Synagogue are located in Woburn House, a number still remain in the East End: the Jewish Board of Guardians, the Federation of Synagogues, the *Beth Din*, the Association for Jewish Youth, and the Association of Jewish Friendly Societies. But neither their honorary officers nor their senior officials live in the area. Synagogues, which ideally should be local institutions, are increasingly coming to be run or supported by men who have moved out of the East End but who keep up their attachment to their old synagogue for sentimental reasons. The Sephardi Synagogue, in Bevis Marks, built in 1701 and the oldest remaining synagogue in Britain to date from the period of the Resettlement, is really a museum piece, with a congregation whose members mainly worship in the Lauderdale Road (Maida Vale) Branch Synagogue. Fortunately, the lovely building in the City, having been scheduled as an ancient monument, will be preserved. Furthermore, as the Jews evacuate Stepney, streets in the district which were once solidly Jewish are being occupied by coloured people. The latter are thus forming another 'ghetto' in the shell of the old.

But the most fundamental index of the decline of the East London ghetto is the widespread agreement in the Jewish world on its low prestige value. A failure is a person who 'can't even get out of the East End.' A person's residence, furthermore, is felt to be an index of the way he can be expected to behave.[1] The importance of this kind of judgment in impersonal relationships is one factor explaining why the quest for the 'right address' has so much significance in big cities. For example:

If you know a person it doesn't make any difference where he

[1] Where this is not true, residence is of little significance in the stratification system. For example, in England regional attributes are of no importance in the status values of the gentry who, having a common style of behaviour and a common type of education, regard themselves (and are regarded as well by other strata) as a thoroughly national or trans-local élite. This is not so, however, among the non-gentry who are the bearers of regional culture in England: accent, manners, and diet. It is also not true in the United States, which lacks a national élite that is as clearly defined as the English gentry. It exhibits, rather, a set of municipal élites who by no means have the same standards or rank each other as equals. V. Cleveland Amory's *Proper Bostonians,* Boston, 1947, to see what Boston society think of the rest of the country.

lives. Would you think any less of one of your friends if he moved to the East End? And if Chaim Weizmann lived in the East End or Golders Green, it wouldn't make any difference. But from an impersonal point of view, I think it does enter into the way you judge people. If you said that you were bringing someone from the East End to dinner I'd sort of expect that he'd be a rougher sort of person or more grob *[coarse]. On an impersonal basis, it does enter in. And I must admit that N.W.11 sounds more affluent and better to me than E.15.*[1]

In the East End today the people are grob, *very rough, swear, don't have any manners. But they can't help it. It's the environment. Among the Gentiles there you'll hear a mother shout to her kid, 'Come 'ere, you.' They drop their aitches. You know it sounds a bit snobby but I went to visit somebody who was sitting* shiva *[mourning] in the East End, very nice people, but I couldn't help thinking how we've grown apart. After all, I lived in the East End, too. And my sister-in-law lives in Stamford Hill; she'd like to move out but she can't on account of my mother. You know how it is with the* shul *[synagogue]. Well, the kid came in and she said, 'Wash your hands before you eat.' And the kid said, ' I don't want to do it. Why should I do it when so-and-so doesn't.' My sister said, ' I don't care. In this house you wash your hands.' Well, here the kids play with the children next door, they speak nicer, they learn from each other. And also, here if a child is going to wash his hands, there's a wash basin right at hand. Stamford Hill is sort of in between the East End and here.*

Q. *Do you feel that one can improve one's social standing by moving?*

A. *Oh, yes. When I buy a parcel in a West End store to be sent, and they ask for the address, I feel much prouder that it goes to N.W.4 than to E.1. It's a nicer feeling.*[2]

On the other hand people in the East End are touchy about living there when they meet people from wealthier districts. Where they do not (or cannot) conceal the fact, they adopt an apologetic and defensive attitude about it. They are anxious to assert that they can actually afford to move to a better neighbourhood but are

[1] Interview with M.F.   [2] Interview with J.G.

prevented from doing so by some factor beyond their control at the present: 'We would like to move but we can't because of the business,' or, 'because of my parents.'[1]

Furthermore, they will, typically, in relations with other East Enders or in fantasy equate themselves with those who have moved upwards. For example:

Let me tell you that 90 per cent, no 99 per cent, of all the Jews in London have come out of the East End.[2]

This equation is likely to take the familiar form of imputing to those who have moved up an unjustified tendency to look down on those who have remained behind. For example:

Q. *How do you regard the Jews in Stamford Hill?*

A. *You mean* schnorrers' *hill? You see, it's only a fourpenny ride from Stamford Hill to here and they think they're a little bit better!*[3]

There is agreement, however, not only on the status of the old Whitechapel ghetto itself. In addition, the pattern of moves North and then towards North-West London is so definitely seen as a 'route' that those who stray from it are somewhat eccentric. For example:

And then there are Jews living south of the river too. But how they got there no one seems to know![4]

The agreement on the prestige value of each area in the hierarchy is, however, a complex matter. To begin with, it can be said that individuals place more importance on residence itself than upon the other things that make up a standard of living. In an upwardly mobile area such as Hendon (N.W.) the incomes of the inhabitants and the standard of living they can enjoy vary a good deal. There is

1 Cf. above, p. 143, interview with J.G.
2 Interview with I.S., who still resides in the East End.
3 Interview with W.A., a resident of Stepney. (Fares have gone up since this interview took place!)
4 Interview with L.R. How the Jews crossed the Thames is, of course, no mystery in reality; what is of interest here is the interviewee's judgment of the southward moves as a deviation from the internal London *pattern*. It is to be noted that the settlements south of the river, in common with the distinctly provincial ones, were geographically isolated from other Jewish settlements. The areas in the main stream of migration, on the other hand, were more or less contiguous with each other.

diversity in types of houses and their size—the difference between a semi-detached and a detached house is an important one—in interior furnishings, car, and recreational pattern. Now it is evident that people in the lower income groups prefer to live at a lower standard in North-West London than at a higher standard in North and East London. At the lowest range one can afford to occupy only part of the dwelling, sub-letting one or two of the rooms.

A further extreme presents itself in the tension which exists in Jewish society between newly rich business men, oriented towards an ostentatious display of splendour, and professionals and ' near professionals '—communal workers with a sense of a career, a certain *esprit de corps,* but no specialised training—of moderate means, oriented towards cultivation and a gracious, though modest, style of life. Yet, these individuals, with divergent standards and who have little respect for each other, are to be found co-existing in almost all the upwardly mobile Jewish areas. That is, they are travelling on the same ' route ' out of the East End, though particularly so in the first moves where the differential in wealth is less of an obstacle. Though the individuals in the latter group feel that ' the only thing that counts around here is money,' they move into and remain in these areas. This is in spite of the fact that, in face-to-face contact with individuals of greater wealth in synagogue and neighbourhood activities, they experience a certain amount of status frustration. On the one hand they lack superior birth qualifications to those in the successful business class. It is of interest to note in this connection the gratification which such individuals derive from their image of the workings of the class system as ' righting ' things at the apex of the hierarchy. For example:

Among the various classes there is the uncouth wealthy, not interested in culture. If these people had no money, they would be brushed aside. As it is, a levelling out takes place at the top ; they aren't accepted by the aristocracy. In this area you could count the highly cultured on the fingers of one hand. They are only interested in bridge. If they come over here, though, they know they're not going to play because they know I don't keep a pack of cards in the house. They certainly can't enter a scientific society.[1]

[1] Interview with G.V.

L

On the other hand, Jewish society (generally, but especially at this level) is so 'small-townish' that a person is aware of the fact that others know within fairly accurate limits, or are constantly speculating about, the size of his income. He is doing the same thing himself. Furthermore, those who have achieved business success not only 'seem to be looking down' on those who have eschewed it (or failed to achieve it) but feel free to point it out to them as a 'proper' goal! For example:

Z . . ., a Jewish millionaire, gives money freely; but if I were to meet him on the street, he wouldn't have any time for me. Do you know what he once told me? 'What are you doing wasting your time with this work? When I was your age, the only thing I thought of was ways to make money.'[1]

Such statements are even more galling to a person when they come from those who in his opinion have defective consumption patterns, who 'don't know how to use their money.'

I once told a man that a friend of mine was going to America on a cargo ship. He said to me, 'Ha, that's goyim naches [*things which only non-Jews would enjoy*].' *They have to go first-class on the 'Mary,' don't call it the Queen. When we travel on the Continent we travel third-class. I suppose they think that's terrible.*[2]

Yet they remain and would be psychologically unprepared to move to a non-Jewish area, such as South Kensington or Chelsea, which would be one way of minimising exposure to these pressures towards business success. Not only do they want to live in a Jewish area for the fellowship with other Jews for themselves and their children which they value, for the emotional security *vis-à-vis* the non-Jewish world, for the services of the communal institutions available, but their status as they see it is a status in a Jewish *milieu*; and within that sector of Jewish society to which they belong residence in South Kensington is meaningless and eccentric. Where a choice becomes more specifically one between a new house in the north-west suburban area and a flat in an old converted town house in South Kensington, the new house is preferred.[3] On the

[1] Interview with C.R., an employee of a communal organisation.
[2] *Ibid.*
[3] The modern blocks of flats in St. John's Wood and the West End are a different matter. These, as I noted previously, have high status significance within this *milieu*.

contrary, residence in an upwardly mobile area, even though one lacks the full complement of symbols of success, gives one a minimal status in this *milieu* which is an important and recurrent source of self-esteem.

But though the agreement on the prestige value of residence in itself may be greater than that on other standard of living symbols, it is far from complete between individuals in different social strata. What is to be found is that individuals in different levels of the status hierarchy have different social horizons. That is, they look up and down in an active way at only a limited sector of a status hierarchy, characteristically at strata which are close to their own. Within these horizons fine social distinctions are drawn which would not be regarded as important or even be perceived by those who belong to other strata. A person in the London working class, for example, would neither be interested in nor know the relative social standing of Oxford Colleges. The existence of the distant social worlds, let alone their internal standards, may not be perceived or be only very dimly thought about. For example:

When you ask me to place people like the Montagus and the Rothschilds, to tell you the truth I never think about them.[1]

Thus, to an individual who after considerable effort has made the move from East to North-West London, this move is important. Furthermore, it is evaluated in this way by individuals to whom he looks for approval. Because this is important it is natural that they should draw a relatively fine distinction between the two areas. They would see things in the migration that others who stood distant from this whole experience would not. For example:

We came from the East End. But when we lived there twenty-five years ago, it was a different place. It was nicer then, the people were more balibatish *[of good standing]. Today, this [Hendon] is like what the East End was.*[2]

Contrast this with the following judgment made by a wealthier person dwelling in Hampstead, with a longer lineage in England:

As far as I can see, Hendon and those places are simply an adjunct of the East End. Not very typical of British Jewry.[3]

1 Interview with A.B.
2 Interview with F.R.
3 Interview with A.A.

In his circle people apologise for living in Hendon, ' explaining ' that they were among the first residents in the area.

One final comment needs to be made here. The opening up of new Jewish areas has often been attributed to the desire of the ' pioneers ' to flee from association with other Jews. Though this motive may exist[1] and though individuals with such propensities may in practice turn out to be models who attract other Jewish residents, it cannot be generalised to explain these movements as a whole—certainly not when the ' pioneers ' in an area are the founders and leaders of synagogues and other communal institutions in the new area. In fact, those individuals who have broken out of the urban pattern altogether and settled in the country have *not* been followed by other Jews in sufficient numbers to form an informal sub-community, let alone communal institutions. Where they have become apprehensive about the Jewishness of their children and, most particularly, the lack of other Jews for them to associate with and to marry, they have in cases felt compelled to move *back* to the metropolitan area.

What appears to be involved here is a mixture of ethnic and social class considerations. Individuals in the middle and lower-middle ranks of the class hierarchy are, as they migrate within London, removing themselves not from Jewish concentrations in themselves but from socially inferior ones. People in the upwardly mobile areas who in one sentence will refer to those whom they left behind as ' Peruvians ' will in the next say, ' We want to live with Jews.' Apart from the services of the communal institutions they can get in a Jewish area, they value the reassurance they get by seeing the faces of other Jews, by knowing that there are Jews near by. Note this, for example, in the following:

I like living here in Golders Green. There's a nice, safe and homely feeling.[2]

It will be recalled that the urge to get out of the East End arises from the fact that it is called the ghetto not only by non-Jews but by Jews as well.[3] In other words it has become inferior within the

[1] A case study of such behaviour is described in Louis Wirth's, *The Ghetto*, Chicago, 1929, p. 264.
[2] Interview with M.F.
[3] An interesting contrast are the cases of non-Jews who had been evacuated from East London during the war and desired to return there

Jewish world. In fact, the ghetto, that is the voluntary ghetto in the technical sociological sense, has not vanished at all. It has simply moved north and north-west to judge by the location of such communal institutions, in addition to synagogues, as kasher restaurants[1] and ritual baths.[2]

If a minimum number of Jews is a pre-requisite for Jewish communal life, how then do excessive concentrations of Jews lower the prestige of an area ? First, as the number of Jews in an area increases, their status attributes will become more heterogeneous. Once the area becomes known (in the Jewish world) as a place to which Jews are moving, at least some of the established Jewish residents are going to feel in the course of time that the ' wrong ' sorts of Jews are moving in, *viz.,* people who are their class inferiors.

Secondly, though the standards of residential quality, to be operative for Jews living in a Jewish society, must be part of the Jewish status system, they are not independent of standards in the non-Jewish world. For ultimately, this sets the tone in these matters. Thus the existence of non-Jews of the 'proper' class position in an area in an indirect way supports the prestige position of the area in the Jewish world. When the concentration of Jews becomes excessive enough for the non-Jews to repudiate the area as a ghetto, this negative evaluation will, in the course of time, find its way into the Jewish status system as well. But there is a time lag between these events.[3] At the same time as non-Jews are repudiating an area, Jews will be moving into it in the belief that it has prestige. But then, at first among the most sensitive and eventually the less, the standards finally cross between the two worlds. For example :

Ha! This isn't such a marvellous place any more. You know what they're calling it now ? Goldstein Green.[4]

at the end of it, who did not want to live anywhere else in London, and who were deeply attached to their local areas. But though the standard of housing in these areas was similar to that in the Jewish parts of East London, the inhabitants of the former did not have the sense of, among other things, living in a ghetto.

[1] V. *The Jewish Chronicle Travel Guide,* 1954, p. 41.
[2] V. *Ibid.,* p. 39.
[3] Gunnar Myrdal has noted the same time lag between the fashions in religious practice of whites and Negroes, Negroes having religious practices which are no longer common among whites but which were prevalent fifty years ago. Cf. his *American Dilemma,* New York, 1944, pp. 858-78.
[4] Interview with S.R., a doctor, who was born in the East End.

Contrast this with the very unqualified pride in residence in the area, in the interview cited with J.G.[1]

The Definition of a Jew

By what criteria does one Jew define another as a Jew?[2] Certainly a great deal of intellectual energy among Jews is taken up with this question. In informal conversation, organised lectures and discussion groups, and in print, themes related to this question frequently arise—' Are the Jews a nation, race, or a religious group ?' In particular, the impact of Zionism and the foundation of the State of Israel has resulted in a flood of self-examination and definition of ' positions,' much of it in controversial terms.

At one extreme are those Jews who hold the view that they are simply one of a multiplicity of religious denominations in a religiously heterogeneous society, comparable to any of the non-conformist groups ; at the other are those to whom the Jews are a nationality, and who at the final extreme advocate the ' liquidation of the exile.'

The stand which individual Jews take in these controversies may bear a certain loose relation to the length of time the individual's forebears have been resident in England. Just as those who hold the former view tend, in the vast majority of cases, to be from Anglo-Jewish families, so those who take the latter standpoint are generally closer to the immigrant generation.

We do not regard ourselves as Englishmen of the Jewish faith. Englishman to us is almost synonymous with Christian. I am a Jew living in Britain or, if you like, a British Jew.[3]

But there are foreign-born Jews, let alone the mass of British-born Jewry of the first and second generations, who simultaneously are identified with Israel and call themselves Englishmen in a more or less untroubled way,[4] yet when they begin to reflect about their status are somewhat puzzled. For example:

The Jewish upper-class are not my type of Jew. I wouldn't feel comfortable with them, feel more as if I'm with an English peer than

[1] Above, p. 143.   [2] See pp. 3-5, 60-63, 201-203.
[3] Interview with E.C., first generation British-born, Right-wing Orthodox.
[4] They are certainly English when they go abroad, even becoming ' Anglo-Saxons ' in Israel.

with my type of Jew. They don't have the homely Jewish traits, are not natural and spontaneous. . . . I consider myself an Englishman of the Jewish persuasion. But still, as long as I think about it, we have a dual obligation. To England, for which we have, if necessary, to lay down our lives, as the country which has taken us in and received us, and to the Jewish nationality—if there is such a thing.[1]

Q. *Do you call yourself an Englishman of the Jewish persuasion, a British Jew, etc. ?*

A. (husband): *Me, I'm a* Yid [*Jew*].

A. (wife): *No, I wouldn't say it quite that way. After all, we're English too, aren't we?*[2]

This unclarity is an indication of their new marginal position, their straddling of two worlds, as contrasted with the outlook of the Jew in the ghetto of the past. He knew, somewhat in the manner of the husband cited above, quite simply what he was. He was a Jew.

As soon as one leaves the world of ideology to examine the norms that actually are operative below the level of explicitness, one discovers the widest agreement on a belief that is essentially by-passed by those preoccupied with defining Jewry as a religious *or* a political entity. This is that Jews are a people between whom there is a biological bond. As such, the only true Jew is one born into the group.[3]

Agreement on this belief is revealed in manifold ways. Jews, wishing to adopt children, want them to be of Jewish birth ; and organised adoption societies have for a long time existed to fulfil this need.[4] Furthermore, Jewish opinion was aroused about the fate of children orphaned during the last war who were concealed from the Nazis by sympathetic Christians and brought up as Christians.[5]

Secondly, from the point of view of the born Jew the rôle of the

---

[1] Interview with M.F.   [2] Interview with J.G.

[3] Cf. Everett C. Hughes and Helen M. Hughes, *Where Peoples Meet*, Glencoe, 1952, p. 120.

[4] By Orthodox Jewish Law the child of a Jewish woman is Jewish ; thus female parentage is a sufficient criterion for those seeking to adopt a Jewish child.

[5] Opinion within the Jewish community on this matter was not unanimous. Those who dissented from the prevailing view that as Jews the children should be returned to Jewish hands did not in fact argue that the children were not Jews. They asserted rather that as the children did not know it, the strain of dislocating them was not worthwhile, etc.

convert to Judaism is eccentric. He would feel restrained, for example, from exhibiting in the latter's presence hostility towards the non-Jewish world.[1] Though it is more difficult to be converted to Orthodox than to Liberal Judaism, both groups place obstacles in the path of the potential convert, pointing out to him the difficulties of being a Jew and the rigour of the training process. In fact it is socially easier for a non-Jew, retaining his identity, to form profound and enduring ties with Jews than to be converted.

The obverse of the above is that to the born Jew persons of Jewish ancestry who no longer regard themselves as Jews are similarly eccentric or marginal because they are in some sense still Jews.[2] Certainly, individuals of this sort who have achieved eminence are liberally identified as Jews within the community. Note the frankness in this respect in the preamble to a list of honours and appointments in *The Jewish Year Book*:

> *The following list has not been limited to members of the synagogue or their children. A wider range has been taken— children and grandchildren of members of the Jewish religious community—themselves, despite their present connections and environment, products of Jewry and of the Synagogue. In these circumstances it is inevitably incomplete.*[3]

Of course, the further back in time that such individuals are (as, for example, Disraeli and Ricardo) the more painlessly can they be re-assimilated into the community. They are simply symbols—well beyond the span of time in which they could have injured the sentiments of anyone alive. Thus, no living member of the community has experienced the bitterness of having the claim that he placed—in his view, rightfully—upon another Jew rejected.

Related to this is the fact that a Jew who drifts away from Jewish society, even going so far as to embrace another religion, can return to it. From the point of view of those in the

[1] This may be due not merely to a lack of confidence in the convert (which can be very high), but to a desire to avoid hurting his feelings.
[2] They are even more eccentric where they have distinctly Jewish names.
[3] *The Jewish Year Book*, 1954, p. 309. Though this corresponds to actual practice, these views have been criticised by those who argue that if a person is not loyal enough to the group to call himself a Jew, he does not deserve to be called one.

group any person born a Jew has a minimal status as such which, except in cases of the most horrifying group disloyalty, he never loses.

A fourth index of the vitality of these ethnic sentiments is the very widespread preference for marriage within the group. In the ghettoes of the past, intermarriage was sadly marked by the same ritual mourning (*shiva*) observed in cases of actual death. Though this is no longer common, survivals of its central symbolism, the writing-off of the transgressor as socially dead, persist. For example:

> *Dr. A.'s brother intermarried, you know. And if you happen to ask him about his brother, he'll say, 'I don't have any brother.'*[1]

Although the personal problems arising from intermarriage are more easily coped with by assimilated Jews, whose association with non-Jews is smooth and easy, even among these individuals, and in spite of their apparently loose attachment to the Jewish community, there exists a definite disdain for intermarriage.[2]

Also of interest is the fascination typically created for Jews by the spectacle of Jews (or so-called Jews) who have obviously different biological characteristics. These would include Negroes, Chinese, Indians, etc.—what are often termed ' exotic ' Jews. They arrest attention in the first instance precisely because there is something ' wrong ' with their rôle-qualifications. One wonders how they were born into Jewry.

Heterogeneity and Cleavage

With the end of mass immigration from Eastern Europe since the First World War, Anglo-Jewry is of necessity becoming more homogeneous as a British-born community. Yet a generation of foreign-born Jews deriving from the mass East European influx is still active economically and a virile element in the social life of the community. On a smaller scale there are small enclaves of

---

[1] Interview with J.G.
[2] But see pp. 92-97. I was acquainted with a Jewish woman in the United States who became a Christian Scientist to cure herself of a tumour, but who was displeased when her son married a Christian.

'exotic' Jews organised in their own groups—the Chassidim in North London, the Sephardim in Manchester and in North London and Holland Park from the Near and Middle East (and who do have organisational ties with the anglicised Sephardim). Somewhat different, yet, in character, was the influx of refugees—primarily German and Austrian—from Hitlerism during the 1930s. Though they still live to a high degree in a social *milieu* composed of other 'Continental' (*i.e.*, Central European Jewish) refugees, they did not form a sub-community within Anglo-Jewry along religious lines.

These diversities in place of origin are symbolically linked, in the eyes of Jews making judgments about one another, to distinctive expectations about behaviour. Certain kinds of judgments between individuals belonging to different groups are, of course, socially inconsequential. These are judgments which essentially demarcate groups rather than rank them. Such, for instance, would be the mutual ridicule of the differences in dialect amongst Yiddish-speaking Jews,[1] or of comments about differences in culinary preferences and skills. To the extent, however, that these expectations have a moral significance, they are a basis of judgments of rank.

For example, amongst East European Jews, 'Litvaks' would typically have regarded Rumanians as too hot-tempered ; Galicians ('Galizianers') as untrustworthy ; Hungarians as less industrious than themselves, the men preferring to sit in coffee houses all day and letting their wives run their businesses. It was most natural for Litvaks to believe that the dream of every Hungarian woman was a Litvak husband.

Many of these stereotypes are simply an ascription of what are regarded as the traits of the host populations to the Jews living amongst them, such as :

There's nothing wrong with the German Jews except that they're exactly like Germans. Real dictators. Prussians. They could push their way in anywhere.[2]

In the peak days of the East London ghetto, group distinctions amongst the immigrants had vitality and implications for social relationships in such matters as the choice of a husband or wife.

[1] Jokes about individuals who cannot pronounce the *sh* sound are still current.   [2] Interview with H.E.

With the gradual anglicisation of the immigrants and their participation in social groups outside the world of the *shtiebel* and *chevra*,
these sentiments have *pari passu* lost these implications. Among
their British-born descendants they persist only as a vestigial basis
of identification with no significant consequences for behaviour.
This is simply another instance of loss of group consciousness
based upon place of origin. For example, the ' Dutch Jews ' of the
late nineteenth and early twentieth centuries are no longer the
entity that they were. Similarly, the social distinction between
Sephardim and Ashkenazim, though by no means extinguished,
hardly has the significance that it had in the seventeenth and
eighteenth centuries.[1]

But the relationships between the Jews whose families were
established in England before the mass influx from Eastern Europe
and those deriving from this influx are still marked by a mutual
sense of the difference in English ancestry. I shall call the former
group the anglicised (or the old) élite and the latter group the Jews
of the newer immigration. At the outset it must be clearly
emphasised that these are not homogeneous groups. Nor are the
group identifications so clear-cut that two distinct, mutually
exclusive groups can readily be seen, with no overlap of persons
and no uncertainty of boundary. But even though these terms are
but generalisations, they are useful as initial reference points
because, to an important extent, they are so used by the individuals
in the minority society themselves.

When the Jews of the newer immigration were massed in the
East End, leadership of the community—the bigger institutions,
and certainly the representative ones—was in the hands of the old
élite. This was a group of families interrelated by marriage which
contained a nucleus of great wealth.[2] Wealth conferred prestige
within the community by virtue of the highly esteemed philanthropy
which it made possible as well as the leadership in communal
institutions which fell to those who heavily supported or, in some
cases, actually founded these institutions.

[1] Cf. Cecil Roth, *A History of the Jews in England,* 2nd edn., London,
1949, p. 197. The fact that some Ashkenazim were welcome at the Sephardi
congregation makes it clear that there was no caste barrier between them
(as is sometimes alleged) and that it was differences of wealth and style
of behaviour that were the basis of differentiation.
[2] *The Jewish Year Book, 1954,* p. 132.

By the time of the mass influx they had acquired not only anglicised patterns of behaviour but symbols of prestige in the non-Jewish world. A small leisure class and a small professional class had made its appearance within this group as evidenced by the founding in 1891 of the Maccabeans as a 'society of Jews and Jewesses consisting primarily of those engaged in professional pursuits.' With respect to Jewish communal life they had already developed within their own families a tradition of communal service. Officials and social workers, who were voluntary and unpaid, were recruited on a basis of kinship. On reaching adulthood children were expected to take up some form of communal work in their spare time.

At the peak of the influx there was essentially little integration between the established Jews living in the West End and the poor immigrants living in the East End. The élite saw themselves as the leaders of the whole of the community. But the mass of the foreign-born, indifferent to the world outside, maintained an autonomous social life withdrawn not only from the non-Jewish world but also from the established Anglo-Jewish élite. The points of contact between the two were maintained mostly through the social work and the philanthropic activities of the élite.[1]

Although considerable distrust of the English Jews existed among foreign-born Jews on the grounds of the former's supposed uncertain piety,[2] the old élite was, on the other hand, highly esteemed for the benefits it conferred upon other Jews. To this day this remains true for the reason that the élite ' plays its part in the Jewish community.' Thus its status within the Jewish community rests mainly upon a history of communal service and leadership.

The Rothschilds, Montagus, Henriques, Sir Robert Waley-Cohen are a group of people who in their lives and in their families have done a lot for the Jewish community. Have always been in the forefront of Jewish philanthropy. Are known in other spheres and intimately connected with other spheres. Have an entrée into circles which others don't have.[3]

[1] Beatrice Potter (Webb), 'The Jewish Community (East London),' in Charles Booth (ed.), *Life and Labour of the People*, 1892, vol. III, p. 171.
[2] Russell and Lewis, *op. cit.*, p. 21.
[3] Interview with S.R.

This pattern of esteem has, of course, undergone certain changes in recent times. First, the greater degree of anglicisation and the rise in the standard of living among the descendants of the newer immigration have served to diminish their sense of social inferiority towards the old élite and have led them to expect a greater proportion of communal offices. Secondly, there has been a change in the kind of leadership demanded, a change requiring from the leadership a greater sense of identification with the mood of the rank and file.

This is seen particularly in connection with the Zionist movement. Of all the many facets of Zionism the most relevant here is the way in which the vision which it presented to the Jewish people—the vision of being no longer a despised minority—captured the imagination of those Jews who stood on the margin of two worlds. It should be recalled that the East European village ghetto was largely hostile to Zionism. How dare one presume to take into one's own hands that which it is prophesied may come about only through Divine agency?[1] The anglicised élite was also hostile or, at best, indifferent. Its members were psychologically incapable of responding to Zionism as either potential emigrants or as people to whom Palestine, and subsequently Israel, was ' their country.'[2] Thus the support which many of the élite *did* give to Zionism did not have an intense emotional attachment to the Zionist symbols underlying it. It was the kind of support which they would have given to any foreign Jewry in distress—a sphere of activity in which indeed the élite had a distinguished record. But to those individuals of the newer immigration whose demands for respect from the non-Jewish world were raised with the assimilation of that world's standards of achievement and who yet were somewhat fearful of it, the nationalist symbols of Zionism were a source of compensatory self-esteem.

Perhaps of more basic importance than the content of the nationalist programme are different conceptions of what are appropriate methods of political action for a minority group. The Jews of the newer immigration, more fearful of the outside world,

[1] There are Jews of this outlook in Israel itself who, waiting for the *Messiah,* do not ' recognise ' Israel as a legitimate nation-State.
[2] Much the same is revealed in the distaste experienced in singing the *Hatikvah* at public functions.

place a premium upon the expression of protest which is in part an end in itself.[1] This end is the reassurance which the very enunciation of this protest creates. Such activity is also of course motivated by the belief in its efficacy. But although a detailed treatment of this point is outside the scope of this essay, it is my impression that its usefulness is exaggerated by those who advocate it. Its sociological significance would appear to lie in the way in which tension produced by an external irritant is reduced in the very process of coming to grips with it; and this remains so whether or not such activity produces any practical results.[2]

The old élite deplored as improper such aggressive self-assertion of the minority in connection with Zionism. Such demands, its members argued, would not be made by a British body primarily identified with Britain. Secondly, they regarded their own methods of seeking political results—methods characterised by the avoidance of public resolutions and a greater emphasis upon high level personal contacts with officials in government departments—as more beneficial for *Jewry*.

In these circumstances the leadership of the élite as suitable guardians of the minority's relations with the host society's political institutions has, in recent times, been to a great extent repudiated on the ground that they are " afraid to stand up for the Jews."

Z . . . has been too pro-British. Because of him we lost Transjordan.[3]

To this extent they have been displaced in esteem as leaders with a community-wide influence by men like the late President Chaim Weizmann or wealthy men stemming from the body of the newer immigration who have given massive financial support to Zionist activities. This has been concretely materialised in the change of power within the Board of Deputies in 1943 when first-generation, pro-Zionist representatives became the majority. The old élite to some extent came to withdraw from this body, though it is still actively identified with political affairs of the Jewish

---

[1] I refer here to protest on the part of leaders or of organised groups. Few in Anglo-Jewry, except perhaps the elderly foreign-born from Eastern Europe, would feel that Jews must turn the other cheek when personally insulted.
[2] It is in this light that much of the activity of Jewish defence organisations could be most properly assessed. [3] Interview with P.G.

community through the Anglo-Jewish Association. The members of the old élite also continue to take a prominent part on the boards of such non-political charities as the Jewish Board of Guardians, the Jewish Orphanage at Norwood, and many cultural bodies, all of which taken together are institutions that Anglo-Jewry could ill afford to lose.

Notwithstanding the status revolt symbolised by the change in power in the Board of Deputies, the old élite is still highly esteemed—for the part which they *do* play in the community, for their family status, and for their anglicised behaviour. Association with them is an active object of social aspiration.

Egalitarianism

Certain sources of the egalitarianism which prevails amongst Jews lie in their historic cultural tradition. Among these is the fact that Judaism, ever since its transformation during the Talmudic period, has been a religion without priestly mediators. The heart of the service is reading a portion of the Law, which any ten men are qualified to carry on.[1] In the Jewries of the past, Talmudical learning was the basis of the highest prestige; and though individuals prided themselves upon descent from distinguished scholars, the scholar-rabbinical élite was one into which a man could ascend by his own aptitudes. A clever but poor youngster was frequently regarded as a good match by the better-off parents of a marriageable girl and maintained by them while he pursued his studies.

It was also in the nature of traditional Jewish educational methods to develop a modicum of anti-authoritarianism. A young man in a *Yeshiva* (rabbinical academy) who could challenge and successfully correct an interpretation of the Law of his older teacher would be admired both by him and by others.[2]

Beyond this, however, there are several aspects of life in a minority social structure that enhance egalitarianism. The first is that being a member of a minority group gives one, to a certain extent, a common status in the host society. Where it is at all

[1] Congregations can thus be independent.
[2] Mark Zborowski and Elizabeth Herzog, *Life is with People ; the Jewish Little-Town of Eastern Europe*, New York, 1952, p. 99.

an inferior status, a ceiling exists upon the legitimate differentiation which can arise between the members of the minority. This
ceiling is reached where an individual appears to disavow his
minority status.

In armies, for example, it is socially difficult to retain an
officer in the same company after he has been promoted from
the ranks. His prior status would cling to him ; the men would
have a difficulty in regarding him in a clear-cut way as an officer.
By the same token Jews who achieve positions of authority in the
host society may mobilise anti-authoritarianism on the part
of those Jews who are placed under them, even though it is not
outwardly expressed.[1]

This anti-authoritarianism is also seen in the more or less
mild ridicule of those who acquire symbols of prestige in the
outside world which are not thought of as conventionally held by
Jews (such, for instance, as becoming an M.F.H.). A more cruel
expression of it is to blame Jews who experience real or fancied
rebuffs in the non-Jewish world for ' pushing themselves where
they're not wanted.'

There is an important implication of the above in the way
in which Jews of the newer immigration view the anglicised élite.
To a significant extent the Jews of the newer immigration do not
regard the élite in a clear-cut way as Jews. Because the élite does
not conform to their own experience of what a Jew is, they are
seen, partly, as being more unequivocally English than members
of the rank and file.

*I was at a meeting when Lord A.... got up and said that he's
a Jew and feels the bond of blood, not in the fascist sense, but
still kinship with other Jews. Well, the very fact that he got up
to say this, the fact that he felt he had to say this, seems to me
that he doesn't really feel it except on the surface. I do not feel
that these are people whom I consider fellow Jews, whom I
could have in for a cup of tea.*[2]

Of interest are *images* that the élite do not behave as Jews (*i.e.*, as
members of a minority) : that they do not have an inferiority

[1] There are Negro domestic servants who refuse to work for other
Negroes, which is a parallel phenomenon.
[2] Interview with P.L.

complex, that they are more ' at home ' with non-Jews than with less anglicised Jews, that they cannot be approached informally.

> *People like Lord K.... regard themselves as Englishmen of the Jewish faith. I'm very sensitive about things that they are not. I'll give you an instance. The other day I was with one of the K....'s and we were getting on a bus. Well the conductor gave the starting signal before K.... had got on and he said, " I'm going to give that conductor a good talking to." I thought to myself the first thing that will happen is that the conductor will call him a Jew and it will be very embarrassing. So I said, ' Don't say anything. Just let it pass.' Well, he was quite furious and determined to call down the conductor because one of his brothers lost his leg in the war and in a similar situation, when a bus was starting, fell flat on his back. So he said to me, ' You're sensitive aren't you?' I said, ' Quite frankly, yes.' You see, they think of themselves as Englishmen.[1]*

> *The anglicised Jews are not my type of Jew. When with them I don't feel as if I'm in the presence of Jews—rather, the aristocracy. The anglicised can intermarry. You don't expect them after five generations not to. But not the foreign-born.[2]*

> *The Monds or the Rothschilds and J....* [a newly rich millionaire] *are miles apart. When one of the Rothschilds comes into our shop, you feel something inside of you. I can't explain it. The Rothschilds are friendly on committees only. If I happen to be on a committee with one of them, and I have done something that draws their attention to me, well, if we meet on the street, it will be, ' Good morning, Mr. S....' But it's always done in a way which means I'm up here and you're down there. Now if J.... was sitting on this committee and I had a business proposition to interest him in, something that would be for his advantage, he would listen and I could talk to him. But I could never approach the Rothschilds about a business matter.[3]*

It often comes as a surprise to first generation Jews to discover

---

[1] Interview with F.J.
[2] Interview with O.S. Though it is widely asserted of anglicised Jews that they marry out more frequently than other kinds of Jews, there is no foundation in fact for this belief in modern times.
[3] Interview with I.S.

M

by personal observation that Jews with a long lineage in this country are, after all, ' really ' Jews :

I was planning a trip with X, who is a member of one of the oldest Jewish families in England, and told him that I would like to bring someone else along. The first thing he asked me, very quickly, was, " Is he a Jew?" Interesting that that was on his mind. I also happen to have learned that he had a very bad time at public school when the Christians beat him up.[1]

One of the conclusions to be drawn from the above expressions of opinion is that the conception of an upper class is equated with the non-Jewish world. It is a basic factor in explaining why no class distinctions are drawn within the society of the Jews of the newer immigration comparable to those drawn between themselves and the anglicised élite. For example:

Q. Would you put Z [first generation communal leader, born in the East End] in the upper class ?

A. No. Well, he's a Jew if you know what I mean. The upper-class are Englishmen who are Jews by religion. They can separate their Jewishness from their Englishness. We can't.[2]

Q. Do you feel that there are any social classes among Jews ?

A. Yes, two, no three. First, the top—those who have culture, learning, breeding, family—people like the Montagus, Lord Justice Cohen, Sir Robert Waley-Cohen, Viscount Samuel. Then the main group—99½ per cent of all the Jews in London. Then, at the bottom, the spivs and parasites (although I must say that I have to admire some of them for getting on).[3]

A second point about the minority society is that offices in communal institutions are highly valued for the prestige they confer, and there is therefore a great demand for them. Of interest is the conception which Jews, and particularly those coming from East European backgrounds, have of themselves as having this demand for prestige :

I work for the Board of Trade and have a good deal to do with Jewish business men in the course of my work. Every so often

[1] Interview with C.R. Anglicised Orthodox informants have told me how recently immigrant Jews cannot believe that they are Orthodox.

[2] Interview with M.B.

[3] Interview with S.R. Note that the lowest class mentioned is a deviant group.

one of them will say to me, 'What is a bright boy like yourself doing in such a job?' I always reply, sort of as a joke, 'Oh, I do it for the coved *[prestige].' This happened recently and the man said to me, 'Well I suppose that's right. A Jew has to have either* coved *or money.'*[1]

Note also the following variation of an anecdote in circulation among Jews :

If five shipwrecked Jews reach a desert island, there will soon be six synagogues, seven rabbis, and eight wardens.

The following statements, with which the respondents often opened their interviews, are common clichés among Jews :

Jews are always running each other down.

You know what they say about Jews, a Jew is his worst enemy.

Also of interest is that Jews are ready to explain the behaviour of other Jews in terms of calculated desires for prestige.[2] It may also be noted how the 'pushiness' of individuals presented itself as a central aspect of their behaviour in interviews cited with H.E.[3] and J.G.[4]

The fact that office in communal institutions is so esteemed and so coveted imparts a certain strain to the workings of Jewish organisations. Among other things it produces a latent tendency towards schism. In the seventeenth century, in the very earliest period of the modern community, there was a succession

[1] Interview with D.S. Note the difference in values on the status of civil service employment.

[2] This is most pronounced of upwardly mobile Jews and is true of upwardly mobile people in general. For example, one hears from middle-class individuals who have, as it were, an open window looking on to the upper class in England that individuals in the latter group dress 'down' and 'thereby show their superiority.' What is of interest here in this 'explanation' is the way in which such behaviour appears to the middle class. In fact, a much simpler and correct explanation of why the upper classes dress 'down,' which they do, particularly when in the country, is that it is 'done' in their circles. They do not want to look 'overdressed,' not in any important respect in order to demonstrate to remote, unknown individuals that they do not need to dress up, but because in their *own* circles this is disapproved of. It is towards the standards of these people that their behaviour is oriented. To explain how this standard arose in their circle one would have to examine the penetration into English culture of Stoic standards, Puritanism, etc. The French aristocracy, it is of interest to note, do not dress 'down.'

[3] Above, p. 154.   [4] Below, p. 180.

of withdrawals from synagogues by those who, unwilling to accept a position in the background, founded new organisations over which they could preside. At first the Ashkenazim withdrew from the established (Sephardi) synagogue, having been relegated to an inferior status within it ;[1] and then there were subsequent schisms within the Ashkenazi community as well.[2] This tendency towards schism is counterbalanced by a spirit of ' clubbiness ' and by the subjectively experienced prestige of belonging to the organisation. The Sephardi group is much more of a ' gentlemen's club ' than any of the Ashkenazi institutions, and the one important schism which did occur in this group, viz., the withdrawal of the reformers in the nineteenth century, was the result of a policy difference. As I have noted in another context (p. 175) the United Synagogue synagogues within the Ashkenazi orthodox camp are fashionable ; and this motivates a desire, if the prestige of office is sought, to seek it within those groups rather than to withdraw and found new ones.

One important sphere in which anti-authoritarian rivalry emerges is in the representation of the community. Here the rivalry is not merely between individuals *per se* but between them as representatives of groups or factions within the community. There has never been a long period in Anglo-Jewish history when there has not been some rivalry of this kind. Even before the community was on a firm legal foundation there was tension between Menasseh ben Israel and the leaders of the cautious party who were afraid that he was proceeding too radically.[3] But when the community was as small and cohesive as it was in the first years after the Resettlement, this was less of a problem. The leaders of the group, who were the wealthy merchants, would very naturally exercise their leadership in a representative capacity as well without arousing protest.

With increasing complexity of the community and division, not only into sub-groups, but sub-communities, the situation in this

[1] Lionel D. Barnett (ed.), *Bevis Marks Records : Being Contributions to the History of the Spanish and Portuguese Congregation of London*, Part I, Oxford, 1940, p. 31, who suggests that the Ashkenazim may have incurred unpopularity by asserting themselves too conspicuously.
[2] Cecil Roth, *A History of the Jews in England*, 2nd edn., London, 1949, p. 197.   [3] Barnett, *op. cit.*, pp. 1-3.

respect changes. For without an authority structure in which not only the internal roles but also the representative ones are given legal form,[1] in terms of the law of the land, leadership in the latter sphere can be usurped. An individual can claim to be a spokesman for Jewry who is hardly regarded as such by other members of the minority. Their reaction is to feel that either they are not being 'properly' represented or not represented at all, especially where their very existence is ignored by the individual or the group which appropriates for itself representative functions.[2]

A concrete example of such tension is that which arose in the eighteenth century in connection with the Coronation. Which group was going to tender the address of loyalty to the Sovereign was an internal 'political' problem. By the time of the eighteenth century the Ashkenazi community contained lay leaders who were in every way as socially qualified to represent the community as were the leaders of the Sephardim; indeed, the former had personal connections with the Royal Family. When on the accession of George III the Sephardim simply ignored them in presenting their Address of Loyalty,[3] their protest led to the founding of the Board of Deputies, i.e., the amalgamation of the representative institutions of the two communities.

Another example of this tension in contemporary times was the dissolution by the Board of Deputies of the Joint Foreign Affairs Committee,[4] on which it had collaborated with the Anglo-Jewish Association. The reason for this action was the Board's fear that it could not count upon the Anglo-Jewish Association to support the demand for a Jewish state in Palestine.

The 'Openness' of the Minority Society

The minority society of the ghetto, corporately organised in relation to the non-Jewish world and more or less uninterested in its culture, has been aptly called by Dr. Parkes 'the closed

---

[1] As contrasted with the situation on the Continent during the period of absolutism. There the court Jews were, in their rôles as the leaders of Jewish communities, royal or princely officials.

[2] In the absence of corporate autonomy the degree to which such spokesmen can effect the material privileges of other Jews is for all practical purposes nil.

[3] Roth, *A History of the Jews in England*, p. 222.   [4] See p. 35.

community.' By contrast a minority may be called ' open ' where the law of the host society operates directly upon the members of the minority, as individuals, who, in addition, freely assimilate the culture of the wider society. It is in this special sense that the term is used below.

Anglo-Jewry, in the first instance, lacks political autonomy. Where Government officials do recognise the Jewish community as an entity and delegate decisions involving Jews to officials of Jewish representative or social service organisations, in general this constitutes informal collaboration. Advice may be needed for which Jewish leaders have to be consulted. For example, when rationing was begun the Ministry of Food collaborated with the leaders of the United Synagogue (who thus assumed leadership in this sphere for the whole community) in developing the system used for kasher food rationing.[1] On a more local and personal level, Jews in the East End who, in the pre-war period, applied to civil magistrates to adjudicate in disputes between themselves were often advised to consult their own rabbi first and so settle the matter by the use of their ' own ' internal methods of adjudication. Juvenile delinquents charged with minor offences, in particular, were, and still may be, ' returned ' to the ' custody ' of Jewish social service organisations.

A second aspect of this openness is that Britain and her culture are profoundly admired by Jews of all walks of life. England, first of all, is regarded very consciously as a symbol of benignity by the immigrant generation, who in the deepest reaches of their minds do not quite take their membership in the society for granted. For example :

During the First World War there was a sign on the offices of The Jewish Chronicle *saying that Jews should do their duty. A certain rabbi got up and said that we had no duty to England, that we were like guests here and that they could turn us out at a moment's notice. Well, no decent Jew would talk like that. After all, they took us in here and let us make a living.*[2]

---

[1] Even this, however, is but a convenience made available to those who wish to use it. It is comparable to the special arrangements made for vegetarians who, from the point of view of the Government (and, in fact) are but a special class, not a minority group.

[2] Interview with S.M.

Though individuals may romantically reminisce about such things as the tranquillity of the Sabbath in the *haim* (Eastern Europe; literally, homeland), its associations are more likely to be unpleasant: crude housing, filthy streets, cruel violence of the non-Jews. This admiration extends equally to the British way of life as opposed to that of Eastern Europe. For example:

I think the Jew should acquire the culture of this country. Twenty years ago if one just talked English, one was looked up to.[1]

When I was a boy in Poland, to speak Polish in a synagogue was considered to defile it. We spoke only Yiddish.[2]

Among the foreign-born the ability to speak English well has always been and is today a source of pride. Individuals feel free to correct one another's mistakes and are looked up to for their superior knowledge. Those who cannot speak any English ' apologise ' for this to the British-born. Jokes ridicule foreign accents and the malapropisms of the foreign-born. The expression ' English type ' is commonly used in tones of approval among the foreign-born, to refer to their children. By the same token much of the respect in which the anglicised élite are held by the Jews of the newer immigration is due to their conformity to the style of behaviour of the English gentleman[3]:

Q. *Do you think the Jewish upper class is too English?*

A. *No, I admire them for their English ways, their politeness. They know how to speak and to act. The trouble with us is that we're too* grob [*vulgar*].[4]

In turn the élite pride themselves upon their superior anglicisation. Some of the concrete criteria, which on the whole have been taken over by less anglicised Jews in drawing distinctions among themselves, will be noted below. One thing, however, is much more prominent in the values of the élite than in that of the less anglicised Jew. This is their distaste for what they regard as the excessive self-enclosure of the foreign-born Jew and certain ghetto traits of

[1] Interview with N.A.   [2] Interview with C.O.
[3] Considerable ambivalence exists towards the anglicised élite as a whole and towards English standards, particularly where conformity is judged as excessive—' aping the Gentiles.' (See below.) The positive esteem for these standards and their assimilation into the behaviour models within the community, however, is important and to be stressed.
[4] Interview with G.V.

behaviour. In the first instance this would be revealed in the mild ridicule of the ' elephant-and-the-Jewish-Question ' mentality—*i.e.*, looking at things only from the point of view of how they affect Jews. Much more serious is disagreement about the terms used to describe non-Jews and about the basic values underlying these terms. The word *Yok*, East End in origin and implying extreme contempt of the non-Jew, is shunned by the anglicised Jew. (Many of them never heard the word until they went to do social work in the East End.) Even the word *goy*, which is a real Hebrew word, produces its troubles. There is, in fact, occasional correspondence in *The Jewish Chronicle* as to its propriety.

The main trait associated with the ghetto which is so unpleasant to anyone who has never lived in one is the suspiciousness and fear of other people.

I do not like the foreign-born Jews too much. So very many have risen above foreign birth, but the majority still think in a foreign way. That is, they have a persecution complex. Very distrustful of another's motives, always thinking that he is trying to get something out of it. Once I did a foreign-born Jew a favour and he later asked somebody why I was doing it for him. This other person said, ' Don't be foolish. He is doing this because you asked him.' That's what I mean.[1]

The openness of Anglo-Jewish society is most fully manifest, however, on yet a third level. This is the desire to ' appear well ' before the non-Jewish world and thus to gain its good opinion for conformity to its standards.

Sometimes in talking with Jews one gets the impression that they think that a gigantic telescope is focused upon them by the non-Jewish world, which does very little else but sit and stare and approve and condemn. Basically this would seem to be a projection of their own sensitivity about themselves on to non-Jews.[2]

[1] Interview with K.M., grandfather born in England.
[2] I was once at a ' Jewish ' evening, *i.e.*, one consisting of an exchange of jokes, stories, and information about Jews, where one of the young men present, as an afterthought following a particularly heavy run of jokes with the Jewish-non-Jewish theme, made the remark: ' You know, I'm sure that Gentiles don't think about us nearly as much as we think about them. A friend of mine told me that they can go for days without even mentioning the word Jew.'

This preoccupation with themselves is not, of course, a distinctively modern characteristic of behaviour among Jews. The leaders of the earliest seventeenth-century congregation were concerned in the highest degree with the prevention of any action by a Jew which, they thought, would provoke the hostility of the non-Jewish world.

These 'political' fears still persist within present-day Anglo-Jewry. (They are also characteristic of other group-conscious but socially insecure minorities such as the American Negroes.) There is still, for example, a strong distaste for the spectacle of two Jews attacking each other before the eyes of the non-Jewish world, such as suing in court. In part this is formulated precisely in the terms of the old 'closed' outlook—*viz.,* that any display of internal disunion will instantaneously be exploited by a hostile environment, and is but an invitation if not to disaster then to trouble.

More fundamentally, however, this distaste would appear to rest upon a sense of the grave impropriety of revealing to outsiders any signs of disloyalty towards fellow-members of the community. There is characteristically a strong sanction within families against 'washing one's dirty linen in public.' This is buttressed by beliefs that the best elements in the non-Jewish world have no respect for a disloyal Jew.

Liberal theologians who, as a result of their criticism of Orthodoxy in their preaching and publications, would feel exposed to this specific charge, have countered in such terms as these :

Some would say Dr. Wiener was putting a weapon in the hands of the antisemites, others that dirty linen must not be washed in public (which means that it must never be washed). At present if any attempt is made within the Jewish community to bring to light a religious evil, we are at once met by the rejoinder : ' Hush, in the face of antisemitism, not a word must be said which could imply that all the Jews are not perfectly united.' Any amount of laxity is of less consequence. Not every Gentile critic of Judaism is an antisemite. Jews are far too ready to assume that this is the case. It is pleasant to avoid the unpleasant task of trying to find out whether there is any truth in any Gentile criticism. Rishuss, antisemitism, we say, and the thing is done. But though the method is easy, it is perilous.[1]

Furthermore, much of the preoccupation with obtaining the good will of the non-Jewish world is formulated in terms of its *political* consequences for the Jewish community as a whole ; it is commonly thought and felt that the esteem of the non-Jewish world for a Jew will *benefit* the community collectively, and that its disapproval will harm. A very crude example of this, in highly utilitarian terms, is the following :

The Rothschilds are useful to have. They are esteemed by non-Jews.[2]

I feel distant from the old English Jews, those whose families have been in this country at least three to five generations. Yet they are a credit to Jewry. They mix with the upper-class Englishmen and dispel antisemitism. I say that every Gentile is a born antisemite, or at least becomes one as soon as he learns to read. Even if he doesn't go to church regularly, if he goes only at Easter, I hear there are some very uncomplimentary things said about Jews in the Easter service. Well, the Englishman looks at these upper-class Jews and sees that they don't have horns. They have their uses, as I said. They are good ambassadors.[3]

One gets the impression from such remarks that it does not matter very much to these individuals why the outside world approves or disapproves of a given set of traits. All that is important is that it has certain standards which have to be taken into account, as facts, if its approval is desired. This utilitarian orientation towards the approval of others is to be contrasted with one where individuals intrinsically value the standards of approval.[4]

---

[1] C. G. Montefiore, ' Dr. Wiener on the Dietary Laws,' a review of *Die jüdischen Speisegesetze nach ihren verschiedehen Gesichtskpunkten zum ersten Male wissenschaftlichmethodisch geordnet und kritisch beleuchtet*, by Dr. A. Wiener, in *Jewish Quarterly Review* (old series), vol. VIII, pp. 392ff. The writer overlooks—as characteristically as do those on the ' right ' whom he criticises—the fact that most Gentiles would be totally uninterested in polemics between Jews about their dietary laws.
[2] Interview with M.F.
[3] Interview with M.B.
[4] *Cf.* David Riesman's comprehensive treatment of this distinction as applied to American sociey in *The Lonely Crowd*, Yale, 1950, and *Faces in the Crowd*, Yale, 1952.

In some cases a very clear-cut classification can be made. With respect to commercial malpractice, such statements as 'Well, everybody does it a little, but you have to keep it quiet'; 'I don't mind a crook, but not a brazen crook,' indicate no great respect for the standard in question. Contrast this with:

I admire a Jew who has made a mark in the world. Someone like Ehrlich. Look what he did for humanity, and a Jew ![1]

But the dividing line between the two orientations is often a subtle one ; and the difficulties are compounded by the facts that the orientations are often mixed and that people deceive themselves somewhat in explaining their own behaviour.

For example, the effort behind the publication of the various lists which have appeared of Jews who have done military service is typically justified by some such assertion as : 'Now the non-Jews should have no reason to doubt that we have done our part.' But this conceals not so much the existence as the primary importance of the intrinsic pride in this achievement felt by individuals who are identified with the host society. In any event, who read these lists ? Non-Jews ? Hardly.[2]

In any event both types of outlook converge in the wide-spread and great esteem given to those who can 'represent' the community, whom Jews are proud to exhibit to the gaze of the non-Jewish world and who, *known as Jews,* have achieved something which (it is believed) is highly valued by the non-Jewish world and who thus 'automatically' attract its approval.[3] This would include political office, titles and degrees, entry into a rôle or the attainment of an honour hitherto not held by Jews.

On the other hand, these same individuals are those who have representative functions (or are envisaged as having them)—people of power and influence in communal organisations—who are felt to be respected by non-Jews for their conformity to models of behaviour esteemed in the outside world.

The changes which have occurred in the rôle of the rabbi neatly reflect the changes in the value system. In the closed phase of Jewish

[1] Interview with H.R.
[2] Would Jews be interested in reading similar lists of Catholics ?
[3] There is a Yiddish term, *shepn naches* (lit., 'gather pleasure '), commonly used to describe this attraction of approval.

society prestige was determined by an internal set of criteria which the outside world did not share : excellence in Talmudical learning, benefits conferred upon other Jews through the uses of wealth or connections with the authorities, and a family background of these traits. The scholar-rabbi, at the apex of the prestige hierarchy, was associated with that part of their cultural tradition that Jews regarded not merely as most sacred but as most distinctive. This was the Law. In this culturally self-sufficient milieu the idea that the rabbi should approximate non-Jewish models of behaviour was preposterous, if not positively insulting—when bad behaviour within the Jewish group itself was characterised as un-Jewish. (In fact, as mentioned previously, the foreign-born rabbi was, up to the present time, a characteristic figure of Anglo-Jewish society throughout its entire history.)

But in the opening up of the closed Jewry, all Jews have come to thrust upon each other the responsibility of becoming ' representative ' in relation to the outside world. Living, as it were, in a sort of glass house, no one is exempt, let alone the rabbi, whom the outside world would very naturally regard as a leader of the community. Note this in the following :

Rabbi X——— has got to be able to speak the King's English because he deals so much with non-Jews. Z——— couldn't but may be above him in learning.[1]

The Chief Rabbi is the Chief Rabbi of the British Empire, and don't forget that he was the Senior Jewish Chaplain of H.M. Forces.[2]

The Chief Rabbi is a very fine type of man. Our mouthpiece to the outside. His own ministers think very well of him. Was army chaplain. He has fluency in English and has to have in order to represent us to the outside. Furthermore, he is quiet, unassuming, gentlemanly, and stands up for other Jews. . . .

I hold a rabbi with an English education higher than the ten-a-penny kind in the East End. I'm taking it for granted that he knows as much about Jewish learning as the East End man. But non-Jews are apt to disparage the latter as foreign, and especially the way they dress.[3]

[1] Interview with B.C.   [2] Interview with S.R.   [3] Interview with M.F.

Compare the above with the following, which does not refer to a rabbi at all :

> *I could look up to Lord Justice Z——— because he is so very upright, so completely unbiased in his administration of justice, the kind of man who is esteemed by Jews and non-Jews alike, the kind of man who won't feel ashamed of being a Jew, if you know what I mean. When he walks by, the non-Jews will admire him and note that he is a man of the Jewish faith or persuasion. We need more types like him.*[1]

This pressure to be a representative places a very serious strain upon the rôle of the traditional, Talmudically trained scholar-rabbi, most marked in the case of the foreign-born rabbi whose command of English is weak. The rank and file of native-born Jews do not regard him as qualified to represent the community—' too foreign, not modern enough, not my type of Jew '; and alienated from the Talmudical tradition, they do not give him the respect to which he would feel entitled by virtue of his scholarship. It is no wonder that he grumbles and is disappointed, surrounded, as he feels, by a mass of ignoramuses (*ame ha-aratzim*) and women who are interested in the voluntary associations attached to the synagogue rather than in study. His frustration is only increased by seeing other rabbis who, to him, are his inferiors in scholarship rise in esteem throughout the community and obtain the leading ecclesiastical appointments simply because they are native-born. Furthermore, he is as exposed as any one to the problems of making ends meet in face of the rising cost of living. One finds him thus withdrawn into enclaves composed of a few other individuals, usually foreign-born, who ' really ' respect his learning.[2]

In the case of the British-born Orthodox rabbi what has evolved is a kind of compromise. Where it is most successful, the rabbi would be respected for his scholarship by the educated and for his

---

[1] Interview with K.M.

[2] Something of the same strain would be experienced by a highly educated Irish Catholic priest, who at the end of a career of seminary work is given a lower middle-class parish and finds it somewhat distasteful to be as ' fatherly ' with his parishioners as they would like him to be. In his case, of course, he does get the respect which his parishioners would be prepared (minimally) to grant any priest, but he knows that they do not really appreciate his learning.

ability to represent the minority (and also to act in its defence) by the community at large. It is of interest to note that in the United Synagogue, which of all the (Ashkenazi) Orthodox bodies is primarily the home of the British-born Jew,[1] certain steps have been taken to make it more ' representative ' in the respects I have indicated. In the first place its organisation is highly bureaucratised. Its ministers wear canonicals in the belief that this gives them more distinction. They also receive their basic salaries directly from the central synagogal organisation (and not from their own synagogues). The United Synagogue has, of course, been subject to criticism from those who feel that it has subordinated learning to ' modern ' administration :

> *The main thing that the United Synagogue is concerned about is that it should not have a deficit.*[2]

It has come in for more bitter attack from those in the Orthodox bodies on the ' right ' of the United Synagogue, *viz.,* the Federation of Synagogues and the Union of Orthodox Hebrew Congregations,[3] who would not only voice such sentiments as those quoted but also feel that there is something suspect about the Orthodoxy of the United Synagogue. Among points of issue would be the fact that some (by no means all) of the synagogues have made slight modification in the *minhag* (service). Perhaps of more fundamental significance is a general distrust of its central leadership, which includes individuals who are not strictly Orthodox in their private lives.

Yet paradoxically enough one hears, even from individuals who have strong reservations about the Orthodoxy of the United Synagogue that it has ' saved Orthodoxy.' And this, I believe, is correct in view of the changing tastes and values of the mass of Jewry. Certainly, the fact that a ' representative ' form of Judaism has emerged within the Orthodox camp is a key factor in explaining its strength compared with those groups which regard themselves as even more representative. The United Synagogue, in fact, has

[1] Certainly of its central leadership. As to the clergy of the functioning constituent synagogues, 13 are British-born and 7 foreign-born [1953].

[2] Interview with A.A.

[3] This body pointedly describes itself as having been founded to protect traditional Judaism.

drawn into it those Jews originating from the East European immigration who, in the United States, were attracted to what is called Conservative Judaism. It is ' fashionable ' to belong to United Synagogue synagogues. (It is also fashionable to belong to the main Sephardi synagogue.) And the explanation of this begins with the intimate connection of the anglicised élite with Orthodox bodies.

The rôle of the rabbi has, however, completely changed in the case of those reforming rabbis who have abandoned not only the Talmudical tradition but serious scholarship altogether.[1] They envisage their rôle quite explicitly as something other than the scholar-teacher—as an ' ambassador to the Gentiles,' or an internal leader along the lines of a parish priest—and justify their abrogation of the tradition in terms of the ' new needs of the times.' In Right-wing Orthodox circles these people are regarded as having usurped the title of rabbi. Within their own groups some of the reforming rabbis enjoy widespread esteem and, in cases, are respected throughout the whole community. But this should not obscure the plight of their rôle. They derive the greatest respect as ' representatives of the community ' from individuals who value such traits but feel that they themselves do not possess them.

But as the community becomes more anglicised this differential becomes smaller. Under these conditions the ability to get positive prestige from being culturally assimilated, from being able to ' get on ' with non-Jews, diminishes as more and more individuals are able to do so, and as this ability comes to be taken for granted. Also, the further that one gets away from Orthodoxy the less dependent is one upon a rabbi for interpretation of the Law. The Liberals, who have rejected not only so many details of the oral Law but also its finality as a corpus, opposing this in their theological writings with the conception of a continuing or progressive revelation of God, pride themselves upon this emancipation from dependence upon the ' authoritative teacher of the Law.'[2] But the upshot of this is that the status of the Liberal minister is much less definite than that of the Orthodox rabbi in a traditional

[1] This is manifestly not true of all. Those who have, however, are sociologically of interest as being the most extreme departure from the traditional (Orthodox) rôle.
[2] Israel I. Mattuck, *The Essentials of Liberal Judaism,* London, 1947, p. 135.

community. It is much more dependent upon personal magnetism, oratorical skills[1] ; and his congregants who, except for a tiny few, are hardly pious in the technical sense, may at times disparage even this.

If the reforming rabbi who takes his rôle as a religious person seriously, furthermore, is irritated by the attacks of the Orthodox for ' aping the Gentiles,' he must be even more so by the tendencies of his followers to regard him not as a man of religion but as a preserver of decorum. In addition to this he must be well aware of the fact that so many of his congregants acquire membership in the group as a status symbol. All this produces a strain in his rôle. Because of this and the recruitment of Liberal ministers from among individuals with a traditional background, there has been a slight retreat in Liberal practice from its original modernisations.

The opposite of the ' representatives of the community ' are those who, by inviting what is regarded by other Jews as the legitimate disapproval of non-Jews, ' disgrace the name of Jewry.' At the root of this is the desire not to be noticed, the touchiness about being singled out as a Jew in anonymous situations, about being ' different ' :

I'm frankly embarrassed when I see a Jew in a long beard and frock coat. But I've analysed this over and over and it's 100 per cent due to our inferiority complex. You know when I grew my beard, I found that people who knew me would refuse to speak to me on the bus. Of course, if I spoke to them, they couldn't help replying.[2]

Sometimes you can see a Jew on a bus reading his Yiddish paper stuck inside the Evening Standard.[3]

One well-known reaction to psychological insecurity is to find some scapegoat. By using the psychological mechanism of rationalisation, one can blame the scapegoat for one's woes.[4] Among Jews living in the open type of minority society—such as present-day Anglo-Jewry—who have accordingly lost the security which the ghetto walls and its cultural tradition conferred, such

---

[1] The sermon was not an integral part of the Orthodox rabbi's rôle.
[2] Interview with G.V., a minister.
[3] Interview with S.R.
[4] This mechanism, far from relieving tension, may, by multiplying the number of hate objects, increase it.

a scapegoat is provided by other Jews who not merely draw the attention of non-Jews but draw it in an unfavourable way : by talking loudly in public, in Yiddish, in a foreign accent, with the flamboyant use of gestures ; by ostentatiously displaying wealth ; by breaking queues.

It seems thus as if the Jewish world were passing the representatives of the community to the outside world for its inspection and approval. But because this outside world is not involved in the Jewish status system, it cannot possibly be as interested as Jews are in their own behaviour. A person who does not in the deepest levels of his personality think or feel himself to be Jewish cannot possibly be as touchy as Jews are about being treated as a Jew, about the doings of other Jews. He cannot feel that a finger points at him when he hears the word ' Jew.'

In fact what is evident is that the members of the minority have taken upon themselves the task of passing the judgments upon each other that the outside world is thought to make.[1] In so doing, they have characteristically distorted the external value system in two ways.

First, Jews are more severe critics of themselves when they deviate from the norms of the host society than are non-Jews in general. Related to this is their image that the outside world has a ' double standard.'

At a seaside resort once there were some Gentiles acting up on top of a bus, of a very common type that we call Yoks. *I said to my wife, ' If they were Jews, think of what would be said.'*[2]

We Jews stand out, and if one does something wrong, then they judge us all by that one. We can't afford to get mixed up in black-market business.[3]

It is worse if a Jew commits a crime. We are such a minority. I

---

[1] Where Jews do get confirmation from non-Jews about how the outside world judges them, it is more likely to be from fanatical antisemites than from anyone else. This, unfortunately, only increases nervousness within the community. Certainly, a non-Jew who is uninterested in the doings of Jews and gives these only transitory attention is not likely to testify to his lack of interest in print or public speeches. Unless one is in personal touch with such individuals, it is easy to lose a sense of proportion and overestimate the strength of antisemitic agitators.

[2] Interview with K.T.

[3] Interview with F.S.

N

don't feel sorry for Stanley. We are like a family and if somebody does something wrong, it hurts the rest of us.[1]

Secondly, achievements in the non-Jewish world have a greater value in the minority than they do outside. Because of the high place which assimilation to the models of the non-Jewish world has in the Jewish value system, occupations, for example, are ranked not only on the basis of such things as the style of behaviour and the income associated with them. They are also judged in terms of the degree to which they upset or confirm negative stereotypes of the occupations of Jews. A Jew who is a professor in a university is not only a professor but, in the Jewish world, a *Jewish* professor. Moneylending and the gown trade, on the other hand, are negative stereotypes. Both, by virtue of this, are held in disesteem by anglicised Jews. The latter, in addition, is associated with the foreign-born and with speculative methods of doing business.

The precise amount of esteem which an occupation or an achievement commands on this basis will vary with its scarcity. The Jew who is the first to win a given honour achieves something spectacular in the Jewish community.

Don't forget Brodetsky was the first Jewish Senior Wrangler at Cambridge. And when I was a boy in the East End and the news came out that he had been made Senior Wrangler, it was on everybody's lips. Today there are so many of them that it doesn't mean the same thing.[2]

There is another reason why there is distortion in prestige values where they are diffused from a group which sets standards to an imitating group. Things which are taken for granted in the former stand out in the latter. On the other hand the residues of an older culture of the minority may diverge from that of the host society. For example, within Anglo-Jewry the social distinction drawn between the ancient universities and the modern universities, though not altogether suppressed, is hardly as heavy as that drawn by the middle and upper classes in British society generally.[3] At root lies a respect for learning.

[1] Interview with W.A.
[2] Interview with S.R. (In fact, the late Professor Brodetsky was not the first Jewish Senior Wrangler.)
[3] The Anglo-Jewish élite has an historical connection with the University of London.

Where people are not members of the same social groups as their models, furthermore, they will fail to acquire that sense of restraint about an honour which their models, taking it much more for granted, have. Why ' play it down ' when it is so profoundly admired in their milieu ?[1]

*　　*　　*　　*

Open though the minority society is, there is still great ambivalence towards the non-Jewish world as a group. One way of putting it is to say that there is a latent tendency to ' draw the line '—to feel hostile towards those who appear to be ashamed of their identity as Jews and their own ways. For example :

I despise ―――. It's not because of his Communist politics but because he called a meeting in the East End on Kol Nidre *night* [*the eve of the Day of Atonement*]. *And any Jew who would do that is the scum of the earth.*[2]

This ambivalence is easily seen in the attitudes of the Jews of the newer immigration towards the old élite who, on the one hand, are admired for their superior anglicisation and, on the other, are felt to be ' too English.' It is seen in the esteem given to those who while being anglicised are not ashamed of being Jews.

When Friday night came Lord Swaythling would light the candles but he wouldn't draw the blinds.[3]

The fact, too, that so many of the old élite have not changed their surnames (even when they have been created peers) is another factor, both in their self-esteem and the esteem in which they are held in the community at large.[4]

---

[1] This discussion applies equally to the relations which exist between the standards of capitals and provinces, mother-countries and colonies, or simply standard-setting societies and their cultural dependencies. H. L. Mencken has an illuminating discussion of the abuse of (English) honours in the United States during the nineteenth century in his *American Language,* 4th edn., New York, 1946, ch. 6, § 5, ' Honorifics,' pp. 271-284.
[2] Interview with M.B.
[3] Interview with K.M. That is, he was not ashamed of revealing to the outside world that he was a Jew.
[4] What is significant is that where changes of surname took place among this stratum, they were made *before* the influx.

As has been argued, the ability to represent the community is the basis of very high prestige in the open type of minority society. Contrasted with this was the internal, protective leader (or the individual who symbolised the highest values of the group, such as the scholar-rabbi) of the closed minority. But if the minority society has any cohesion at all, it is to some degree closed. Unless its members have a conception of it as a group towards which they have some obligations, such as standing up for it when it is attacked, there can be no minority society. Thus the rôle with the highest prestige will have to combine both types of attributes.

The specific attributes that make up this combination can vary. The more distinguished and respected a man is in public life, the more is his obligation to the minority fulfilled in simply maintaining his identity as a Jew. The less his achievement in public life, the more, as it were, is expected of him in communal work.

In the conflicts that exist within Anglo-Jewry today what is at issue are the details of this combination, not the desirability of the combination itself. Because both the élite and the rank and file of Jewry esteem achievements in the non-Jewish world as well as action on behalf of the minority, Anglo-Jewry is more integrated than these conflicts might suggest. Note in the following how respect is granted both for the expressive action, on a minor scale, discussed earlier, as well as for symbolic achievements in British society.

Dr. A―――― is a person I greatly admire. I would call him a balibuss [*a man of substance and character*]. *He was born in very poor circumstances. His family lived near us in two rooms in the East End. He put himself through university entirely by scholarship; and when he moved up here, he brought his parents to live with him. And no matter who comes into the house, he introduces them. He isn't ashamed of the fact that his parents speak English with a foreign accent. He is a wonderful son. Furthermore, he is the doctor of an English association. His name is right on the letter-head; and if they picked a Jew, he must have been respected by the Gentiles as well. He is also on the Board of Deputies. And one thing about him, he is not afraid of the* Goyim.[1]

―――――
[1] Interview with J.G.

The Maintenance of Group Solidarity

A DISTINCTIVE CULTURE

No society could for long endure whose members regarded an alien system as so greatly superior to their own that they wished to join it and had the means to do so. This is seen as a social problem in Anglo-Jewry. Leaders of Orthodoxy are apprehensive about the flight from the traditional religion, particularly among the younger generation. They are also concerned about the difficulty of inducing enough students to become candidates for the ministry to fill future needs. There are even ministerial posts at the present time which remain vacant. Liberal Judaism justifies its modifications of Orthodoxy partly in the belief of its success in retaining within the community Jews who would otherwise have totally abandoned it. Jewish historians are frankly pessimistic about the outlook of the survival of the community in a hundred years time, and one view is that it would not have survived to the present time had it not been for the constant influx of immigrants from Central and Eastern Europe.

The process of generating sufficient attachment to a group and its ways to counteract defection takes place in the first instance within families. Through the process of identification of the child with his parents (or parent figures), group loyalties are developed and held in place through personal loyalties. The ultimate restraint upon intermarriage, for example, is the desire not to injure one's parents who would feel disgraced before the eyes of the community.[1] In addition, the family is also a group in which conceptions of membership of wider groups and sentiments of loyalty towards them are developed. The class consciousness of a child may begin, for example, with his mother's suggestions about the choice of appropriate playmates. The family is also the primary unit for the transmission of the distinctive culture of the wider group of which it is a part. Furthermore, the family develops a desire among its members to participate in voluntary institutions which perpetuate a

---

[1] As interesting as statistics of intermarriage in general would be statistics of those cases which are initially concealed from the Jewish parents in the hope of eventually obtaining parental acceptance *post factum*.

distinctive culture—such as the educational institutions of Orthodox Judaism.[1]

The importance of a distinctive culture or style of life for a minority (or social class) lies, in the present context, in its function as a centripetal force. It achieves this, in the first instance, by comprising a set of behaviour patterns which, when followed, result in approval and self-esteem. The individual thus, in sociological terms, becomes involved in the minority system. Secondly, a culture comprises a set of group activities (such as ceremonial and play activities) which are emotionally and æsthetically gratifying.

It seems to be a serious distortion of Jewish history to regard the cohesion of Jewish society solely as a consequence of the hostility of the external environment. It is hardly believable that without their internal culture—their belief in God and their conception of themselves as a Chosen People—which enabled Jews to turn so emphatically inward, they would have survived as a communal entity for more than a few generations. This is especially so in view of the lack of any important racial characteristics differentiating them from the people among whom they lived and in view of the latter's pressure to obtain converts to their own faith. Though a slight increase of hostility from the non-Jewish world may intensify a sense of identification with the group, especially in Jewish communities other than the one immediately subject to the specific threat, an organised community can function as such only with a minimal level of security. Excessive fear would make a normal communal life impossible.

In the (Orthodox) Jewish life of the *Diaspora* ritual in the synagogue and the home provided a periodic flow of æsthetic gratification—'high points' of the week and the year—in contrast to which the life of the non-Jew seemed empty. This was perfectly realised in the East European small town (*shtetl*):

> *On the Sabbath the* shtetl *feels most strongly and most gladly that ' it is good to be a Jew.' . . . As the family groups return through the unpaved* shtetl *streets, they see about them the other members of the community, the non-Jews,* goyim, *going about their business*

1 See discussion of the methods of these educational institutions, the way in which they moulded behaviour and their function in the minority social structure in Zborowski and Herzog, *op. cit.*, pp. 88-105.

as usual, the children running barefoot through the mud. And as they see, they pity the barefoot goyim, *deprived of the Covenant, the Law, and the joy of Sabbath. True, they will have their own kind of Sabbath on the following day. But it is a different kind, 'something else again.' Moreover, for the devout members of the* shtetl, *Sunday is part of the week and no true Sabbath at all. 'We thought they were unfortunate. They had no enjoyment . . . no Sabbath . . . no fun. . . . They'd drink a lot and you couldn't blame them, their lives were so miserable.'*[1]

With the secularisation of Jews in an urban social environment, so much of the things that were once pleasurable now appear tedious or constricting. Synagogue attendance is uneven during the year. At the annual holy-days of the New Year and the Day of Atonement the demand for synagogue seats is so great among those who attend only at this time that overflow halls have to be hired.

In this process of secularisation such institutions as youth clubs and community centres have emerged, rivalling the synagogue in the importance which they have for their members. Essentially, these organisations do nothing distinctively Jewish (are indeed modelled after social service organisations, such as the Y.M.C.A., Boys' Brigade). They are regarded as Jewish only because they are composed exclusively of Jews.[2] The benevolent attitude of communal leaders to such organisations is, in part, determined by a feeling that they help to arrest the drift from the community. Support for them is marshalled with the common-sense point that unless the attractions which they provide are not available within a Jewish milieu, they will be sought elsewhere. Furthermore, activities within these organisations have a Jewish 'cast' in two respects. The first comprise such elements of Jewish culture as prayers and study of Jewish history which are linked up with the aims of the organisation. The second consists of intellectual activities within the groups which keep the members 'thinking as Jews.' But a fundamental impetus to membership in such groups is the desire for the fellowship of other Jews *per se*; parents, in particular, are anxious that their children remain connected within the community. As such, these

[1] Zborowski and Herzog, *op. cit.*, pp. 48, 57.
[2] Secular in general character, these organisations are recurrently faced with the question of 'Shall we admit our non-Jewish friends?' (Some, in fact, do.)

organisations parallel the community as a whole, which is marked by a decline in the cultural consensus. For this reason they are the most characteristic organisations of present-day Anglo-Jewish society.

It may be of interest to point out certain brakes on the decay of the cultural tradition which, in spite of secularisation, emerge from the transformation into tastes of traditional taboos which used to be associated with religious sanctions.

The behaviour of Jews with respect to the dietary taboos of Orthodoxy (the rules of Kashrut) may serve as an example. All that need be said here is that certain foods regarded as unclean are forbidden altogether, forbidden foods must not come into contact with permitted ones, meat which is permitted must be slaughtered ritually and its distribution supervised by Jewish religious officials, and within the home separate dishes and utensils are required for meat and milk foods. The psychological experience, for one raised in an Orthodox Jewish home, of eating forbidden food for the first time can be quite terrifying, producing severe visceral reactions. In between those Jews who will eat no food that is not strictly *kasher*, and is served either in private homes that they trust[1] or in restaurants certified by a Kashrus Commission and those who completely disregard these rules are Jews who deviate partially, in a sequence of stages which forms a characteristic pattern.[2]

First there is the individual who, while maintaining a *kasher* home, deviates outside, such deviation taking the form of eating food which, while not intrinsically forbidden (*e.g.,* vegetables, fish, tea, coffee, etc.), is nevertheless cooked in a ritually unacceptable kitchen[3] ; eating beef and other permitted meat which has not been

[1] It is not uncommon for strictly conforming Orthodox Jews to refuse all but the slightest refreshment in the homes of relatives whom they either suspect or know to deviate more or less from the dietary laws. This does not necessarily result in any friction. Similarly, Jews who are lax in these matters but who respect the strict habits of conforming relatives whom they wish to invite for meals may keep on hand a few special dishes and saucepans reserved for their exclusive use.

[2] To a pious Orthodox Jew, of course, one either conforms entirely or does not: there are no 'degrees' of laxity, since nothing less than full conformity is acceptable. I am concerned here, however, merely with shifts in taste.

[3] This is not forbidden by the Law, which explicitly makes allowances in a common-sense way for emergencies. In case of serious illness a Jew would be both exempt from the injunction to fast and be permitted to eat forbidden foods were it necessary for his recovery.

ritually slaughtered ; eating bacon, ham, and other pork products, as well as crustaceans and game. Then there are those who within their homes abandon the injunction to maintain separate vessels and utensils for meat and milk foods within the household. Others consume at home non-kasher meat, *i.e.*, meat bought from a non-kasher butcher. Finally, come those who consume bacon,[1] etc., within the home.

Thus the specific complex of culturally distinctive behaviour, originating in a taboo, is preserved in degrees (far more so than Sabbath worship) among those to whom it has lost its connection, not only with religion, but even with the sanction of communal disapproval. The source of restraint is experienced as purely personalised taste. This can be justified in terms of statements about health (*e.g.*, that pork can cause trichinosis, typically coupled with pride in the reflection that the early Jews ' really knew what they were talking . about ') or asserted simply as a gastronomical preference *per se*.

Yes, I do eat bacon but I draw the line at rabbit. I cannot bear to look at it hanging in the shops.

Of late, restaurants, delicatessen shops, and hotels (at holiday resorts) which are not strictly kasher but offer a bill of fare that includes Jewish specialities have become fairly common. These are patronised by, among others, that type of not entirely ' dejudaised ' Jew, who is sometimes called the ' Bauch Jude ' or ' the chopped liver and pickled onions Jew.'

COMMUNAL ACTIVITY

One aspect of such activities as charity and communal work is that they result in preoccupation with the community. It is important for its cohesion that there be things for Jews to do which enhance their sense of being part of the group. One such type of task is collective work on behalf of the community. Another would be activities which maintain relationships with other individual Jews as persons who have special claims upon one's resources, energy, and affection by virtue of their being fellow-Jews.

---

[1] Bacon and ham, as cured meats, seem to be separable from pork in general. For some curious reason bacon is less objectionable than ham in the United States. This may be partially due to the therapeutic properties associated with bacon in popular medical beliefs.

It is thus very important for the cohesion of the society that charity commands the prestige which it does in the Jewish value system. In the *shtetl* and earlier periods of Anglo-Jewry, charity was more personalised than it is today. With the growth in size of the community the administration of philanthropy has become centralised and organised. This by no means, however, excludes gifts from individuals.

Such charitable activities have been to some extent limited in recent times partly by the rise in the average standard of living among the community. The main work of the Jewish Board of Guardians, for example, has been increasingly less concerned with philanthropy and more with such activities as apprenticing boys and social welfare work generally. This tendency has, however, been offset by charitable activities concerned with the new State of Israel. Fund-raising and communal work on behalf of the new State are an important source of prestige. Thus, in addition to the gratification which Jews derive from the existence of Israel as a symbol which is an important substitute for the loss, in varying degrees, of the traditional religious gratifications, fund-raising on its behalf has given Jews something to do as Jews. As such it is of great sociological importance for the solidarity of Anglo-Jewry and of other Diaspora communities in similar circumstances.

EXEMPLARY INDIVIDUALS

I refer here to those individuals within a group who are regarded by its members as distinctly above the average in their devotion to the group. The activities which command this esteem may indeed be such things as fund-raising and voluntary administration which are necessary for the smooth functioning of the group. However, it is the symbolic significance of this action upon those who observe it which is of interest at this point.

Just as individual rule-breaking propensities arise when it is felt that standards are collapsing, these individuals, as exemplary models of devotion, reassure one in vivid ways about the behaviour of others, increase respect for the group, and thus help to counteract centrifugal tendencies. Symbols of solidarity, they are thus equivalent to the heroes which a more self-sufficient society requires mainly in periods of emergency.

An auxiliary aspect of their rôle in the minority is that their own achievements entitle them to address explicit demands to 'slackers' for effort on behalf of the group. They are also direct models of approved behaviour in the status system which confers high rewards for this behaviour.

In the light of the above the continued membership of Anglo-Jewish society of the (culturally) assimilated élite who, in addition, have achieved eminence in the country's public life generally has important symbolic significance for less anglicised Jews. In the minds of the latter the more anglicised Jews are people 'who could have left the community but didn't.'

Yet, indicative of the distress in Anglo-Jewish society which rapid secularisation and unloosening of the class structure, among other things, have brought about is a readiness to impute selfish motives to such behaviour. As a first instance, ambivalence exists towards the anglicised élite ; and competing with the respect accorded them are such judgments as :

The only reason they call themselves Jews is because the non-Jews do.

They are only interested in running Jewish organisations so that they can control the masses.

A second instance is the yearning for the standards of the past —a 'golden age of social solidarity'—by those who have moved up in the world :

In the East End (or in the haim[1]*) a friend was really a friend.*

In contrast to this, so much of the charity and the communal work that goes on is devalued in such terms as : 'They are only doing it for *coved* (prestige).' For example :

In this area there are no balibatishe Yidden [*Jews of substance, standing, and character—literally, householders*]. *It stinks with social climbers. You see people here joining clubs, attending meetings, getting on to organisations to meet people and for* coved. *Real* balibatim *are in St. John's Wood. Here they have friends, but they want to meet people who they think are higher up. I think more of the people in Stamford Hill than I do of those here. There is more learning in Stamford Hill, more polish. I'll tell you something. It is*

---

[1] The place of origin in Eastern Europe.

the custom to give the minister presents on a Yontif [*religious holiday*]. *Well this is a rich congregation and you'd think the minister would be showered with gifts. Well, they are so tight-fisted, unless their name is called up and they can be noticed for it.*[1]

Conclusion

The distinction which has been made in this essay between the closed and open minority society has been fundamental in this analysis.

The closed Jewry, the classical ghetto of the Diaspora, was a corporately organised community whose members were separated from the outside world by their ritual rules. These communities were sustained by their religious and intellectual tradition, which was, in effect, a whole way of life. It embraced a scheme of values by which they could differentiate themselves from the surrounding population, who even when benign could be pitied for their lack of the Law. Apart from this self-enclosure, there was also the hostility of the non-Jewish world which pressed for the compulsory segregation of the Jews in its midst. In concrete terms this was symbolised by the ghetto wall; but it was, nevertheless, a late development in the history of the Diaspora and by itself cannot account either for the cohesion or the survival of the community in the Exile.

At the apex of its prestige hierarchy was the scholar-rabbi. His authority in settling disputes was universally recognised. Also his status was confirmed by a practical dependence upon him for decisions about what, in any case of uncertainty, was the ritually correct line of action. In addition, knowledge of the Law was respected as an end in itself. It was also felt that the greater one's knowledge of the Law, of what was right, the better would one be—that deviation from the rules was the result of ignorance.

At the base of the prestige hierarchy, on the other hand, were the unlettered, the *ame ha-aratzim*. Originally this meant simply men of the land. It came to connote, however, not merely ignorance

[1] Interview with M.B., foreign-born, a resident in a North-West London suburb.

but also lesser degrees of what were regarded as the best human qualities: kindness, an open house and an openness of spirit, respect for others and, of course, respect for the Law. The traits which conferred prestige, furthermore, became associated with family lines. To come from a good family in this culture meant descent from a long line of rabbis.

High prestige was also conferred for exemplary behaviour on behalf of other members of this very tightly knit community or of the group as a whole. To be charitable and hospitable to the limit of one's resources and to defend the interests of the community was a standard of conduct for all to follow. Wealth was respected in so far as it made possible a signally impressive mark in this sphere of action and was a normal basis of the communal leadership, the *balabatim* (householders, men of substance).

Poverty and the pursuit of certain occupations, such as heavy manual labour, had low prestige because they prevented one from studying and were associated with ignorance and brutality. Poverty also meant dependence on others, which in an egalitarian milieu was particularly unattractive. Furthermore, as in most societies, wealth, apart from the estimable qualities such as generosity and independence associated with its possession, naturally commanded from the less wealthy some respect for its own sake.

In a consideration of the main institutions of the society,[1] primary importance rested with those which perpetuated the way of life established by religious tradition: the Synagogue and educational institutions. The rôle of the rabbi, both as a symbol of all that was best and as an arbiter of the Law, has already been noted. The services of various ritual functionaries, such as the teacher, synagogue reader, ritual slaughterer—sometimes all these services were performed by a single individual—were also indispensable; and they would be found in all communities above a certain size.

Ultimately, however, the criterion of the self-sufficiency of a community was the quality of its rabbi's learning. A community, whose rabbi would consult, for the solution of a religious problem, the rabbi of another community as a man of greater learning, depended upon this second community. It may thus be argued that

[1] V. Israel Abrahams, *Jewish Life in the Middle Ages*, London, 1932.

the survival of Jewry depended, ultimately, upon the *chochma* ('wisdom') of its greatest scholars.[1]

In addition to such religious activities, there were others concerned primarily with the organisational problems that face any highly knit minority group. Such, for example, were the relations of the community with the non-Jewish world. It was, of course, vitally important for the survival of the community that it should prevent its members from causing the kind of trouble that would provoke retaliation by the non-Jewish world against the group as a whole. Sometimes when this was not possible, the community would disown the recalcitrant:

The Jews in Amsterdam had every reason to excommunicate Spinoza. They were afraid that when the Christians would read his books they would expel the whole community.[2]

It was also important to keep internal quarrels—hardly to be avoided in such an ingrown setting—from making themselves felt outside the boundaries of the community. What was most feared in the closed community was the renegade or informer—that a Jew in his anger at another (or, perhaps, in his self-hatred projected upon the group)—might enlist the aid of non-Jews.

Underlying this fear was the premise that the non-Jewish world was waiting to pounce upon the Jewish community and that the tales spread by such renegades or informers would furnish convenient pretexts for wholesale destruction. It may be questioned whether this was universally true, though Jewish history is dotted with tales of informers who were responsible for disaster. What is certainly true, however, is that the morale of the closed community depended upon the conviction that its members presented a united front to the outside world. The ordinances passed by the seventeenth-century *Mahamad* (executive body of the Sephardi synagogue) in London are interesting examples of internal police regulations concerned with maintaining the equilibrium which had been achieved with the non-Jewish world.

It was also necessary for the functioning of the community to have plenipotentiaries to represent it in its corporate capacity in dealings with the non-Jewish world. (Conversely it was expected

[1] Cf. the literature of rabbinical *responsa*.
[2] Interview with N.A.

that a member of the minority should not use his relations with non-Jews to obtain advantages as against other Jews.) It is of interest that the rôle with the highest internal prestige, the scholar-rabbi, did not necessarily entail these representative duties. In Eastern Europe, where the Jews in their village communities spoke their own language amongst themselves, the rabbi might not even have known the vernacular of the non-Jews. It is thus that these representative tasks would normally fall to the better off merchants who would have the experience of dealing with non-Jews in their everyday affairs. This is the pattern which also became established in the early seventeenth-century community in England. One can hardly overlook, however, the extraordinary mission of that most devoted servant of his people, Rabbi Manasseh ben Israel, who took it upon himself to plead for the readmission of Jews to England.

A second type of institution concerned with organisational problems sustained the purely social ties between Jews—as members of a cohesive community who had a right to each other's help. Examples would be a group devoted to convivial activities, a philanthropic institution, or one (such as a mutual benefit society) which combined rational financial pursuits with social ends. Here too, however, ritual considerations had their place. Jewish orphans could not be turned over to non-Jewish agencies because, at the very least, it was necessary that they be served with food prepared by Jews (or under Jewish direction) in the ritual manner.

These institutions existed in a society where bonds between kinsfolk were strong and in which the family, with its warmth of human relationships, played a role which can hardly be over-emphasised. In the absence of a political structure having the force of law the importance of kinship ties for the cohesion of a group was very great ; for it was through such ties that pressures for conformity to the rules of the group could be effectively exerted. These communities, then, may be said to have been held together by common religious values, a strong sense of brotherhood—of particular importance for individuals moving between these communities—and the strength of family bonds.

When one comes to summarise the details of the structure of contemporary Anglo-Jewry, the first fact that strikes the observer

191

is how much of this classic structure and the spirit behind it is still in existence. It is true, of course, that Jewish society as a whole is not a legal corporate entity. No official of the Jewish community has authority over other Jews conferred upon him by the non-Jewish world, such as, for example, that possessed by the Crown Rabbis of the seventeenth-century continental absolutisms (an authority, incidentally, which, in the Jewish world, was not really regarded as legitimate). But though today the association is voluntary, there does exist a considerable degree of corporate organisation in Anglo-Jewish institutions and likewise, as evidenced in such conceptions as 'the good name of Jewry,' a sense of corporate autonomy.

Furthermore, there is still an active religious life. If I have called attention to the weakening of attachment to the ancestral religious-intellectual tradition, it is only to highlight the central importance—from the point of view of what keeps the society in existence—of the synagogue and all the related communal institutions which maintain the Jewish way of life.

In addition to the synagogue there is the same array of representative and social institutions. Many of the concrete changes in their structure, as compared with those of an earlier epoch, constitute no departure in principle but merely an adaptation to a new age and new conditions. Such changes, for example, can be seen in the grouping of synagogues in federal organisations, the full-time specialisation of such functionaries as the circumcisors, the institution of *kashrut* commissions, and the growth of a professional secretariat in the communal organisations.

But if much of the fabric of the older structure persists, there have been important changes in the system of values—varying, to be sure, in intensity in different parts of the society. These changes underlie some of the conflicts in the society and also account for certain modifications in its institutions. They constitute what I have called above the opening of the ghetto community: the loss of cultural self-sufficiency, the assimilation of standards of prestige of the non-Jewish world explicitly into the Jewish value system, the preoccupation with conformity to that world's standards with the object of obtaining its approval, and finally, the demand to be treated with respect by that world.

At root here is the impact of the secular philosophy evolved since the seventeenth century which has affected the assumptions not merely of Jewish but of West European thought generally. It is hardly conceivable in this day and age, for example, that an Amsterdam rabbi could effectively persuade the English Government to permit the resettlement of Jews, on the grounds that by so doing they would enable a Biblical prophecy to be fulfilled. Secularism has also resulted in the abolition of religious qualifications for full membership in the political society. This has made it possible for the modern Jew to identify himself with his host society in a way which would have been impossible for his medieval ancestor.

The result of all this is that a schizoid quality has been injected into the system of values, a condition which arises wherever individuals are faced with the problem of harmonising loyalties to the standards and the symbols of different groups.

A second aspect of the value system is that the emphasis on wealth has got out of hand. Wealth, of course, and the worldly comforts which it could purchase were never repudiated in the talmudical tradition, which was not an ascetic one. It is this outlook which informants expressed when they would state in a matter-of-fact way, ' Of course, every Jew likes to live well.' But in the older structure there were restraints within the prestige system upon the respect which would be granted to wealth and its enjoyment as ends in themselves. The wealthy man was expected to use his wealth for the good of the community, to support scholarship, and to elevate his own dignity by the further study that his leisure might permit him. Where, however, the acquisition of wealth has been very rapid and coincided, more or less, with growing laxity in the observance of ritual, the result has sometimes been to produce an inversion in the scale of values, and even to lead to the spurning of scholarly activities among some on the ground that they are ' unprofitable.'

This change is not restricted to the ' new rich.' Even scholars may be sensitive to pressures to maintain a higher standard of living than they can afford—how painful, indeed, when the pressures come from within their own families. Perhaps the saddest casualty of this whole process is the rise of the essentially uneducated

O

professional man who, in sharp contrast to the typical Jewish professional of the period before the First World War, is bent above all on personal gain.

Undoubtedly, much of this shift in values is but temporary, the usual concomitant of a first generation's rapid rise in wealth. Moreover, account must be taken of the fact that though the old respect for learning seems to be suffering an eclipse in certain quarters, that respect is far from being extinguished even among those very elements which appear to spurn it. The surface flashiness is easier to see than the moral integrity which may remain hidden underneath. Again, there exists a widespread respect for the good breeding of the educated English gentleman, respect akin in some ways to that which in the older tradition would have been given to the learned *fainer mann* (' gentleman ').

A third aspect of the Anglo-Jewish value system arises from the fact that the minority society has been populated by immigration from abroad. This accounts for the importance assigned to the length of time that a family has been resident in Britain—' who arrived first ?' This, incidentally, is very much the case in the United States, not only among Jews, but in the population at large. When associated with other qualities, such as leadership, wealth, and the assimilation of English habits and behaviour, such considerations have played a part in laying down a pattern in the social stratification of Anglo-Jewry.

As for the main disunities within Anglo-Jewry, the first to be cited is that which exists between those who are ashamed of being Jews and those who are proud of being Jews, a conflict which exists not merely between individuals but also, to a great extent, within their own personalities. Somewhat related to this is the disagreement between those who stand for ' positive' Jewishness, on religious, cultural, or nationalist grounds, and those whose Jewishness, in the opinion of the former, is exhausted in an empty preoccupation with the status of the Jewish community in the eyes of the non-Jewish world. Also related to this are disagreements which arise over what is felt to be the proper balance between the two worlds, on religious, cultural, or political grounds, with the extremes regarding one another respectively as too assimilated and too self-enclosed. The explicit claim of the orthodox members of the older Anglo-Jewish leadership was, indeed, that they were not extremists, that they were able to maintain a high degree of participation in English life without compromising their loyalty to the ancestral tradition.[1]

Issues in this sphere are constantly arising. One such, for example, is over the merits of instituting Jewish public schools, which would be viewed as excessive self-enclosure by those who oppose them. But this would become a painful disloyalty issue within the community only where supporters of such schools felt that their opponents were attacking them in the eyes of the non-Jewish world. Within the community it can be reasonably discussed; and even where no unity is reached, a courteous agreement to disagree can be achieved.

But where matters do not become ' political ' issues, a much greater degree of agreement is discernible in the society. Note, for example, the following testimony of a man whose son is a pupil at one of the Jewish day schools and who himself is an active member of several Zionist organisations:

My son has a talent for languages and I want him to have the best of both worlds—a good classical education and a good Hebrew education.[2]

On religious grounds conflict exists between those who conform strictly to traditional orthodoxy and those who have modified it. This is, however, not simply a religious controversy, but one involving the question of adequate group loyalty. Supporters of right-wing orthodoxy who are also Zionists would be prepared to overlook the non-conformity of the Zionist leaders whom they esteem in a way in which the orthodox members of the anglicised élite would not. To such men some at least of the Liberal Jewish leaders have, by their explicit departure from orthodoxy, manifested disloyalty to Judaism, a charge which they could not possibly direct against the Zionist leaders.

The conflict over Zionism itself has, of course, with the establishment of the State of Israel, changed its terms. The principal point at issue which still survives from that controversy is a

[1] V. Dr. Cecil Roth's article, 'The Collapse of English Jewry,' *Jewish Monthly*, July, 1947.
[2] Interview with Z.K.

difference in the conception of the appropriate methods of political action of a minority group.

Other conflicts, both overt and covert, exist between scholars and those whose Jewishness is limited—more or less exclusively— either to piety without learning or, alternatively, to the strictly practical aspects of communal work. From this originates some of the estrangement between the foreign-born scholar and those members of the anglicised élite who have lost the ancestral passion for learning. Friction can be discerned between those who are *feine* ('refined' or 'gentle') and those who are *grob* ('coarse'):

I used to live in Stamford Hill. But when Channa ' X ' would come out in her dressing-gown to run across the street and call on her friend, I decided that I could not live there any more, that I had to move. But, of course, if a person is feine, would you think any the less of him if he lived in Stamford Hill ?[1]

When the disunities are examined from the point of view of the organisational structure, the most notable event of recent years was the split between the Anglo-Jewish Association and the Board of Deputies. Here considerations of social class were present to complicate policy differences. The extent of cleavage due to policy differences, however, may be somewhat over-estimated. Cutting across such differences there are common cultural interests and common religious values. The truly educated, as in all civilised societies, can talk to each other.

As to the institutions of the open minority society, the main facts can be summarised as follows: first, there has been a change in the way the function of representing the community is conceived, in the sense that those who perform this function are expected to follow the best standards of behaviour in the non-Jewish world ; secondly, there has been the rise of what might be termed the ' protest leader ' and of institutions the object of which is to combat public expressions of antisemitism, while attempts are made to ' police ' the community, bringing pressure to bear upon individuals who appear to provoke anti-Jewish feelings to mend their ways—an activity reminiscent of that performed by the seventeenth-century *Mahamad* ; thirdly, there is the relative rise in importance of institutions with a purely social significance—as contrasted with

[1] Interview with N.A.

ritual institutions—to hold in place relationships between individual members of the minority society.

To conclude, the synagogue and the related educational institutions still are, and must continue to be, the central institutions of the community. For without a belief in the intrinsic value of the intellectual-religious tradition there would come a point in the history of the group where there would no longer be any object in Jews retaining those qualities, habits, and ways of life which distinguish them from their non-Jewish neighbours and cause them to recognise themselves as a distinct community. This is true notwithstanding influences working for the solidarity of the group emerging from quasi-nationalist or racial sentiments.

Just as a single institution can be seen to depend essentially on the labours of a small core of devoted workers, so is a whole society dependent upon the life which goes on within certain of its component institutions. From this point of view those Jews who do not support religious life but who desire some group activity as Jews are, so to speak, parasites upon the inner core, a core consisting of institutions and people firmly wedded to the Jewish religious tradition. It follows that, without the survival of Judaism in its deepest religious sense, groups within the community which are largely secular—Jewish social clubs, for example—would be bound to disintegrate in time. In a very real sense the Jewish social club depends for its survival on the living synagogue, on faith illuminated by learning.

PART FOUR

Jews in the Society of Britain

MAURICE FREEDMAN, M.A.

Jews in the Society of Britain

SIR OLIVER SURFACE: "I'll accompany you as soon as
you please, Moses.—But hold! I have forgot one
thing—how the plague shall I be able to pass for
a Jew ?"

MOSES: "There's no need—the principal is Christian."
The School for Scandal, III, 1.

Jews as a Minority

OF the red herrings which confuse discussion of the place
of Jews in European society none is more wearying than
the question of race. This is certainly not because the
racial origin of the Jews and the present-day racial composition of
the populations called Jewish are uninteresting ; for, working with
a physical anthropologist's definition of race and following his
methods of study, we may learn much that is of scientific importance
about the bodily endowment of people said to be Jews. But what
the physical anthropologist has to tell us is of limited relevance to
the task of marking out the categories of individuals who are
labelled the Jews of this or that European country and of understanding their position in these societies. Jews certainly sometimes
think of themselves as a race and others often similarly conceive
them, but their social and cultural separateness does not rest on
any homogeneity of physical characters.[1]

Yet paradoxically, at first sight, there is something to be gained
from bringing the study of Jewry under the heading of Race
Relations.[2] The U.S.A., in wrestling with its domestic problems of
minority groups, among which the Negroes have enjoyed an

[1] I may cite two somewhat differing expert views of the physical
anthropology of the Jews, both of which, however, place stress on the rôle
of culturally determined characteristics in the common-sense sorting of
Jews from Gentiles. C. S. Coon, *The Races of Europe*, New York, 1939 ;
pp. 441-444 and pp. 644-646. C. C. Seltzer, 'The Jew—His Racial Status '
(1939) in *This Is Race*, ed. E. W. Count, New York, 1950 ; especially
pp. 616-618.   [2] See pp. 3-5, 60-63, 150-153.

unenviable pride of place, has produced a vast body of literature
devoted to the adjustments and maladjustments of minorities of
various kinds to the wider society in which they live as types of
American citizen. In Britain, where the melting-pot has been
simmering longer and less evidently to the casual eye of today,
the study of Race Relations has awaited a later flowering of
sociological activity and has taken its tone from more recent
urgencies. In late years there has been a series of investigations
concerned with the latter-day colour problem of this country.[1] It
is yet too early to see how the study of Jews will be integrated with
that of coloured people (and perhaps minorities of other sorts) to
produce something in the way of a theory of the position of minority
groups in Britain, but it is to this that we must look forward.[2] In
some respects Jews and their problems may be unique, but Anglo-
Jewry is no more to be isolated from a general scheme of
sociological study than it is from British society. The temptation is
always with us to treat Jews as unique, to think, for example, of
the Jewish business man and the déraciné middle-class Jew as
Jews rather than as types of a common feature of society at large.
Only the careful and constant study of society in Britain will keep
us from falling into the fallacy of the uniqueness of Jews and their
problems.

The Jewish problem is often posed as one of assimilation, but
when we look closely at this term we see that it does little more
than restate the problem without sharpening it. For assimilation
may signify a number of different things, changing its meaning as
we shift our point of view from one position to another in society.
Legal and political assimilation exist as a formal fact; there are

[1] The most important of these studies is *Negroes in Britain*, by K. L.
Little, London, 1948. Among other publications I may draw attention to
Michael Banton, ' Negro Workers in Britain,' *Twentieth Century*, Jan., 1952,
and S. F. Collins, ' Social Processes Integrating Coloured People in Britain,'
British Journal of Sociology, vol. III, No. 1, 1952. A. H. Richmond,
' Social Scientists in Action,' *Science News 27* (Penguin Books), London,
1953, discusses the work done in this field, and in *Colour Prejudice in
Britain*, London, 1954, gives an account of his own research in Liverpool.
[2] The beginnings of a scientific study of antisemitism in Britain may be
seen in a piece of research which has not yet been published: J. Robb,
A Study of Anti-Semitism in a Working Class Area, Ph.D. thesis, University
of London, 1950. A brief note on this research is to be found in
Quarterly Bulletin of the British Psychological Society, vol. III, No. 16,
April, 1952, p. 46.

no barriers to the established rights that follow from British citizenship. Yet full equality before the law, enfranchisement, and eligibility for public office are only one possible set of criteria for assimilation. The man who sets himself up as an English gentleman of the Jewish persuasion may be thought of as a remarkably fine product of the process of adjustment, with all but an adherence to a modernised Judaism ironed out by a public school education and acceptance in upper-class social life. Can this be what is meant by assimilation for Jews in Britain as a whole ? The sense of being both British and a Jew, which is clearly the aim of many—witness the fervent identification with the symbols of both—measures the degree to which Jews have been assimilated only if we know how far the world of non-Jews accepts the combination. It is even possible to argue that assimilation is only perfect when an erstwhile minority fades as a separable entity ; if this is so, there may never be a complete absorption of Jews in Britain as long as the Jewish religion exists.

It is comparatively easy to find out how Jews see themselves in relation to the wider society. How do we know, on the other hand, where, in the minds of non-Jews, there are barriers to acceptance ? Antisemitism in this country is not an unexplored phenomenon, but between the unusual extremes of love and hate there are many points at which Jews may be accepted in different senses and in different contexts. It may well be that the use of the word ' British ' is itself a trap, for on too casual an attribution of meaning we might assume that a Jew called British by non-Jews is freely taken into the wider fold. There are distinctions made between British, on the one hand, and English, Welsh, Scottish, and Irish, on the other, which may allow a Jew the political description while withholding the cultural. Of course, the adjective British is not devoid of cultural meaning, and such expressions as the ' British way of life ' may point to an increasing diffusion of its significance; but discomfort at the French usage of *anglais* and *britannique,* when the first word is often made to do service for what the second seems to imply, and American freedom with ' British,' suggest that there are native discriminations which need careful scrutiny. Perhaps Jews are the losers by these subtleties. To be a citizen of the U.S.A., we are told, is to be unequivocally an American. A British passport makes a man British ; it does not follow that he is accepted as an Englishman. I find that Mr. Mikes, in his sparkling anatomy of 'alienship,' has made a similar point with respect to immigrants. 'It is a shame and bad taste,' he writes, ' to be an alien, and it is no use pretending otherwise. . . . Once a foreigner, always a foreigner. There is no way out for him. He may become British ; he can never become English.'[1]

English society, during its long history of absorbing diverse elements, has shown itself capable of turning foreigners into Englishmen and of congratulating itself upon its success. The very multiplicity of its ' racial ' origins has been used as an argument for its strength when other European nations have tried to live by the myth of the racially monolithic community. Along with the gradual amalgamation of alien elements there has been a firm resistance to the foreigner who is readily identifiable as such ; to the man, that is to say, who has not yet acquired all the marks, of language, bearing, and manner, which act as the badge of member-ship. While it is true that many individual Jews, by taking on the necessary marks, have qualified for membership in this way, there often seems to exist in the minds of Englishmen the idea that there is a more or less undifferentiated category called Jews who, besides being an aberrant religious community, are also, as a group, foreigners.

The imputed foreignness of Jews does, of course, rest on some ground of fact. It is only some seventy years since the mass immi-gration from Eastern Europe began, and within that time, although evolving from tight settlements of a highly idiosyncratic nature into more dispersed urban and suburban pockets, Jews of this origin have retained many cultural distinctions. As far as London is concerned, for example, they have become Cockneys and members of the middle class, but they still often wear their badges with a difference. Perhaps Jews themselves are more sensitive than others to the nuances in speech and manner which seem to mark them off from general London society, but one may suggest, in the absence of proper scientific evidence, that the phonetic changes in English often made by the London-born Jew (even with only a few Yiddish words at his command), and an exotic use of the body in

[1] George Mikes, *How To Be An Alien*, London, 1946, p. 8.

posture, gesture, and gait, are not without their effect in suggesting to the English ear and eye a marginal Englishness and partial foreignness.

However, the foreignness of Jews is not based merely on such differences in superficial behaviour. Somewhere near the heart of the problem lies the exotic nature of the religion in terms of which Jews are defined in the first place. This religion is not only alien—as are, for example, Islam and Hinduism—but it stands in a special relationship to the religion of the vast majority of the population. Stemming from a common source and confronting one another for nearly two millennia, Judaism and Christianity have often created serious problems for Jews and Christians in their dealings with one another. The modern secularisation of thought in this country has perhaps reduced the possibilities of religious tension, but the values of religion are still important in English life, and the symbols of Judaism and Christianity, however unfanatically employed, continue to oppose one another. The fact that the Jews have been thought of as a people of the Book has at times stood them in good stead with Puritan Englishmen ; the friendly collaboration of churchmen and Jewish religious leaders in such bodies as the Council of Christians and Jews[1] at the present time means that harmony can be established even within the framework of doctrinal differences ; yet the stiff-necked rôle of the Jew in Christian history and the network of popular myth which connects the Jews of today directly with the active opponents of Christ, makes it possible for the Jews to be treated as ritual oddities. Jews can be tolerated in a Christian nation, but the values of the dominant faith may reinforce the alien quality of the nation's Jewish citizens with the strangeness attaching to the other religion of the Bible.

Of other aspects of the attributed homogeneity of Jews as a marginal group perhaps the most striking is the economic. Anti-semitic propaganda classically makes free with indiscriminate accusations of wholesale Communism and bloodsucking capitalism, but the minds of ordinary Englishmen, resistant enough to the lunatic fringe of anti-Jewishness, seem often to be captured by the economic peculiarity of Jews. The stereotyped Jew is no longer the usurer, but as a business man of one sort and another he seems

[1] See p. 50f.

to reflect a drive for economic well-being and the efficient exploitation of his environment alien to the ideally more staid behaviour of the Englishman. The apparent devotion of Jewry to the cause of self-betterment may sometimes find the bitter commentary of *auri sacra fames* in the mouths of outsiders, but, whatever its wording, there is a common English view of the Jews as a whole pushing their way to success with the maximum effort.

The Anglo-Jewish Community

Because of the penumbra of meaning which surrounds the name Jew, there are many ways of defining the entity with which a study of Anglo-Jewry is to concern itself. Essentially, however, all such definitions fall into one or other of two classes. In so far as there is a set of institutions, ritual and secular, which mark out a distinct sphere of Jewish social life, there exists a Jewish community. On the other hand, to the extent that there is a body of individuals who, on the basis of a number of cultural criteria, are called Jews, then there is for the investigator only a vague category within which he must find what order and regularity he may. To limit one's attention to the Jewish community, institutionally defined, is to think of Jews only as persons participating in a specifically Jewish area of society. In attempting to deal with all those individuals who are in some sense Jews, one is thrown beyond the boundaries of organised Jewry into the confused territory where it is an exacting task to decide what consequences follow from the Jewishness attributed to one's subjects. Both approaches would have their place in a comprehensive study of Anglo-Jewry, but it is the former which must command, initially at least, the greater attention.

A first glance at organised Jewish life in Britain, with its network of associations, might suggest that we have to deal with a kind of tightly integrated structure fit to stand alongside the types of Diaspora communities through which Jewry in exile has, surprisingly to many observers, been able to preserve itself intact. Above the level of local communities, expressing their solidarity around the foci of synagogues, religious schools, cemeteries, clubs, youth organisations, and voluntary bodies of one sort and another, there appears to be a complex of institutions at the national level which binds Anglo-Jewry together into a distinct segment of British life. Synagogues band themselves into unions which, at various points along the scale from extreme traditionalism to modern experimentation, allow of unified control and a centralised expression of religious opinion. The Beth Din and the Chief Rabbi seem to stand at the apex of religious organisation with the air of the final authority in things ritually Jewish. The Board of Deputies of British Jews and the Anglo-Jewish Association emerge as the representatives of an Anglo-Jewish community politically organised. A complex of friendly societies, charitable bodies, and education committees appear to co-ordinate a nation-wide Jewish attempt at solidarity within the sphere of social welfare. A weekly newspaper with a large circulation caters nationally for Jews by its specialist treatment of news and publicity of Jewish affairs. In modern times, too, the various ramifications of Zionism have added further strands to the web of Jewish society in Britain.

And yet, despite appearances, we know that much of this co-ordination, ritual and political, is illusory. A problem for future research workers is to establish, not merely from formal constitutions but from the day-to-day functioning of nation-wide bodies, the extent to which they have relevance for the solidarity of the Anglo-Jewish community. If, for example, we look at the two political associations, the Board of Deputies and the Anglo-Jewish Association, which claim to speak for large bodies of opinion, we must know not only the provisions they make for their recruitment and their stated sets of rules and aims, but also how the reality of their working reflects the distribution of political interests and power within Jewry. In form the aims of these two organisations do not to any considerable extent overlap, but to the outsider it may seem significant that at times, while both including eminent spokesmen of Anglo-Jewry at large, they appear to come into conflict and arrive at compromise in the adjustment of their rôles as representative institutions. With such pointers to the problems of organised Jewish life a disinterested study of Anglo-Jewish institutions might be able to throw light on the developments of a minority passing through crises of antisemitism, ' assimilation,' and nationalism.

Similarly, within the ritual sphere, a bald statement of the religious and legal functions of the Beth Din and Chief Rabbinate and of their relations with the complex of synagogues tells us little about the actual way in which the behaviour of Jews formally attached to religious organisations is regulated by the structure so patiently contrived. It must, for example, be a measure of the self-containedness of the Jewish minority that a number of its matrimonial disputes are brought before the religious Court (some of them ending in traditional divorce) and that some civil disputes between Jews, outside the range of marriage law, are voluntarily submitted for the Court's arbitration. But what is the extent of the Beth Din's implication in the process of maintaining order, and how does its rôle shift with changes in the secularisation of the community and in its socio-economic structure ?

Minority status built on a distinctive religion and, through Zionism and concern for world Jewish problems, connected to some extent with extra-national political activities, must naturally express its individual character in institutions springing from its special needs. A religious court, an organ for the ritual supervision of food, sectarian schools, and associations of many kinds maintain that which is specifically Jewish in Jewish life. But beyond this field there is a network of associations of another order, which, in contrast, does not relate so much to the satisfaction of Jewish needs as to the setting up within Jewry of organisations which parallel those of the wider, non-Jewish, world. The Jewishness of these bodies lies rather in their exclusive recruitment of Jews than in their pursuit of peculiarly Jewish aims. The Association of Jewish Ex-Service Men and Women, the Jewish Peace Society, the Jewish Psychic Society, a proliferation of social clubs and literary societies, testify to the existence of a minority society within which the purposes of the wider society are reproduced in little. Of course, the activity of such bodies is by no means always devoid of specifically Jewish content, but it is on their function of grouping Jews with Jews that one ought to concentrate one's attention in order to understand the mechanisms which help to perpetuate a minority in a free society.[1] Once more, how these parallel institutions vary in importance from one local community to another, and how they change over time in response to

[1] Cf. p. 183.

shifts in the status of Anglo-Jewry, are matters that need to be studied with care.

One set of functions performed by organised Jewry is concerned with the interesting phenomenon of defence. There is perhaps no surer test of the impact on Anglo-Jewry of both outright antisemitism and the milder criticism which is levelled, or thought to be levelled, at it, than the formalised attempts to explain, justify, exculpate, and protect. The nature and effectiveness of this counter-propaganda are clearly problems of the first order and must fall squarely within the scope of any comprehensive study of the Jewish community in its relations with the Gentile world. However, while some aspects of this question will be touched on later in this essay, I do not propose to make any general statement on it except the obvious remark that it is clear that much defence work is carried out in ignorance of its precise effects on the people who are addressed, harangued, instructed, admonished, and cajoled. As for the internal structure of the Jewish community, defence work speaks for the view which a minority group holds of itself and its responsibilities for and towards its members. When, for example, Jews fear for the consequences of the criminal behaviour of individual Jews and adopt the cause of easing the strains set up by economic rivalries which seem to fall along the lines dividing Jews from their non-Jewish neighbours, we are clearly in the presence of a typical expression of minority spirit. In the give and take of public life in this country there are strong inhibitions against the collective damning of groups and sections of the nation other than those competing directly for political support—and even here the canons of good taste can be invoked to prevent excesses of abuse. Yet the suspected innuendo in the special mention of a shady character with an exotic name sets up anxieties which may find organised expression in bodies devoted to ensuring fair play for Jews.

The most obvious feature of Anglo-Jewry, and one which may be overlooked by traditionalists in whom the nostalgia for a closed Jewish world is strong, is its complete reliance on the principle of voluntary grouping. The state, while making some concessions to Jews, as in oath-taking and marriage forms, submits them to the law of the land as ordinary citizens. The Board of Deputies has some official status as spokesman for the Anglo-Jewish community,

P

and the Beth Din, in the exercise of its ecclesiastical functions, can look to be supported in the courts, but whatever is found in organised Jewish life in this country is essentially the result of the elaboration of voluntary grouping and the free adherence to rules. In the time of Charles II a memorial was drawn up to suggest the segregation of Jews under the control of a Justiciar who would be 'responsible for the collection of taxes and to supervise their relations with the Crown.' Charles submitted the memorial to the Privy Council; it was dropped.[1] At the Resettlement, of course, Jews had expected that they would be given a special status as a group.[2] At the beginning of the nineteenth century the Jew Van Oven tried to get legislation for a Jewish governing body to collect poor rates and dispense relief ; it came to nothing.[3] In Britain, whatever exclusion from public privilege their religion may have earned them in the past, Jews have not been treated as a special social problem or entity. Salo Wittmayer Baron, as a student of Jewish communal life, has stressed the lack of interference by British authority in Jewish affairs ; his respect for the voluntary construction of communal bodies in the Anglo-Jewry of an earlier day is perhaps not misplaced. He says that it is difficult to imagine now the 'courage, determination, and persistence' of British Jewry in building up its institutions when the law of the land tried to ignore them.[4]

Having survived so large a measure of official neutrality so long, Anglo-Jewry may have benefited by developing a communal structure strong enough to maintain a core of Jews wholehearted in their Jewishness and weak enough to let its marginal members drift easily between the Jewish and non-Jewish worlds. The tightly knit Jewish community which has emerged at different times and places in the Diaspora, marking off Jews unequivocally from the people among whom they lived, owed its compactness and isolation to no small extent to the policy of Gentile rulers intent on cutting

[1] Cecil Roth, *A History of the Jews in England*, 2nd ed., Oxford, 1949, pp. 181f.   [2] Cf. p. 11 above.
[3] Roth, *op. cit.*, pp. 234ff. J. Rumyaneck (*The Social and Economic Development of the Jews in England, 1730-1860*, unpublished Ph.D. thesis, Univ. of London, 1933, pp. 87-109) points out that the success of Van Oven's scheme would have radically changed the nature and status of Jewry in this country.
[4] S. W. Baron, *The Jewish Community : Its History and Structure to the American Revolution* (3 vols.), The Jewish Publication Society of America, Philadelphia, 1942, vol. II, p. 364.

off their alien subjects from the main body of society and controlling them fiscally and politically through the agency of a closed group. Even in circumstances where Jewish life has been more diffused through society at large but where the State has intervened only to control ecclesiastical matters there has, for that reason, been a clearer line drawn between the Jew in the fullest sense and his fellow withdrawn from religious activity, and the possibility of a more centralised control of specifically Jewish affairs by Jews.

Anyone casting an eye over a list of the multifarious associations of Anglo-Jewish society[1] must be impressed by their variety and scope; he will perhaps be reminded of a similar efflorescence of voluntary groupings among other minorities. There are many aspects of the development of associations in sections of a society which are underprivileged or undervalued, but one of these aspects may help to illuminate a phenomenon which some self-conscious Jews are apt to think a peculiarity of their own minority. The *macher*, the pushful individual seeking status through a somewthat too overt manipulation of his membership of associations, has long been a figure of fun in the gallery of Jewish self-criticism. He has even been made the centre of a Potteresque technique called *machmanship*. In an article under this name Mr. Witriol has with much wit defined *machmanship* as ' the art of getting elected to Synagogue Boards of Management without Actually Asking People to vote for you . . . ' and gone on to stress the fruitful field open to the *macher* in Zionist activity.[2] The breaking up of minority society into a multitude of parts, within each of which prestige-bearing offices are made available, reflects a status-system not closely linked with that of the wider society. In some cases it may argue severe deprivation in the wider society, but, whether or not this is the case, the extent to which ambitious Jews seek, as Mr. Witriol might say, to *mach* themselves into men of importance within the confines of Jewry is a measure of the degree to which Jewish society stands on its own. When we know who the men are who climb the Jewish ladder, we gain some insight into the way in which Anglo-Jewry is moving towards its future adjustment to society in Britain.

[1] See, *e.g., The Jewish Year Book, 1954,* London, 1953, pp. 52-186.
[2] *The Jewish Chronicle,* Oct. 19, 1951.

Jews and Economic Life

The uncertain boundaries of modern Anglo-Jewry do not prevent many people from thinking of it as a kind of corporate entity the members of which are responsible for one another. This is to be seen particularly in the field of economic affairs where some Jews assume that the community must take responsibility for the impact made by Jewish business men on the wider society in order to preserve the good name of the community and the good will of Gentiles. It may be doubtful whether non-Jews generally think that Jews ought to be held responsible for one another, but some of their generalising prejudices against Jews in economic life seem to stimulate the latter to answer for their fellows.

Accusations of unfair dealing, commercial immorality, and unrestrained cut-throat competition are, of course, likely to appear where the interests of a minority are to a considerable degree bound up with business. Before asking whether such attacks are justified, it is wise to consider the possibility that it is the marginal position of the minority which encourages the accusations, and that they may be made on assumptions which presuppose the undesirability and unworthiness of the minority. The accusations, as it were, may merely document a prior hostility. MacCrone's paradoxical dictum puts the view with most point: ' It is not because of their economic competition that Jews and Japanese excite hostility, but it is because they are Jews and Japanese that their competition is unfair, or underhand, or an offence to those who are neither Jews nor Japanese.'[1]

There are, then, two quite different problems facing an inquirer into this aspect of the economic relations between Jews and their neighbours. The first of these is the extent to which it is true that Jewish behaviour deviates from that of the general society. The other problem is to decide why, whether accusations against individual Jews are true or false, they are sometimes made the basis for attack on Jewry as a whole and defence by Jewry as a body. The disposal of the first problem lies at the heart of Jewish defence activities, which, while sometimes stressing the outstanding contributions made by Jewry to the world, at other times appear to lean

[1] I. D. MacCrone, *Race Attitudes in South Africa*, London, 1937, p. 254.

JEWS IN THE SOCIETY OF BRITAIN

over backwards in the effort to prove that Jews are just the same as other people. It is not my intention to discuss this matter at length, but it is perhaps worth saying that, in view of the quite recent standing in this country of a considerable proportion of Jewish business men, it might well be that their methods of doing business differed somewhat from general methods. But whether such differences really amount to ' unfair practices ' is another question.

The classical attempt to refute accusations of Jewish dishonesty was that made during the war by the Trades Advisory Council, an organisation the general significance of which I shall discuss later,[1] when it undertook to examine the evidence concerning Jewish participation in the black market. Its report, which has had a very limited circulation, has not been made public, but I am able to summarise the inquiry here with the permission of the Council, to which I am indebted for this and other courtesies. During the period 1942 to 1944 records of prosecutions kept in various Ministries were examined and the incidence of offences by Jews compared with the proportions of Jewish firms which, on the basis of another investigation, appeared to participate in the relevant trades. Within the limits of its method, the inquiry seems to have established that, at a time when some unfair publicity to Jewish offenders was creating the impression that Jews were prominent in the black market, there was not in fact a disproportionate number of Jews involved in crimes of this sort.

But what is it, more specifically, that Jews are said to do or to fail to do that excites opposition and hostility on the part of non-Jews in Britain ? Vague, general notions about sharp practice, which are to a great extent the heritage of older ideas about the place of Jews in economic society, mark out only the haziest of public profiles. Among the direct competitors of Jews in specific fields of economic activity, on the other hand, more clearly formulated prejudices emerge. And these prejudices sometimes lead to action which reinforces the conception of Anglo-Jewry as a kind of corporate body answerable for the behaviour of its members.

There is an interesting example of such prejudice and the reaction to it to be found in the field of the retail grocery trade, and it seems useful to go into this in a little detail. In the grocery trade, during

[1] See pp. 217ff.

the last few decades, Jewish shopkeepers have sometimes seemed to their non-Jewish competitors to have employed methods of doing business which run counter to the principles of correct dealing and are detrimental to the interests of the trade as a whole. The delinquency—if delinquency it is—is to a large extent summed up in one word: price-cutting.[1] Accusations against price-cutters in general came before those levelled at Jewish price-cutters, and certainly by no means all grocers have singled out Jews as the villains ; but, at least in some areas, the Jewish grocer has at times incurred the hostility of his competitors on the grounds that he sold below prices that were thought fair.[2] It is necessary to understand that, in the context of the grocery trade before the war, price-cutting referred to the sale of goods below their ' price-maintained ' prices, in the case of some brands, but below ' recognised ' or ' suggested ' prices in the majority of cases.

The reaction to price-cutting in large sections of the grocery trade seems to have taken an antisemitic turn in the 'twenties, and by the time of the establishment of Nazism in Germany there appears to have been strong feeling generated in some quarters against Jewish competitors.[3] The small, independent tradesman, pressed by competition from several sources which he thought unfair, was able to furnish a good target for the propaganda of England's own brand

[1] My attention to the significance of the grocery trade in this connection was drawn by my colleague Mr. Basil Yamey, to whom I am also indebted for the guidance he has generously given me.

[2] Cf. an editorial statement in *The Grocer and Oil Trade Review*, 9/12/33, p. 63: ' In view of the fact that Jews are often alleged to be the principal price cutters, readers will learn with interest . . .' of the report that Jewish traders in the Stamford Hill district had formed themselves into an anti-price-cutting association.

I should like to stress that my citation in what follows of antisemitic words and formulae from the pages of *The Grocer* must in no way be taken as a reflection on the editorial policy of that journal. Indeed, it is my impression that it reported fairly and performed its function in the trade without bias.

[3] Cf. the last footnote. In September, 1935, a Stoke Newington representative at a gathering of the Greater London Council of Grocers' Associations spoke of the menace of the aliens ' who were cutting the throats of the legitimate traders ' and pointed out that his association had decided against the admission of Jews. A Hackney representative replied that it was better to get the Jews into the associations in order to control them. See *The Grocer*, 7/9/35, p. 93. Early in 1936 a correspondent wrote to stress that the cutters were nearly all Jews (*The Grocer*, 1/2/36, p. 37). He was answered by another letter-writer, who insisted that cutting was not confined to the Jews (*The Grocer*, 8/2/36, p. 47).

of fascism, and the opportunity does not seem to have been missed.[1] An illuminating report of a grocers' association meeting in 1936, which was addressed by a leading member of Sir Oswald Mosley's staff, brings out clearly the economic tensions which found their expression partly in anti-Jewish feeling.[2] It is worth considering at some length.

A ' largely attended meeting of grocers and other traders ' was held in Stoke Newington in November, 1936, to hear Mr. Raven Thompson, ' director of policy of Sir Oswald Mosley's Party.' Introducing the speaker, the chairman, who was president of the local association, spoke of the difficulties facing the retail trader and enumerated three problems, in their order of importance. The first of these problems was the Jewish cut-price trader, the second the chain store, and the third co-operative trading. Of the forms of competition with which traders had to contend, cutting was the most cowardly. ' As Britishers they were used to fair play. That was their one aim, and to be able to meet their creditors and pay 20s. in the £. Unfortunately that did not apply to the Jewish competitor they were up against.' As for the chain stores, the majority of them were owned by foreign interests. The meeting would be interested to hear Mr. Thompson, since the fascists were known to have a policy in these matters.

The fascist speaker, ' who met with a cordial reception,' outlined at length the measures proposed to protect the small trader. About Jewish competition, he said that ' they had got to face the fact that Jews had an entirely different standard of moral values from the Englishman's. . . . The Jew was the man who was prepared to buy up bankrupt stocks—possibly from a member of his own family— and he opened a cut-price shop, traded for a few months, and then off he went.' This could be stopped only with the help of fascism in laying down ' a by-law forbidding such trading.'

This occasion seems to have been of considerable importance historically in that it provoked a reaction from the Board of Deputies which was to flower later into a co-operation with the grocery trade to avoid the troubles alluded to. A letter from the Board is reported to have said : ' We are concerned at the nature of these allegations,

[1] Cf. F. Mullally, *Fascism Inside England,* London, 1946, p. 66.
[2] *The Grocer,* 7/11/36, pp. 88f.

and would gladly do all that we can by way of exercise of moral influence to eliminate such practices.'[1] The letter was considered ' an olive branch ' and an augur of good things to come by a spokesman of the Stoke Newington Grocers' Association. Meetings with the Secretary of the Board of Deputies were arranged, and these produced a statement that ' the Board of Deputies of British Jews, recognising that a substantial proportion of the community it represents is engaged in trade,' and being concerned for the maintenance of good trading practices, ' will continue to assist, by the exercise of its influence, all efforts such as yours, to prevent any defection, no matter how small the numbers of individuals concerned, from those high standards set by British custom and tradition.'[2]

In this case the premier secular body of Anglo-Jewry was involved in a trade dispute between Jews and non-Jews at a time when politically organised antisemitism could draw inspiration and comfort from Germany. The war ended this chapter of anti-Jewish activity but brought other economic problems to exercise the concern of those Jews who took it upon themselves to stand as mediators between their own community and the greater society. Price-cutting was no longer a live issue (although there were those who looked forward with misgivings to possibilities of its return after the war[3]), but there came more sinister accusations. In a severely rationed and restricted economy Jews were sometimes said to be prominent in

[1] *The Grocer,* 16/1/37, p. 99.

[2] *The Grocer,* 6/2/37, p. 43. This letter was reported in connection with the Grocery Proprietary Articles Council, and presumably refers to co-operation to prevent cutting in the prices of goods with fixed prices.
   In July and August, 1938, there was a lively correspondence in *The Grocer* on the Jewish question, which includes, as a jewel of antisemitica, a letter from a commercial traveller attacking under the improbable *nom de guerre* of Ipso Facta [*sic*]. In reply to a Jewish trader protesting against anti-Jewish accusations, he wrote: ' The antagonistic feeling against Semitism mentioned is very real, and growing stronger every day among " the sweated " and everywhere else, and if Mr. —— has not heard of it yet, he will do.' (6/8/38, p. 32).

[3] Cf. General Secretary's Report of the work of the Council, quoted at p. 8 of *T.A.C. The Monthly Bulletin of The Trades Advisory Council* (hereafter cited as *T.A.C.*), vol. II, No. 8 (May/June, 1943): ' We are endeavouring, for instance, to see that the charge that Jews are price-cutters shall not be sustained after this war.' It is interesting to speculate on the light which might be thrown on the position of the Jewish shopkeeper by a study of, say, Welsh grocers in England. Indeed, a study of anti-Welsh behaviour would be a useful parallel to the study of antisemitism.

the ranks of the black marketeers.[1] From the tensions of the immediate pre-war period and the special circumstances of the war arose what was to become one of the most interesting of Anglo-Jewish institutions.

The neutrally named Trades Advisory Council traces its origin to the year 1938, when a committee was set up to advise the Defence Committee of the Board of Deputies, but it took more formal shape under its present name in 1940 to act as a specialist body operating under the auspices of the Board. Its preoccupations emerge clearly enough from its statements of policy. ' The principal aim of the Council is the avoidance of friction and misunderstanding in the economic field which endangers the maintenance of harmonious relations between Jew and non-Jew in trade and industry. It is concerned with the good name of Jewry in the business world, and in its efforts to preserve this it deals impartially with offenders within its ranks and defamers without.'[2] ' The Trades Advisory Council is an association of Jewish business and professional men and women, which aims at maintaining the highest ethical standards in the conduct of business. It seeks to increase good will between Jew and non-Jew, to protect the good name of Jewry, and to combat antisemitism arising out of trade, commerce, and industry.'[3]

In mid-1943 membership of the Council stood at something over 3,700 ; by 1947 it had exceeded 8,000 ; at this latter figure it apparently maintained itself for some time, although in more recent times it seems somewhat to have declined. According to the Council's own analysis, its 8,000 members represented about one-third of ' Britain's Jewish traders and businessmen,'[4] and, while from the point of view of the organisation itself, this was not a sufficiently high proportion of the Anglo-Jewish business world to allow it to function as it wished, nevertheless, to the outsider it may seem a surprisingly large mobilisation of Jewish interests in the cause of defence in the economic field.

To carry out its chosen task of easing the relations between Jews and their neighbours in the realms of trade and industry, the Council set up various regional committees and trade sections. The London

[1] Cf. p. 213, above.
[2] Back cover, *Annual Report of the Trades Advisory Council, 1942-43.*
[3] Back cover, *Annual Report of the Trades Advisory Council, 1947-8-9.*
[4] See *T.A.C.*, vol. VIII, No. 5, p. 4.

Administrative Committee had eighteen Trade Sections in 1943 and twenty-seven in 1946.[1] Operating from its various centres, the Council has tried to fulfil what are clearly its two main objects: the investigation and correction of improper economic behaviour on the part of Jews, and the protection of Jews from discrimination in the realms of business and employment. The categories into which the Council places the cases it has dealt with, however, suggest a somewhat wider field of activity. From April to December, 1952, for example, a total of 110 resolved cases were analysed under the following heads[2]:

Type	Number
Discrimination in employment, lettings, insurance, etc.	18
Unethical conduct	31
Jew v. Jew (business disputes)	25
Jew v. non-Jew	10
Formal arbitrations	2
Trade practices	24

That Jews, as members of a minority, however ill-defined, should have recourse to the services of a body which sets out to protect them from discrimination as seekers after employment and in such fields as insurance, is not difficult to understand. It is perhaps more striking that the same agency should assume the burden of shielding the wider society from alleged malpractices and shortcomings of members of the minority in order to ensure its good name. And it is this latter aspect of the Council's work which has apparently been uppermost. The language used to describe action taken against ' offenders ' within the ranks of Jewry and to elaborate the principle lying behind it surround the Council's work with an air of self-assurance and moral rectitude which leaves the

[1] The Trade Sections clearly attempt to take in the range of economic activity within which Jews hold a significant place. These various trades include: antiques and art ; chemical and pharmaceutical goods ; china, glass, and earthenware ; clothing ; confectionery ; engineering ; estate management ; food ; footwear ; furs ; furniture and timber ; insurance ; hairdressing ; jewellery ; leather and fancy goods ; licensed victuallers ; radio and electrical goods ; textiles, draperies, and fashion goods ; wines and spirits ; waste and scrap dealing ; bakers ; films ; hair and bristle trade ; millinery ; optical and photographic trade ; and publishing. (See *Annual Reports* for 1945-46 and 1946-47.)
[2] *T.A.C.*, January, 1953. In the years 1946 to 1949, 803 cases were dealt with (*Annual Report* for 1947-48-49). The precise boundaries between the different categories are not clear to me.

observer with no doubt concerning the organisation's conception of a mission to protect Jewry as a whole.

The sensitiveness to criticism from the non-Jewish world and the determination to eradicate what are thought to be some of the causes of antisemitic feeling in Britain are eloquently displayed. One editorial of the Monthly Bulletin speaks of ' a widespread demand ' which is growing ' for the imposition of some kind of sanctions against members of the community whose conduct brings discredit to the Jewish name.'[1] ' The slogan [" It all depends on you "] has a special application to Jewry in the present situation. Firstly as a reminder that each and every single Jew has within his own hands the power to add glory or dishonour to the Jewish name.'[2] ' The Trades Advisory Council carries a responsibility the importance of which cannot be over-estimated. The Jewish community in this as in other countries is to a large extent engaged in trade and industry. . . . The Jewish trader is therefore exposed not only to more temptation, but is far more open to criticism and the essential need for the maintenance of a high standard of commercial practice becomes more and more vital.'[3] Even that the over-elaboration of Jewish festivities in times of food shortage should offer a cause for criticism becomes a matter of concern.[4]

A more recent exposition of the theme of corporate responsibility was given in an article by the President of the Board of Deputies in 1953. ' The doctrine that " all Jews are answerable to one another " has always been considered a cardinal principle regulating Jewish life. . . . It is an undeniable fact that Jews are all in one boat and the whole community is affected by the conduct of the few. . . . [The life of the Jew] is not his own because it is inextricably bound up with that of his fellow-Jews as their life is bound up with his. Especially true is this in his relationship with his Gentile neighbours, and this relationship is largely concerned with his business activities.'[5]

[1] *T.A.C.*, vol. II, No. 1, Feb., 1942, p. 1.   [2] *Ibid.*, p. 2.
[3] *T.A.C.*, vol. II, No. 8, May/June, 1943.
[4] See *Annual Report f*or 1946-7.
[5] *T.A.C.*, January, 1953. One of the more interesting consequences of the Jewish determination to keep its name clean is the occasional plea that, because Jews are so liable to criticism, they ought in fact to behave *better* than other people. Whether this penalty is unnecessarily self-imposed or is a reasonable response to prejudice could be debated! It certainly argues a profound anxiety.

Admonishing the erring Jewish brother, remonstrating with the prejudiced non-Jew, the Council has been an institutional expression of some of the stock traits of the minority in an uneasy position: sensitiveness, fear of public criticism, and the feeling that in bad conduct the many are made to answer for the few. The antisemitism and economic stresses of the 'thirties and 'forties produced in the Trades Advisory Council an organised response which, even if its influence and effectiveness can too easily be exaggerated, has been tangible proof that, in some degree, Jews and non-Jews regard Jewry in Britain as an isolable segment of society the representatives of which can speak for—and against—its members to the outside world. One must not, of course, overlook the probability that the image in some Jewish minds of a minority constantly under the critical scrutiny of the Gentiles has no close parallel in the minds of the latter. Is it a fact that the delinquencies of individual Jews consistently produce the unfair generalisations from which Jewry has to be protected ? There can be no doubt that in many important respects this is the case, but we obviously need to know very much more about the variations and limitations of such generalised prejudices.

How does the Trades Advisory Council bring recalcitrant Jews into line in its efforts to preserve the good name of Jewry ? What sanctions does it apply and how effective are they ? If we could answer these questions we should know a great deal about the internal working of Anglo-Jewry. What pressures, economic and non-economic, can be brought to bear systematically on the man who seems to be prejudicing the status of the ' community ' ? On the face of it, it must seem that the extremely loose organisation of Jewry in Britain would make it very difficult for effective sanctions to be applied, but it must rest with the social historian of a few generations hence, who has access to the records, to say definitely how correct an assumption this is.

That Jews worry about the consequences of their economic relations with non-Jews follows in part from their rôle as businessmen and traders. When members of an alien group function as intermediaries, standing between producers and consumers, their position *vis-à-vis* the majority is likely to be delicate. The conception of the Jew as an economic parasite, producing little but earning much with the fruits of the labour of others, is part of a worldwide stereotype which is of great convenience to antisemites of all shades of political thought. It has happened that when other minority groups have occupied a similar economic position they have found a ready honorary title in the name Jew. Chinese, for example, have been abused as the Jews of Thailand ; the economic resentments built up against them have found a European imagery to hand.

But how far is it true that the Jews of Britain at the present time are significantly concerned with commerce and trade of one sort and another ? The Trades Advisory Council's estimate of their 8,000 members as a third of Anglo-Jewish traders and businessmen implies, on the basis of Dr. Neustatter's figures, that some seventh of the Jewish male population over the age of fifteen falls within this category. The Council's pamphlet on economic matters prepared by Dr. Barou gives between fifteen and twenty per cent as the proportion of gainfully occupied Jews who are in trades and industries on their own account.[1] It may well be, as Dr. Neustatter's material seems to suggest,[2] that this proportion is an understatement of the extent to which Anglo-Jewry is composed of independent economic agents, and there is certainly a large enough contingent of traders and businessmen, particularly in the smaller settlements in the provinces, to lend the community a specifically commercial air in the sight of the nation. Certainly, when the face-to-face relations between Jews and their neighbours have their setting in the market-place, Jewry as a whole may attract some of the attitudes more specifically directed towards tradesmen. The complicated and ambivalent appraisals made of shopkeepers and businessmen in our society may have a special bearing on the position of the Jews. It is by now a commonplace in the analysis of the Jews in western society to say that they have found their way into niches of the economy where they have had to bear the strain of economic antagonisms. To have moved in popular thought from moneylender to businessman is an advance, but it is not a progress into complete security.

If we believe that the relations between Jews and non-Jews turn significantly upon the nature of Jewish economic pursuits, we

[1] N. Barou, *The Jews in Work and Trade*, Trades Advisory Council, London, 3rd. ed., 1948, p. 7.   [2] See p. 127.

must obviously ask whether there are likely to be any changes in these pursuits which could materially affect the position of Jewry. According to the kind of analysis made by the Trades Advisory Council, the Jewish businessman has it in his hands to affect for good or ill the standing of the community. What if other types of Jewish occupation were to come to the fore? Very probably the majority of gainfully occupied Jews in Britain are wage and salary earners, and it is possible that the ranks of the Jewish working-class population may come to be swollen if there is any contraction in the businessman's opportunities. Jewish workers, however, are concentrated in a fairly narrow range of occupations,[1] and if they were to stay generally within this orbit no new frictions would be likely to appear. But the work of the Trades Advisory Council in fact suggests that Jews often try to get employment in areas of the economy where there are resistances to their acceptance by non-Jewish employers reluctant to make the innovation. The position is, of course, a difficult one, for, while over-specialisation is often thought undesirable, it may in practice be maintained by barriers of prejudice to a widening of the field of employment. Once more one needs to draw attention to an aspect of Jewish life which calls for careful investigation. How, in fact, are the limits set to the diversification of Jewish callings?

In addition to the Jewish businessman, industrialist, shop-keeper, and worker, there is the professional man to be considered. Everyday observation, supported by the kind of material adduced by Dr. Neustatter,[2] suggests that the tempo of professionalisation in Anglo-Jewry may be tending to specialise Jewish economic life in yet another direction. The stress on higher secular education and training for the professions, which seems to characterise Jewry when it finds itself in the relatively open social atmosphere of Western Europe and America, has clearly converted a considerable element of locally born Jews into a professional class. Within this class there appear to be strong accents on medicine and the law. While

[1] The tailoring trade is a prominent example of the specialisation of Jewish workers. Barou, *op. cit.*, p. 9, says that in 1932 there were some 40,000 Jewish workers in the clothing industry, about half of whom were men. According to a letter in *The Jewish Chronicle*, 14/10/49, the total membership of the National Union of Tailors and Garment Workers was at that time 140,000, of whom roughly 15 per cent were Jewish.
[2] See pp. 130ff.

these two callings are perhaps channels of progress more exclusive in popular thought than in reality, they at least seem to be common routes of ascent. Jewish doctors, dentists, barristers, and solicitors may be forming a new face for a minority whose atypical occupational structure changes without losing its peculiarity.

While Jews who find their way into the Who's Who included in *The Jewish Year Book* are very far from being a category necessarily representative even of the upper layers of Anglo-Jewish society—apart from their prominence, the men and women who appear in the Who's Who are also senior in age as well as status—the bias shown in their professional qualifications may have some small significance for Anglo-Jewry at large. Of some 550 Jews listed in 1953[1] who were born in Great Britain and Northern Ireland and who appear to be resident there at present, over 90 have legal qualifications of one kind and another (although, of course, by no means all of them have practised the law), and some 50 are qualified in medicine. Apart from the religious ministry and the teaching profession (which is a very mixed category of callings), no other professional bias emerges so clearly. Engineers, architects, artists, musicians, accountants, and the like form only a small proportion of those selected for their eminence. In the non-eminent majority of professional Anglo-Jewry they may well bulk larger.[2]

Prejudice and its Forms

We know that Jews regard their economic position as an important factor in the making or exacerbation of antisemitism, that, in some degree, they are conscious of the constraining influences of prejudice around them, and that they take institutional action against many forms of anti-Jewish utterance and deed. The Defence Committee of the Board of Deputies, the Trades Advisory Council, and the Association of Jewish Ex-Service Men and Women all apply their skills to the combating of antisemitism in Britain. It is characteristic of our state of knowledge of Jewish life that the counteraction emerges more clearly than the stimuli to which it responds, and that the Jewish fear of antisemitism is more easily documented than anti-Jewish action and prejudice themselves.

[1] *The Jewish Year Book, 1953*, London, 1952.
[2] Cf. the distribution of professions given in Table XII, Appendix, p. 255.

Outside the field of politically organised antisemitism there is indeed little generally known of the precise nature and extent of prejudiced behaviour towards Jews. It is to be found certainly among some employers faced with a Jewish candidate. It has taken specific forms, as we have seen, in some economic fields where Jewish competition has been resented. Again in economic life, it has strikingly appeared as a reluctance to accept Jews as risks in business insurance.[1] But over the whole field of social intercourse between Jews and non-Jews in Britain it is very difficult to get a clear idea of the types of situation in which Jews find themselves resisted, rejected, and excluded.

From time to time advertisements and notices appear which make it evident that some seaside resort hotels and London landlords refuse accommodation to Jews. Jews have been known to find it difficult to get membership of certain clubs. On the other hand, so little is anti-Jewish discrimination systematised in public life that Jews appear to find little difficulty in getting themselves elected to Parliament, appointed in the various public services, accepted in the universities, and honoured for their work for the nation. There is, however, perhaps no great contradiction between the myriad pinpricks and minor exclusions, on the one hand, and the major acceptances, on the other. For the personal prejudices which can operate in private life, where individuals are relatively free from the inhibiting influence of wider public opinion, may tend to be suppressed in deference to the rules of the greater institutions. A particular civil servant may dislike Jews and fend them off in the privacy of his ordinary life, but if he attempts to carry over his prejudice actively into his bureaucratic duties he is liable to run foul of the rules against discriminatory behaviour. The members of a club may keep Jews firmly from their door, but as individuals participating in many other forms of social life they adhere to the principles of fair treatment. The prejudices of sub-editors and reporters may sometimes find expression in the (perhaps unconsciously) biased presentation of news ; on the whole, the national press is careful to avoid giving offence.

While this dualism is perceptible in the case of Jews, it is more

[1] The Trades Advisory Council appears to have been particularly successful in combating this form of discrimination.

striking in areas where stronger prejudices are involved. Against coloured people in Britain there are antipathies which are reflected in severe exclusions. Some landladies put up a stiff resistance to accepting coloured lodgers and boarders, who are then exploited by having to pay high rents for inferior quarters. The coloured man is often kept at a social distance from his white neighbour. He runs the risk of coming up against brutal expressions of the doctrine of white supremacy. Yet officially he is treated with equality, and in public life can move with the freedom of any other man of similar means and accomplishments.

From such differences in the expression of prejudice at different levels of social life we may conclude that, in order to understand the position of Jews in British society and the pressures to which they are subject, we must do something more than simply measure the incidence of antisemitic feeling in the general population. What we need to know is the way in which Jews are accepted and rejected in various institutional contexts. We might, for example, find from a simple opinion poll that a high proportion of English people manifest some significant degree of antisemitism, but this would not be a satisfactory guide to the manner in which Jews are actually treated in the many phases of their contacts with their non-Jewish neighbours. The expression of hostility towards Jews by a collection of individuals treated as units in a poll is one thing ; quite another is the variation in prejudiced behaviour of the same individuals acting in specific social situations involving Jews. The Jew who is able to say that some of his best friends are antisemites points the moral that there is a world of difference between discrimination against real people and actual groups, on the one hand, and hostile stereotypes against hypothetical Jews, on the other hand.

A recent book by Dr. H. J. Eysenck[1] makes it clear enough that antisemitism, in the sense of an attitude unfavourable to Jews which can be elicited from informants on the basis of questionnaires, is very general in Britain.[2] It can be no comfort to Jews to learn that, as far as the United States and this country are concerned, only a quarter of the total population is devoid of unfavourable attitudes towards them. Yet, even when this large antisemitic population is

[1] *Uses and Abuses of Psychology*, Penguin Books, Harmondsworth, Middlesex, 1953. (See chapter 14: 'The Psychology of Anti-Semitism.')
[2] *Ibid.*, p. 261.

Q

broken down into the sub-categories of lesser and greater antisemites by the developed techniques of social psychology, and the fanatics sorted from the milder Jew-haters, what have we learned about the treatment of Jews by the Gentile world? It seems to me that the insidious attraction of easily quantifiable data may too easily divert the attention of students of antisemitism from the examination of institutional behaviour to the collection of measured attitudes.

Dr. Eysenck himself is well aware of the need for other than psychological studies of antisemitism,[1] but he is concerned to defend the social psychologists' work in this field against the charge that it deals with words and not with actions. However, his rejoinder that, while verbal statements may not always accurately reflect individual attitudes, ' . . . actions also may give an entirely false impression '[2] does not appear to meet the criticism that institutional discrimination, that is, how people are treated unfairly in organised social life, is not necessarily illumined by a study of personal prejudices.

Two of the interesting aspects of studies in antisemitism to which Dr. Eysenck draws attention in order to demonstrate the usefulness of psychology are, firstly, the relation between antisemitic attitudes and other ethnocentric attitudes within the same individual, and, secondly, the connection between antisemitism and certain types of rigid personality structures.[3] Yet, once more, we must ask ourselves about the contribution which these studies make to an understanding of antisemitism in society. To put one major objection very crudely, does it help us to know that antisemitism may be nothing more than a substitute for many other kinds of prejudiced thinking and that some kinds of unfortunate individuals are, as it were, pushed into antisemitism by the shape of their personalities? *Why the Jews?* This last question, if it can be answered at all, will be answered by an analysis of the social relations in which Jews are involved as members of society in Britain.[4]

[1] *Uses and Abuses of Psychology*, Penguin Books, Harmondsworth, Middlesex, 1953, p. 261.   [2] *Ibid.*, p. 280.   [3] *Ibid.*, pp. 268-278.
[4] I have avoided here the usually vague and over-generalised 'theories' of antisemitism, with which the literature on 'the Jewish question' is well stocked. I ought, however, to take this opportunity of pointing out that nearly all that can be usefully said on antisemitism in a general way has been said by Professor Morris Ginsberg in his essay, 'Anti-Semitism' (1943), which appears in his book, *Reason and Unreason in Society*, London, 1947.

The Processes of Assimilation

It might be argued that any activity, such as that conducted by the Trades Advisory Council, which stresses the separateness of Jews by treating them as a special group with special needs impedes the assimilation of Jewry to the greater society. In this sense assimilation would imply the breaking down of the distinctiveness of Jews. But there are other possible meanings to be given to the term, and it is important to try to understand how Jews themselves use the word 'assimilation' to express both their view of an existing state of affairs and a programme for the future.

Among Orthodox Jews there is no possibility of compromise with the way of life of the majority to the extent of allowing them to behave in public and private intercourse simply as Englishmen, Scotsmen, Welshmen, or Irishmen. Jews whose religion prevents them from behaving on Saturday as their fellow citizens behave, who cannot indulge themselves in one of the most potent symbols of fraternity, commensalism, who see themselves as bearers of a faith which destines them to stand aloof in many ways from Gentiles, can mean by assimilation—if, indeed, they approve it in any way—only some harmonious adjustment of their behaviour which might better be called accommodation. Orthodoxy encourages Jews to be good citizens; it cannot allow them to pass over the line dividing Jew and non-Jew which was elaborately fortified in the old ghetto world. To be an Orthodox Jew in Eastern Europe was to move within boundaries sanctioned not only by Judaism but supported by the social and political segregation implicit in the relations between Jews and their non-Jewish political masters. It is perhaps not a general decline in religious attachment in Britain in modern times which has, for most Jews, broken the back of a rigid Orthodoxy, so much as the difficulty of harmonising the separatist precepts of Eastern European Judaism with the demands of a new situation in which Jews feel themselves obliged to come closer to national standards.

As soon as we pass from the smaller sector of Anglo-Jewry which still adheres to the most traditionalist Judaism we are in the large field where religion has ceased to be a total framework for social life to become rather the matter of conscience and occasional conformity which is thought to be characteristic of most Christians in Britain. To be an Englishman and a Jew, which is probably the aim of a very large proportion of Jews born in England, depresses Judaism to the level of one faith among many in a predominantly secular society. Here assimilation implies the state in which Jew, Protestant, and Catholic stand in similar relationship to the social entity which comprises them all. It is debatable whether Jews have in fact reached this kind of position ; I have already suggested that there may be resistances among non-Jews which hinder the acceptance of Jews as simply another religious community within the nation ; but there is no doubt that there is a large number of Jews who speak as though this were their conception of the ideal integration of Jewry into British society.

Flanking the Jewish Englishman is, as it were, the Englishman of Jewish extraction. Assimilation, for unbelieving Jews, is a process by which they merge into the life of the country, dropping nearly everything which marks them as Jews except the avowed fact of their origin. There are, of course, men and women who seek to evade even this residue of un-Englishness, and for them assimilation means the erasure of anything which suggests a Jewish descent, but —and this is a matter which some non-Jews find puzzling—the category of Englishmen of Jewish extraction is a lively and apparently populous margin around the Anglo-Jewish world. It is represented by the agnostic who paradoxically answers ' Jew ' when the recruiting sergeant asks his religion ; by the man who goes out of his way to announce the fact that he is a Jew when he is noted for his anti-religious bias ; by the man who allows his name to stand in the Jewish Who's Who while professing anti-religious or no religious views.[1]

The compulsion felt by many men and women to maintain this minimal identity with Jewry speaks for the existence of an ethnic Jewishness which is easy enough to understand in some other contexts—Communist authorities in Eastern Europe, while frustrat-

[1] To an outsider to the Jewish world unfamiliar with the intergrading of the ethnic and religious senses of ' Jew,' the criteria by which men and women are chosen for inclusion in the Who's Who must seem confused. The preamble to the lists of Honours and Appointments and the Obituary section in *The Jewish Year Book* may serve to show how the compilers of such lists see the problem. (See p. 152, above.)

ing religion, can sometimes make a reasonable case for treating Jews as a cultural minority—but is apt to be bewildering in Britain. One might say, of course, that, fundamentally, the marginal Jews of this type exist only by virtue of the centre round which they are the periphery. Judaism fades among many of the children and grand-children of ' the Synagogue,' but while ' the Synagogue ' lasts Jewry is able to keep its unbelieving offspring on ethnic strings.

The variety of meanings to be attributed to the term assimilation, then, must warn us against asking over-simplified questions of the order of : Are the Jews of Britain becoming assimilated ? We can pose fruitful questions only by asking concrete questions about the social, cultural, and religious persistencies which carry down the significance of Jew from generation to generation. Socially, the varied institutions of Anglo-Jewry have undergone change in the three centuries since the Resettlement and have involved differing degrees of participation by Jews. No crude total of the membership of Jewish Friendly Societies,[1] clubs, Zionist organisations, and the associations of many kinds, even if we knew it accurately, would be able to tell us enough about the present-day implication of Jews in a Jewish social life ; for we have still to understand the less formal organisation of Jewish activities exemplified by such things as suburban cliques and seaside hotels.[2] Similarly, the cultural survivals in diet, language, and manners cannot be gauged from the know-ledge we have at the present time.

Obviously a study of the persistence of religious Jewry must stand at the centre of an inquiry into the changes in Jewish life, and on this subject, because of the crucial rôle of the synagogue in Judaism, it is possible that some significant generalisations can be made. We can, in the first place, answer approximately the question about the extent to which Jews in Britain are sufficiently attached to their religion to be members of synagogues. (Of course, if we

[1] *The Jewish Year Book, 1954*, p. 81, estimates the total membership of Friendly Societies at about 30,000. The Friendly Societies are a form of organisation which has apparently much declined in recent times. The growth of alternative types of social insurance has presumably been one of the factors contributing to this decline.

[2] It is a matter of common observation that holiday-making Jews tend to cluster in certain popular resorts and patronise special hotels—which are not all strictly kasher, *The Jewish Chronicle Travel Guide, 1954* (compiled by ' Green Flag '), lists, *e.g.*, 20 hotels in Bournemouth, 15 in Brighton and Hove, 13 in Margate, and 13 in Southend and Westcliff.

could measure the attendance at New Year and Day of Atonement services we should have an index of something else.) Within the category of practising Jews we can look to see how the movement towards the creation of Englishmen of the Jewish persuasion is reflected in changes in ritual and the allegiances which ritual variants command. If traditionalist Orthodoxy impedes anglicisation then Jews aspiring to be Englishmen must modify their religious practices. This modification is, in fact, achieved in two different ways. Many Jews remain members of synagogues of an Orthodox complexion and put in sporadic appearances at services, while working on the Sabbath, eating non-kasher food, and otherwise diverging from the principles on which the synagogue is based. On the other hand, new types of synagogue have emerged to effect a more open compromise between Judaism and the demands of conformity to national life.

In the country as a whole perhaps something like 80,000 individuals are members of synagogues, and the rough significance of this figure seems to be that between a third and a half of all Jewish adult men are members.[1] In the Greater London area at the present time there are, from the worshippers in the small front-room synagogue to those in the most imposing ecclesiastical structure, something like two hundred congregations. The United Synagogue has sixty-one synagogues in this area (the building of one of these is out of use) ; the Federation of Synagogues has sixty-two; the Union of Orthodox Hebrew Congregations of Great Britain and the Commonwealth has forty-three; the Sephardi section of London Jewry has five synagogues. There are, in addition, nine Liberal, five Reform, and twenty-one independent congregations.[2] The United Synagogue as a whole seems to have a total membership of some 31,000, most of which is in the London area. The Federation of Synagogues, again for the most part in London, numbers some 17,000 ' families.' The Union of Orthodox Congregations has some 3,000 members.

These last three groups together represent by far the greater part of synagogue membership in London and comprise most of the institutional forms of Orthodox Ashkenazi Judaism. While traditional religion is a common basis for all these groups of

[1] But see p. 112 above, where the 1950 figures seem to show a much smaller membership.
[2] See *The Jewish Year Book, 1953,* pp. 92-120.

congregations, each group nevertheless stands for a different type of adjustment to the English environment. The orthodoxy of the United Synagogue, which is organisationally at the centre of Judaism in this country, furnishing the Beth Din and being largely responsible for the maintenance of the Chief Rabbinate, has been able to accommodate sermons in English, stained-glass windows, organ music, choirs, and ministers in distinctly untraditional clerical garb.[1] Historically it represents an early adjustment to the needs of Jews in England,[2] and at the present time appears to stand out as the main symbol of the adaptation made by the typical middle-class religious Jew. The other Orthodox synagogues stem from later influxes from the Eastern European source of Ashkenazi tradition and seem to express much smaller modifications of original forms.

To a considerable extent the siting of different types of synagogue in this general category of Orthodox Ashkenazi institutions reflects the way in which different social elements of Jewry are distributed over the London area. The United Synagogue congregations are spread very widely over the region of London where Jews are to be found, although their distribution shows some bias in favour of west and north-west London.[3] On the other hand, there is a concen-

---

[1] The assimilation of the titles and appearance of the rabbi to that of the Christian clergyman causes some astonishment to Jews unfamiliar with anglicised Jewry. I have heard it said that the man with a distinctly Jewish name but wearing a clerical collar and calling himself Reverend is apt, in some parts of the world, to be mistaken for a converted Jew shamelessly profiting from his new religion.

[2] See p. 26.

[3] United Synagogue congregations, the numbers of which are indicated, are found in the following postal districts:

District	Number	District	Number	District	Number	District	Number
N.1	1	E.1	1	S.W.11	1	Edgware	1
N.2	1	E.3	1	S.W.16	1	Hounslow	1
N.3	1	E.4	1	W.1	1	Harrow	1
N.4	1	E.6	1	W.2	2	Kenton	1
N.5	1	E.7	1	W.5	1	Pinner	1
N.6	1	E.8	1	W.6	1	Stanmore	1
N.8	1	E.9	1	N.W.2	3	Wembley	1
N.10	1	E.12	1	N.W.3	1	Becontree	1
N.11	1	E.C.3	1	N.W.4	1	Ilford	1
N.12	1	S.E.6	1	N.W.6	2	Romford	2
N.14	1	S.E.14	1	N.W.7	1	Wanstead	1
N.15	1	S.E.17	1	N.W.8	1	Richmond	1
N.16	1	S.W.2	1	N.W.9	1	Surbiton	1
N.17	1	S.W.3	1	N.W.11	1		

One synagogue without premises of its own is not included in this analysis.

tration of Federation synagogues in East London,[1] while a high proportion of Union congregations are to be found in the Stamford Hill (N.16) area.[2] This last area is an earlier point on the route of the movement from the East End to the north, and the siting of the Federation and Union synagogues seems to stress the general link between the maintenance of the more traditionalist forms of Judaism and residence in the older and on the whole poorer and less prestige-bearing areas of London Jewish settlement.

At the other end of religious Jewry stand the Reform and Liberal congregations which have consciously striven to adapt their ritual behaviour to the needs of a modernised life. Reform Judaism came into being over a century ago. In 1840 the founders of the West London Synagogue of British Jews set out to establish a place of worship ' where a revised service may be performed at hours more suited to our habits and in a manner more calculated to inspire feelings of devotion, where religious instruction may be afforded by competent persons, and where, to effect these purposes, Jews may form a united congregation under the denomination of British Jews.'[3] The Liberal movement, a much more recent and extreme attempt at reform, has gone to the extent of relying to a great degree on English as a ritual language, of dispensing with head-covering, and of removing the old stringencies from the laws associated with the observance of the Sabbath and the food taboos. (An analysis of the theological adjustments or shifts made in reformed Judaism would throw some light on the changes in ritual

[1] Federation congregations, the numbers of which are indicated, are found in the following postal districts:

District	Number	District	Number	District	Number	District	Number
N.16	1	E.11	1	W.6	1	N.W.11	2
N.17	1	E.13	1	W.9	1	Edgware	1
E.1	30	E.14	1	W.11	1	Greenford	1
E.3	1	E.17	1	W.C.1	1	Ilford	1
E.5	2	S.E.16	1	N.W.2	1	Loughton	1
E.8	3	S.E.18	1	N.W.3	1	Croydon	2
E.9	1	S.W.6	1	N.W.10	2		

[2] Union congregations, the numbers of which are indicated, are found in the following postal districts:

District	Number	District	Number	District	Number	District	Number
N.4	1	E.5	4	N.W.2	1	N.W.10	1
N.5	1	E.8	1	N.W.4	4	N.W.11	7
N.16	17	E.9	1	N.W.6	1	Edgware	1
E.1	3						

[3] See *The Jewish Year Book,* 1954, p. 122.

and ideas as they accommodate to the needs of anglicised Jews.) The synagogues of these two classes are to be found in areas of London which suggest a relative prosperity and solidity of social status. The Reform congregations are one in each of the following districts: W.1, N.W.4, N.W.11, S.W.19, and Edgware. (The first of these congregations, the oldest, has a membership of about 2,000. The total membership of the Association of Synagogues in Great Britain, of which the West London Synagogue is a constituent, is approximately 11,500.) The Liberal synagogues are one in each of: N.14, N.16, E.1, S.W.16, W.2, W.5, N.W.3, N.W.8, and Wembley.[1]

'Assimilation,' which is approved by many Jews as the name for one or other of the types of successful integration into the life of Britain, has also its woeful usage in the protests against the collapse of Jewry. Many threats are seen under the heading of assimilation, but the most formidable assault on the integrity of Jewry is inter-marriage. Although conversion to Christianity might in theory have been a rival to intermarriage as a solvent of Jewish unity, religious defections from the ranks of Anglo-Jewry, despite some picturesque missionary work from time to time, does not seem to have been of any importance in recent decades. Jews have certainly ceased in considerable numbers to be religious Jews, but an ethnic Jewry is not robbed by this type of backsliding ; conversion to Christianity on any appreciable scale would have been a loss of a much more serious nature.

The threat of intermarriage is enhanced by the pressures which urge the Jew wishing to marry a Christian to abandon his faith. For, although there are in fact conversions of

---

[1] The Liberal synagogue in East London (E.1), which seems a contra-diction to the general relation between middle-class status and adherence to modernised Judaism, is the St. George's Settlement Synagogue, founded in 1925 under the auspices of the West London and Liberal Jewish Synagogues. The total membership of the Union of Liberal and Progressive Synagogues (Jewish Religious Union) throughout Great Britain and Ireland is 8,350.

To complete the picture of the distribution of synagogues in London, it may be useful to give the locations of the Sephardi and independent congregations. Sephardi: one congregation in each of W.9 and W.11 and two congregations in N.16. (Nine Sephardi synagogues in England have a total membership of 2,000 'families.') Independent: one congregation in each of N.16, E.5, E.8, E.17, N.W.2, N.W.5, N.W.6, and N,W,11, two in E.2, and nine in E.1. (The Sephardi synagogue in E.C.3, the Sephardi 'cathedral synagogue,' has now no active congregation.)

non-Jewish men and women to Judaism, the religious obstacles raised to this preliminary to intermarriage are formidable. Orthodox Jewry is not merely a community of the freely adhering faithful; it looks only to the children of its members for its recruitment. It eschews proselytising and accepts the outsider with the greatest reluctance. As a result it is not a simple solution for the Jew or Jewess wishing to marry out to bring his or her partner into the religious fold of Jewry. On the other hand, the strong resistance to conversion from Judaism inhibits the use of Christian rites as a common means of entering into a mixed marriage, and the register office seems to be the ordinary setting for the formation of unions of Jews with non-Jews.

Between two categories of the population, Jews and non-Jews, neither of which is homogeneous and which do not stand in a simple relation of social dominance one to another, the circumstances and direction of intermarriage are not regular and the social filiation of children of mixed unions becomes complex. The only feature discernible in the crude information we now have is that Jews seem to marry out more than Jewesses,[1] and this fact, presumably, reflects the differential social freedom of the sexes among Jews. In earlier phases of Anglo-Jewish history Jews of higher social status seem to have married out more than their fellows lower in the social scale. Nowadays Jews of the upper social strata and upwardly mobile Jews do not appear to be disposed to marrying out more than other kinds of Jews, and, while this witnesses an increase in the contacts between Jews and non-Jews at the lower-class levels, it also points to changes in the routes to assimilation. For in nineteenth-century conditions conversion and marriage out could remove barriers to acceptance in English society which today are not so formidable. To be a peer, judge, or high-ranking soldier at the present time a Jew need not attempt to conceal his ethnic attachments, even to the extent of changing his surname.

Any programme of systematic research into Jewish problems in this country must have in the forefront a study of intermarriage and the social position and connections of the offspring of mixed unions. Brought up as Jews, Christians, or neither, the web of their social relations, their degrees of acceptance by Jews and non-Jews,

[1] Cf. p. 92f.

and the kinds of self-identification which they make, may be able to underline for us the shifts which are taking place in the status of Anglo-Jewry and the degrees of tolerance in the wider society. Is there, for example, any tendency for mixed marriages to produce less children than more conventional unions such that one might infer anxieties and strains set up by the anomalous family? Are there ambiguities in the status of the half-Jew which impede his development as an Englishman?

There is a further aspect of Jewish assimilation in Britain which requires the most careful study. With the rise of Zionism in European Jewry there has been the tendency to oppose the 'assimilationists' to those Jews standing in the nationalist camp. From the Zionist point of view, however, policies of assimilation into the nations of the Gentile world have seemed unrealistic and unlikely to be successful. At least for some Zionists the ingathering of the Jews from the Diaspora has appeared to be the only happy solution, in the long run, to the world-wide Jewish problem. Within the ranks of Anglo-Jewry the debate on Zionism has been largely stilled by the establishment of the State of Israel, which, emerging from vision to reality, has rapidly outpaced academic discussions about possibilities, difficulties, and dangers. Cleavages certainly exist in Jewish attitudes to the State as a homeland for world Jewry, but there can be little doubt that among most of the Jewish population of Britain there is at the present time a positive attachment to the Jewish State, at least in the form of a special interest and affection directed towards a nation of Jews.

Using the superficial evidence of a network of Zionist organisations and an abundant display of support for and good will towards Israel, and reasoning from other situations in which minority groups take eagerly to a nationalism centred on an overseas homeland, an observer might jump to the conclusion that Zionism in Anglo-Jewry is a simple index of the failure of Jews to find a satisfactory place for themselves in British life. At a deeper level of inquiry it might still seem that Zionism in Britain is at least a factor impeding the gradual amalgamation of Jews in the wider society.

A simple numbering of the Jews actively concerned with Zionist work in this country suggests, in the first place, a low degree of political involvement.[1] Perhaps thirty per cent of Jews in Britain are directly connected with Zionism either as contributors to the Joint Palestine Appeal or in some other way. On the other hand, the penetration of the values of Zionism into many Anglo-Jewish institutions, from synagogues to bodies at the national level, means that this percentage does not sufficiently express the importance of Zionist opinion and interest in the community at large. It becomes a problem to understand what, in the wide field of Jewish behaviour oriented towards Israel, is relevant to the assimilation of Jews to British life.

There are other 'diasporas,' notably those of the Chinese and the Indians, in which it is common to find the overseas sojourners accused of trying to maintain an *imperium in imperio,* of fostering a separatist educational system, of breaking the loyalty of citizens to the land of their birth by stimulating the use of a foreign language and by inculcating the political and cultural values of a nation across the seas. There are, to use the term which J. S. Furnivall has given us, many plural societies which have to face the difficulty of keeping within one political system social entities of divergent cultures and aims. Is there a hint of this undesirable situation in the position of Anglo-Jewry under the impact of Zionism? The fear of disrupted loyalties seems to have played some part in the resistance of Jews to the Zionist programme in earlier days. The organisation of Zionist youth movements, the drive to use Hebrew as a living secular language, and propaganda to stress the peculiar position of the Jew might be made to appear to run the risk of increasing the ambiguity of Jewish status in Britain.

Yet analogies with other 'diasporas' are not altogether satisfactory. Since 'return' to the homeland stands at the centre of Zionist thought and policy, the fully indoctrinated nationalist is likely to remove himself to the State, and even the convinced Zionists who do not, for the moment, go to Israel, reckon with the possibility of an early withdrawal from the Diaspora. We know, however, that this wing of the Zionist Movement is relatively unimportant in Britain, but we must still ask whether Zionism has the effect on the bulk of Anglo-Jewry of setting up resistances to assimilation to the wider society.

[1] Cf. p. 122 above.

236

No answer can be given to the question with confidence until much careful research has been carried out, but it is at least plain that fears of 'disrupted loyalties' are largely misplaced. As is frequently suggested, what passes for Zionist activity is very much a charitable support for a Jewish cause. Jews in Britain give money for Jews in Israel. They take part in Zionist-organised meetings and festivities as they participate in many other kinds of functions —a word and activity much loved in the community—concerned with Jewish matters. It may very well be that Zionism, by strengthening the bases of Anglo-Jewish life and enriching its cultural content, has contributed, in this sense, to the hindrance of assimilation ; but it is very doubtful whether it could be reasonably said that, by orienting interests and sympathies outside the country of their birth, Zionism has seriously deflected the main body of the Jewish community from its aim of finding a suitable adjustment in terms of full citizenship within British society.

However, it is important to realise that part of the very process of finding this suitable adjustment may entail some sort of Zionist alignment, for it is clear that, at least in the case of some Jews, there is a great deal of self-respect and sense of security to be derived from an identification with the Jewish State. Moreover, common observation suggests that in the last few years, during which Israel has become an established feature of the international landscape, formal ties with organisations centred on Israel have become ' respectable ' in Anglo-Jewry at large, unlike the links with Zionism in the days before the State came into being. It is quite possible, indeed, that Zionist activity, measured in the broadest terms, is increasing at the present time and will continue to grow in the immediate future ; but the significance of this increase will lie not so much in the evidence it affords of a resurgence of nationalist spirit as in the light it throws on attempts by some sections of the Anglo-Jewish minority to iron out the uncertainties of their position by association with Zionism. It is certainly true that Zionist nationalism has not provided, and cannot provide, for Anglo-Jewry the basic and all-embracing solidarity once given by the Jewish religion, but when Jews in modern Britain feel the need for the assertion of some Jewishness, activity in relation to Israel may be a suitable idiom of expression for them.

As a set of ideas Zionism is at many points separable from Judaism, and its rôle in fostering nationalism among Jewish children can be studied to some extent apart from the question of the religious indoctrination of the young. It would not, however, be enough to take the small participation of Jewish boys and girls in formal Zionist activities as a measure of the effect of Zionist influence on them, for within the setting of some of the religious schools, which exist to equip children in doctrinal and ritual knowledge, elements of Zionism appear to have been introduced in recent decades. The language which was for long used for sacred purposes only and the land which for most Jews remained unapproachably remote through the ages have taken on, even in the context of the religious schools, a new significance.

There appears, for example, to have been some trend in recent years to replace the traditional Ashkenazi pronunciation of Hebrew by that used in Israel (which is based on the Sephardi values). The permeation of contemporary Judaism by Zionist ideas is to be seen in other ways. A prayer for Israel, after that for the Royal Family, has been introduced in the synagogues on the instructions of the Chief Rabbi. Some Holy-day services have been used as occasions for collecting money for Israel. The United Synagogue— its constitution rules out political activity—is not formally linked to Zionist activity, but the Federation of Synagogues has Zionist affiliations. In the 1934 revision of the Federation's statement of objects there occurs the following: ' To further the upbuilding of Eretz Yisrael and thereby create a haven of rest there for our brethren who are persecuted because of their race and religion in many countries.'[1]

On the other hand, the rôle of the religious schools in creating among children a specifically Jewish orientation, of a Zionist complexion or not, is limited by two factors. In the first place, Jewish religious education is confined to a fairly small section of the community.[2] In the second place, religious education as it is conducted appears to be ineffective over a considerable area of its

[1] *The Jewish Year Book, 1954,* p. 109.
[2] See p. 118f. above.

endeavour. Apart from a few schools which provide a whole-time rounded education, comprising both secular and religious teaching,[1] Jewish schools are establishments to which children go after their ordinary school hours for instruction in Hebrew and religious subjects. They are, on a somewhat more extensive scale, the rough equivalent of Sunday schools in the Christian churches. Since, however, many of them seem to rely on poor teaching staffs and unsuitable buildings, and because their primary function appears to be the cramming of boys for their *barmitzvah* at the age of thirteen, there seems a probability that their effect on Jewish youth is not so important as at first sight might appear. No dogmatic statement of such a kind will do ; we clearly need a careful and impartial assessment of the social and cultural consequences of religious instruction ; but it seems unlikely that the religious schools contribute very much to the making of an intensively Jewish life.

There is one further aspect of Jewish religious education which needs to be considered. It is clear that for a considerable number of Jews, who are neither Zionist nor reluctant to take advantage of every opportunity they see to live the life of an Englishman, the perpetuation of some specifically Jewish culture is an indispensable element in the adjustment of Jewry to the wider society. When this notion is fully rationalised, it takes the form of a statement that Jews in Britain, unless they have some kind of Jewish culture by which to make a stand, run the grave danger of finding themselves well and truly between two stools. If they abandon the cultural support provided by the synagogue and the religious school they will be neither Jews nor yet real Englishmen, floundering as piteous ' marginal men ' in the rough seas of ambiguous status. It is, on this view, only confidence in their own culture that can preserve Jews from this perilous position.

Of course, what precisely is meant by Jewish culture, what minimum amount of Jewish culture will guarantee the kind of security sought, and how the preservation of Jewish culture affects the more general question of assimilation, are all problems which

---

[1] See *The Jewish Year Book, 1954*, pp. 124f. for a list of such schools in the London area.

are both difficult to deal with and important to answer. They can, in fact, be satisfactorily approached only on the basis of very detailed study of concrete data ; but there is one preliminary point of theory which may be worth the statement here. The process by which a minority group finds a place for itself in the wider society may be said to be one both of assimilation and accultura-tion. By the use of the former term we may undertake an analysis of the way in which the minority becomes incorporated into the system of social relations which constitutes the greater society. Employing the second term, we may study how the cultural characteristics of the minority change in response to those of the surrounding majority.

It is evident that the two kinds of things studied under the two different headings are not of the same order, and yet they are very intimately linked. Progressive assimilation, by which members of a minority become diffused within the larger society, must entail a measure of acculturation ; and acculturation, whereby members of a minority come to act in ways similar to those of the majority, involves some assimilation. It is impossible, for example, for a Jew who maintains a large measure of the ghetto culture of Eastern Europe, speaking only broken English and behaving in others ways which from an English point of view are exotic, to assimilate in English society. A Jew who maintains social relations which are characteristically those of an Englishman, and is so assimilated, must be acculturated at least to the extent that nothing un-English remains in his behaviour to act as a barrier to his acceptance.

But before the precise relationship between assimilation and acculturation can be understood in any particular context, we need to know which elements of cultural behaviour are the most relevant for assimilation. It is obvious that, as far as the position in England is concerned, the speaking of broken English is of considerably more importance as a cultural hindrance to assimilation than, for example, eating a Jewish diet or specialising in the retailing of Jewish jokes. How relevant is the hard core of religious behaviour which the Jew, anxious to avoid becoming a ' marginal man,' seeks to preserve? This is a question we cannot answer from first principles. We need to look more closely at reality.

Jews and Non-Jews

When Jews commune with Jews in private life the outer world is still often that of the *goyim,* even on lips innocent of a language other than English. Looking beyond his own immediate horizon, the Jew who tries to give a neutral and unemotional term to his neighbours as a class must use ' Christians,' ' Gentiles,' or the somewhat ethnocentric ' non-Jews.' When (particularly immigrant) Jews avoid all these terms and couch their polite reference to the great majority in the simple word ' English ' they are documenting the first approach in the adjustment of an ethnic and religious group to a predominantly secular society.

But whatever labels we may use for the two categories of citizens, Jews and non-Jews, and however difficult it may be to draw clear lines to divide them, there is an impact of one on the other which needs to be studied as a case of culture contact. Assimilation and acculturation, whatever precise meaning we may give them, assume the approximation of Jews to a set of national norms. Have the others—the Christians, the Gentiles, the non-Jews, the ' English '—been affected? There is play here for both anti- and philo-semites. A particular contribution to British life made by Jews, from the vocabulary of Jewish music hall comedians to the rationalisation of the clothing industry and the stimulation of cheap but lush restaurants in the metropolis, may be seen as an affront and corruption or a joyous enhancement of public amenities. But to a large extent what is Jewish is exotic, and an adjustment to it on the part of the wider society is an exercise in toleration.

Apart from what it takes from Jews for itself British social life makes adjustments in the interests of Jewry. It makes them concessions and grants them privileges. Kasher kitchens are provided on ocean-going liners. Shopkeepers unwilling to trade on Saturday may open on Sunday. The machinery of food rationing is modified to allow Jews to enjoy ritually slaughtered meat and compensate them for their abstention from bacon and lard. Jewish children are let out of school in time to observe the Sabbath eve and Jewish employees in the public services indulged at the times of the great Holy-days. The *shabbas goy* (the ' Jew's poker,' as he was called at an earlier date) hovers about the Orthodox household unable to

241

R

kindle it own fires on the Sabbath. Shops and stores bid for Jewish trade with a flourish of 'Kosher for Passover' labels. Such accommodations are signs of a broad toleration, and as they ease the path of the religiously conforming Jew they lend a gracious air to the 'British way of life.' On the other hand, the toleration of social eccentricity sometimes encourages it to persist. Quite apart from any pressures generated within Jewish society, many Jews appear to assume an outward conformity to their religion in direct response to the special provisions made for them. The Yom Kippur (Day of Atonement) Jews, who pack the overflow services in their annual devotions, often excite ridicule ; that they are able to live on the margins of religious Jewry and well within the limits of an ethnic Jewry may be at once a reflection of British tolerance and an index of British resistance to the outsider.

Tolerance and resistance are, after all, not such strange bedfellows, for what is not taken into intimacy may be encouraged to have its own identity. It is not uncommon for Jews to discover that Gentiles respect them more for abstaining from bacon and for going to the synagogue than for trying to be the complete Englishman without taboos and odd religious commitments. And there may be a feature in this which is paralleled in the experience of colonials who learn that, in British eyes, they are better as self-respecting natives, firmly established in their own culture, than as would-be Europeans. The French, it is said, have a different sense of social and cultural inclusiveness, welcoming the gallicised foreigner and colonial, and offering them rewards for their imitation of French models. The British—or is it the English in this case ?— recruit within narrower limits. They resist outsiders somewhat as Judaism resists converts. We shall know whether this is a correct characterisation of attitudes only when we have looked more closely at the position of all minority groups in British society.

APPENDIX I

Tables
By H. Neustatter

SURVEY OF THE JEWISH POPULATION IN GREAT BRITAIN

Sample Page
including those questions used in this Survey

QUESTIONNAIRE A.J.S.-1

NAME AND ADDRESS OF ORGANISATION ....

....

  I *Estimate of total Jewish population* ....

      Of which .... not associated with any Jewish Organisation

 II *Average number of persons in each Jewish family* ....

III *Number of births* in 1945 .... 1946 .... 1947 ....
                      1948 .... 1949 ....

IV *Number of deaths* in 1945 .... 1946 .... 1947 ....
                      1948 .... 1949 ....

  V *Jewish Schools :*

      (1) Total number 1950 .... and 1945 ....

      (2) Number of religious schools ....

      (3) Number of secular schools ....

      (4) Number of pupils attending ....

         (a) Religious schools ....

         (b) Secular schools ....

THE JEWIS

SURVEY OF THE JEWISH P

Ques

ADDRESS (See Note † below) ....

NUMBER OF PERSONS IN HOUSEHOLD (including Boarders).....................

PERSONAL DATA

SURNAME (See Note † below)	Initials	Relation to House-holder (e.g. wife, son, lodger etc.)	Sex	BORN AT		Married or Single ? (See Note * below)	N/
				Place	Date		At b
1.							
2.							
3.							
4.							
5.							
6.							

NOTES * If married, please enter "M"
      If single   „   „   "B" or bachelor
                          "S" „   spinster   } whichever applicable
                          "D" „   divorced
                          "W" „   widowed

† Names and addresses requested *only in order
to prevent duplication in compiling the Survey*

HRONICLE

ATION OF GREAT BRITAIN

e A/J/S-2

OCCUPATION											
OWN ACCOUNT				EMPLOYED					What University Degree or Professional Qualifications do you hold ?
Profession or Trade (Please specify e.g. Medicine, Law, Grocery, Tailoring, etc.)	Please put tick in appropriate column below if applicable			Profession or Trade (Please specify e.g. Civil Service, Banking, Motor Industry, Radio Manufacture, etc.)	Please put tick in appropriate column below				
	Manufacture	Wholesale	Retail		Managerial	Professional or Technical	Clerical	Manual	

REMARKS. (i.e. add relevant supplementary information, if any)

....

....

....

....

247

TABLE I

A.J.S.-2 Questionnaires Completed and Returned (1952)

Area	Number of forms returned	Number of individuals covered
Derby	46	135
Glasgow	32	111
Grimsby and Cleethorpes ...	56	162
Hull	464	1342
Leeds	107	366
Liverpool and Southport ...	210	686
Greater London ...	362	1191
Sheffield	247	763
Sunderland	35	126
Torquay and Paignton ...	56	176
Wolverhampton ...	20	67
Miscellaneous ...	32	100
Totals ...	1667	5225

TABLE II

Naturalisation of Jewish Aliens by Area of Residence

Year	London	Manchester	Leeds	Glasgow	Birmingham	Miscellaneous	Total
1938	532	30	11	16	12	108	709
1942	485	21	12	11	13	187	729
1944	88	8	3	3	1	83	186
1945	94	4	3	2	3	66	172
1946	302	13	3	12	8	138	476
1947	6150	436	238	166	300	5699	12989
1948	6469	437	204	137	166	2684	10097
Total	14120	949	474	347	503	8965	25358
Allowance for married women 20 % *	2824	189	95	69	101	1793	5071
Total	16944	1138	569	416	604	10758	
Grand Total	...	...	...	...	...	...	30429

* Married women naturalised together with their husbands are not separately enumerated in the Home Office White Papers on Naturalisation of Aliens.

TABLE III—A.J.S.-1

	Estimated Jewish population	Estimated average size of family		Estimated Jewish population	Estimated average size of family
Aberavon	44	3.0	Nottingham	2500	4.0
Bangor	54	3.5	Oxford	500	4.0
Barrow-in-Furness	78	3.0	Peterborough	118	3.0
Belfast	1800	4.0	Pontypridd	110	4.0
Birmingham (*Mr. Prais's estimate*)	6300	3.6	Preston	160	4.0
Blackpool	1500	3.0	Ramsgate	106	2.0
Bournemouth	1500	2.5	Reading	500	4.0
Brighton & Hove	4500	3.0	Ruislip	750	3.0
Bristol	410	3.5	St. Annes-on-Sea	375	3.0
Brynmawr	45	4.0	Sheffield (revised estimate)	1850	3.2
Chester	30	3.0	Southampton	150	3.5
Darlington	195	3.0	Southend	3500	4.0
Derby	205	3.3	South Shields	115	3.4
Dundee	100	3.0	Staines	500	3.5
Durham	6	2.0	Sunderland	1050	4.0
Eastbourne	60	3.0	Swindon	30	3.0
Glasgow	15000	5.0	Torquay	183	3.0
Harrogate	385	3.0	Tredegar	27	4.0
Hayes (Middlesex)	145	4.0	Wallasey	280	3.0
Hull	2000	3.0	Walsall	21	3.0
Leeds	25000	4.0	Welwyn Gdn. City	195	3.5
Letchworth	150	4.0	West Hartlepool	80	4.0
Liverpool	7500	4.0	Whitley Bay	175	4.0
Luton	800	3.0	Wolverhampton	230	2.5
Newcastle-on-Tyne	2100	3.0	Worcester	45	3.0
Norwich	135	3.0	York	30	4.0

Total estimated population and average size of family   83622   3.4

TABLE IV—A.J.S.-2

AGE AND SEX DISTRIBUTION

Age	Males	Females	Total both sexes	Age	Males	Females	Total both sexes
0- 4	186	216	402	45-49	245	196	441
5- 9	177	147	324	50-54	193	191	384
10-14	150	137	287	55-59	138	119	257
15-19	148	153	301	60-64	110	120	230
20-24	159	148	307	65-69	85	99	184
25-29	149	181	330	70-74	60	73	133
30-34	163	185	348	75 & over	39	40	79
35-39	232	231	463	Age			
40-44	270	238	508	unknown	105	142	247
Total					2609	2616	5225

249

TABLE V—A.J.S.-1

Jews not Affiliated to any Jewish Organisations

	Estimated Jewish pop.	Not affiliated	Not affiliated %		Estimated Jewish pop.	Not affiliated	Not affiliated %
Bangor	54	25	46.3	Merthyr Tydfil	198	10	5.0
Barrow-in-				Newcastle ...	2100	50	2.4
Furness ...	78	24	30.8	Nottingham ...	2500	500	20.0
Belfast	1800	50	2.8	Oxford	500	40	8.0
Birmingham				Peterborough ...	118	5	4.2
(*Mr. Prais's*				Pontypridd ...	110	5	4.5
estimates)	6300	1260	20.0	Reading	500	100	20.0
Blackpool ...	1500	250	16.7	St. Annes-on-Sea	375	10	2.7
Bournemouth ...	1500	500	33.3	Sheffield ...	1600*	200	12.5
Brighton &				Southampton ...	150	40	26.7
Hove ...	4500	450	10.0	Southend ...	3500	100	2.9
Brynmawr ...	45	—	—	Staines	500	10	2.0
Cambridge ...	200	50	25.0	Sunderland ...	1050	10	1.0
Darlington ...	195	18	9.2	Torquay ...	183	10	5.5
Derby	205	28	13.7	Wallasey ...	280	15	5.4
Dundee	100	2	2.0	Welwyn Garden			
Durham	6	2	33.3	City	195	93	47.7
Eastbourne ...	60	6	10.0	West Hartlepool	80	6	7.5
Harrogate ...	385	24	6.2	Whitley Bay ...	175	12	6.9
Hull	2000	30	1.5	Wolverhampton	230	30	13.0
Letchworth ...	150	50	33.3	Worcester ...	45	3	6.7
Liverpool ...	7500	1500	20.0	York	30	15	50.0
Luton	800	200	25.0				
Total					41797	5733	13.7

* First estimate later increased to 1850; *no estimate for people not affiliated given with latter estimate.*

Note : We conclude from this table that a percentage of 15 for Jews not affiliated to any Jewish organisation for the country as a whole is a very conservative estimate, as, with the exception of Liverpool, none of the large Jewish centres, *e.g.,* Leeds, Manchester, and Glasgow, has replied to this question, and the proportion of the relevant group in the total Jewish population can be presumed to be the greater the larger the local Jewish population.

TABLE VI—A.J.S.-1
AVERAGE NUMBER OF JEWISH BIRTHS, 1945-1949

	Estimated Jewish population	5 years' average No. of births		Estimated Jewish population	5 years' average No. of births
Aberavon	44	0.2	Norwich	135	2.8
Bangor	54	0.8	Oxford	500	2.4
Barrow-in-			Peterborough ...	118	1.8
Furness ...	78	0.8	Plymouth	350	4.6
Belfast	1800	20.0	Pontypridd ...	110	0.2
Birmingham ...	5500	51.6	Preston	160	2.2
Bristol	410	2.0	St. Annes-on-Sea	375	5.7
Cambridge	200	0.8	Southampton ...	150	2.0
Chester	30	0.6	South Shields ...	115	1.8
Darlington ...	195	1.2	Sunderland ...	1050	28.0
Derby	205	1.0	Tredegar	27	0.2
Dundee	100	1.8	Wallasey	280	9.0
Durham	6	0.2	Walsall	21	0.2
Eastbourne ...	60	0.6	Welwyn Garden		
Harrogate	385	3.6	City	195	2.6
Hayes (Middlesex)	145	0.6	West Hartlepool	80	0.6
Hull	2000	15.0	Whitley Bay ...	175	2.0
Letchworth ...	150	1.4	Worcester	45	0.6
Luton	800	17.4	York	30	0.8
Total				16078	187.1

Birth-rate : 11.6 per thousand

TABLE VII—A.J.S.-2
MARITAL CONDITION

Age	MALES B	M	D	W	U	Total	FEMALES S	M	D	W	U	Total	Total both sexes
0- 4	186	—	—	—	—	186	216	—	—	—	—	216	402
5- 9	177	—	—	—	—	177	147	—	—	—	—	147	324
10-14	150	—	—	—	—	150	137	—	—	—	—	137	287
15-19	148	—	—	—	—	148	152	1	—	—	—	153	301
20-24	147	11	—	—	1	159	93	54	1	—	—	148	307
25-29	80	67	—	2	—	149	55	124	—	1	1	181	330
30-34	40	121	—	1	1	163	38	145	2	—	—	185	348
35-39	36	195	—	1	—	232	30	198	—	3	—	231	463
40-44	41	224	2	1	2	270	30	201	5	2	—	238	508
45-49	29	215	—	—	1	245	18	171	4	3	—	196	441
50-54	14	170	4	3	2	193	16	162	—	11	2	191	384
55-59	10	118	—	8	2	138	11	81	—	26	1	119	257
60-64	12	93	—	4	1	110	10	77	—	29	4	120	230
65-69	6	67	—	12	—	85	7	56	—	32	4	99	184
70-74	1	45	1	11	2	60	7	18	—	48	—	73	133
75 & over	1	25	1	10	2	39	2	15	—	23	—	40	79
Unknown	30	61	1	5	8	105	36	74	—	17	15	142	247
Totals	1108	1412	9	58	22	2609	1005	1377	12	195	27	2616	5225

Key : B=bachelor ; S=spinster ; M=married ; D=divorced ;
W=widowed ; U=unknown, i.e., no information entered

Among explanations of there being more married men than women are : intermarriage ; completion of forms by collectors, instead of householders, who filled in known data leaving other questions blank ; and optimism as to the fate of marriage partners stranded in Europe during the war.

TABLE VIII—A.J.S.-1
AVERAGE ANNUAL NUMBER OF JEWISH DEATHS, 1945-1949

	Estimated Jewish Population	5 years' average number of deaths		Estimated Jewish Population	5 years' average number of deaths
Aberavon	44	0.4	Norwich	135	2.4
Bangor	54	0.2	Oxford	500	1.8
Barrow-in-Furness	78	0.6	Peterborough	118	0.4
Belfast	1800	16.5	Plymouth	350	7.4
Birmingham	5500	72.6	Pontypridd	110	2.0
Blackpool	1500	14.5	Preston	160	1.0
Brighton and Hove	4500	92.0	Ramsgate	106	1.4
Bristol	410	3.2	St. Annes-on-Sea	375	5.3
Cambridge	200	1.6	Sheffield	1850	18.1
Chester	30	0.8	Southend	1200	1.8
Darlington	195	0.8	South Shields	•115	1.4
Derby	205	2.2	Sunderland	1050	12.8
Dundee	100	1.5	Tredegar	27	0.2
Durham	6	0.0	Wallasey	280	7.2
Eastbourne	60	1.0	Walsall	21	0.0
Harrogate	385	4.8	Welwyn Garden City	195	1.0
Hayes (Middlesex)	145	0.2	West Hartlepool	80	0.8
Hull	2000	25.0	Whitley Bay	175	3.0
Letchworth	150	0.6	Worcester	45	0.2
Liverpool	7500	115.8	York	30	0.4
Luton	800	8.2			
Total				32584	431.1

Death-rate : 13.2 per thousand

TABLE IX—A.J.S.-2
NATIONALITY AT BIRTH AND AT PRESENT

Age	MALES British	For-eign	Un-known	Total	N/N	FEMALES British	For-eign	Un-kn'n	Total	N/N	Both sexes Grand Total
0- 4	186	—	—	186	—	215	1	—	216	1	402
5- 9	177	—	—	177	—	147	—	—	147	—	324
10-14	150	—	—	150	—	135	2	—	137	1	287
15-19	143	5	—	148	1	144	9	—	153	1	301
20-24	154	5	—	159	1	135	13	—	148	3	307
25-29	135	14	—	149	4	164	17	—	181	1	330
30-34	155	8	—	163	2	174	11	—	185	3	348
35-39	219	13	—	232	2	220	11	—	231	—	463
40-44	247	23	—	270	2	207	31	—	238	—	508
45-49	221	24	—	245	3	166	30	—	196	3	441
50-54	154	39	—	193	7	148	42	1	191	11	384
55-59	93	45	—	138	14	76	43	—	119	10	257
60-64	51	59	—	110	15	70	50	—	120	15	230
65-69	34	51	—	85	9	54	44	1	99	13	184
70-74	20	40	—	60	11	18	55	—	73	25	133
75 & over	12	27	—	39	9	19	21	—	40	11	79
Unkn'n	71	31	3	105	3	99	37	6	142	11	247
Total	2222	384	3	2609	83	2191	417	8	2616	109	5225

Key : British=British born ; Foreign=Foreign born ; Unknown=Not indicated ; N/N=Not naturalised

252

TABLE X—A.J.S.-1

JEWISH CHILDREN OF SCHOOL AGE RECEIVING ORGANISED JEWISH EDUCATION

(Age group 5 to 15 represents about 14 per cent of total U.K. population)

Area	Estimated Jewish population	Number of children receiving Jewish religious education	Per cent of Jewish population
Aberavon	44	5	11.3
Barrow-in-Furness	78	2	2.6
Belfast	1800	120	6.7
Birmingham	5500	300	5.5
Blackpool	1500	70	4.7
Bournemouth	1500	70	4.7
Darlington	195	10	5.1
Dundee	100	10	10.0
Eastbourne	60	8	13.3
Exeter	30	4	13.3
Glasgow	15000	1085*	7.2
Harrogate	385	28	7.3
Hayes (Middlesex)	145	9	6.2
Hull	2000	80	4.0
Liverpool	7500	760	10.1
Luton	800	60	7.5
Merthyr Tydfil	198	25	12.6
Newcastle upon Tyne	2100	100	4.8
Nottingham	2500	80	3.2
Oxford	500	20	4.0
Plymouth	350	16	4.6
Pontypridd	110	6	5.5
Preston	160	16	10.0
Reading	500	50	10.0
St. Annes	375	34	9.1
Sheffield	1850	150	8.1
Sunderland	1050	105	10.0
Torquay	183	26	14.2
Wallasey	280	6	2.1
West Hartlepool	80	6	7.5
Whitley Bay	175	24	13.7
Worcester	45	6	13.3
Total average percentage ...	47093	3291	7.0†

* *The figure entered on our A.J.S.-1 is 536, owing to a misunderstanding. The figure of 1085 has been repeatedly published from various authoritative quarters.*

† *This 7 per cent may be compared with an average percentage of 7.7 arrived at by the Jewish Memorial Council for 1952.*

TABLE XI—A.J.S.-2

OCCUPATIONS ALL AREAS : MALES

Trade	Marital Status B	M	D	W	U	Own Account	Em-ployed	Kind of Employment Mana-gerial	Tech. Prof.	Cleri-cal	Man-ual	Nationality at Birth British	For-eign	Un-known	Nationality at Present Not British
(1) Books and allied trades	5	10	—	—	—	9	6	3	2	1	—	14	1	—	—
(2) Boots and Shoes	3	15	1	2	—	18	3	3	—	—	—	18	3	—	—
(3) Builders and allied trades	4	16	—	—	—	16	4	1	1	—	2	19	1	—	—
(4) Clothing, tailoring, etc ...	54	271	5	14	—	271	73	27	19	3	24	272	72	—	21
(5) Drapery, textile, fashion	11	88	—	6	—	89	16	11	2	2	1	74	31	1	1
(6) Fancy goods	4	20	—	2	—	23	3	3	—	—	—	23	3	—	—
(7) Food—(a) Miscellaneous	11	34	—	2	—	42	5	3	1	—	2	37	10	—	2
(b) Bakers	2	10	—	—	—	9	3	—	1	—	2	8	4	—	—
(c) Butchers	3	14	—	—	—	13	4	2	1	—	1	13	4	—	—
(d) Caterers	5	17	—	—	—	17	5	4	1	—	—	17	5	—	—
(e) Grocers	5	34	—	—	—	35	4	3	—	1	—	32	7	—	—
(8) Film	1	6	—	—	—	2	5	5	—	—	—	6	1	—	—
(9) Fur	7	16	—	1	—	16	8	2	2	1	3	21	3	—	1
(10) Furniture	26	82	1	1	2	80	32	15	3	3	11	87	23	2	5
(11) Glass and china, etc.	1	10	—	—	—	10	1	1	—	—	—	9	2	—	—
(12) Hairdressing	9	48	—	—	—	45	12	2	4	—	6	47	10	1	1
(13) Insurance	1	12	—	—	—	8	5	1	2	2	—	11	2	—	—
(14) Jewellery	12	27	—	3	—	35	7	2	4	—	2	33	9	—	—
(15) Metal	3	17	—	—	—	17	4	2	—	3	2	18	3	—	—
(16) Motor and allied trades	10	24	—	—	—	19	15	2	3	2	7	28	6	—	—
(17) Shipping	3	6	—	1	—	1	8	—	—	—	4	8	1	—	—
(18) Stockbrokers	1	5	—	—	—	5	2	—	1	—	1	7	—	—	—
(19) Tobacco	2	12	—	—	—	14	—	—	—	1	—	12	2	—	—
(20) Wines	3	1	1	—	—	1	3	1	—	—	1	4	—	—	—
(21) Miscellaneous trades	62	157	1	1	—	126	95	23	8	34	30	180	39	2	6
Total	248	952	8	34	2	921	323	117	54	53	99	998	242	4	37

254

TABLE XII—A.J.S.-2

PROFESSIONS ALL AREAS: MALES

Profession	B	Marital Status M	D	W	U	Own account	Employed	Mana-gers	Prof. Tech.	Cleri. cal	Man-ual	British	For-eign	Un-known
(1) Accountants	17	17	—	—	1	11	24	2	18	4	—	35	—	—
(2) Archæologists	1	—	—	—	—	1	—	—	—	—	—	1	—	—
(3) Architects	—	4	—	—	—	3	2	—	2	—	—	4	1	—
(4) Artists	2	2	—	2	—	3	1	—	1	—	—	3	5	—
(5) Chemists	10	21	—	—	—	13	20	5	13	2	—	28	—	—
(6) Civil Servants	8	9	—	—	—	—	17	3	6	8	—	17	—	—
(7) Dentists, Dental Surgeons, & Dental Mechs.	4	15	—	—	—	16	3	—	3	—	—	17	2	—
(8) Engineers (Electrical, Mechanical, etc.)	16	16	—	—	—	11	21	4	10	—	6	26	6	—
(9) Estate Agents	2	13	—	—	—	12	3	—	3	1	—	13	2	—
(10) Law	10	22	—	—	—	27	5	—	5	—	—	32	—	—
(11) Mathematics	—	1	—	—	—	—	1	—	1	—	—	1	1	—
(12) Medicine	14	56	—	2	—	53	19	1	18	—	—	65	6	—
(13) Ministers of Religion	1	11	—	—	—	2	10	—	10	—	—	10	2	—
(14) Communal Workers	—	—	—	—	—	—	6	2	1	2	1	6	—	—
(15) Musicians	3	6	—	—	—	7	1	—	1	—	—	7	1	—
(16) Optical and Photographical	4	5	—	—	—	—	3	—	3	—	—	12	2	—
(17) Physicists	1	10	—	—	—	9	5	2	—	—	—	1	—	—
(18) Publicity (Press, Advertising, etc.)	—	—	—	—	—	—	1	1	2	1	—	6	—	—
(19) Teachers	7	5	—	—	—	3	3	—	25	1	—	25	1	—
(20) Miscel. Professions	2	19	—	—	—	1	3	—	3	—	—	3	1	1
Total	103	234	—	4	1	171	171	20	125	19	7	312	29	1

* All now British (1952)

255

TABLE XIII—A.J.S.-2

OCCUPATIONS ALL AREAS: FEMALES

Trade	Male Index No.	Marital Status					Kind of Employment						Nationality at Birth			Nationality at present
		B	M	D	W	U	Own account	Employed	Managerial	Tech. Prof.	Clerical	Manual	British	Foreign	Unknown	Not British
Books & allied trades	(1)	1	1	—	—	—	2	—	—	—	—	—	1	1	—	1
Boots & shoes	(2)	1	—	—	—	—	1	—	—	—	—	—	1	—	—	—
Clothing	(4)	18	6	—	1	—	7	18	1	1	4	12	20	5	—	1
Drapery, etc.	(5)	14	11	—	6	—	19	12	2	—	8	2	28	3	—	1
Fancy goods	(6)	1	1	—	—	—	2	—	—	—	—	—	2	—	—	—
Food—Butchers	(7c)	1	—	—	—	—	1	—	—	—	—	—	—	1	—	—
Catering	(7d)	3	2	—	1	—	3	3	1	—	—	2	4	2	—	1
Grocers	(7e)	3	1	—	1	—	5	—	—	—	—	—	4	1	—	—
Fur	(9)	1	1	—	—	—	1	1	—	—	1	—	2	—	—	—
Furniture	(10)	3	2	—	—	—	2	3	—	—	3	—	5	—	—	—
Hairdressing	(12)	2	2	—	—	—	4	—	—	—	—	—	4	—	—	—
Insurance	(13)	1	1	—	—	—	—	2	—	—	2	—	—	2	—	—
Jewellers	(14)	1	1	—	1	—	2	1	—	—	1	—	2	1	—	—
Metal, etc.	(15)	1	—	—	1	—	—	2	—	—	1	1	2	—	—	—
Motor, etc.	(16)	1	—	—	—	—	—	1	—	—	1	—	1	—	—	—
Stockbrokers	(18)	1	—	—	—	—	—	1	—	—	1	—	1	—	—	—
Domestic Service	(21)	4	2	—	1	—	—	7	1	—	2	4	5	2	—	—
Miscellaneous		66	12	—	3	—	16	65	8	10	39	8	74	7	—	1
All Females in Trades & Services ...		123	43	—	15	—	65	116	13	11	63	29	156	25	—	4

TABLE XIV—A.J.S.-2

PROFESSIONS ALL AREAS: FEMALES

Profession	Male Index No.	Marital Status					Kind of Employment						Nationality at Birth*		
		S	M	D	W	U	Own account	Employed	Mana-gers	Prof. Tech.	Cleri. cal	Man-ual	British	For-eign	Un-known
Accountants	(1)	4	1	—	—	—	—	5	—	—	5	—	5	—	—
Architects	(3)	1	1	—	—	—	1	1	—	1	—	—	1	1	—
Artists	(4)	4	2	—	—	—	2	4	—	4	—	—	6	—	—
Chemists	(5)	1	1	—	—	—	—	2	—	—	2	—	2	—	—
Civil Servants	(6)	2	—	—	—	—	2	—	—	—	—	—	2	—	—
Dentistry	(7)	—	1	—	1	—	—	2	—	2	—	—	2	—	—
Engineering	(8)	1	1	—	—	—	1	1	—	—	1	—	2	—	—
Law	(10)	1	2	—	—	—	2	1	—	1	—	—	2	1	—
Medicine	(12)	3	2	—	—	—	—	5	1	4	—	—	5	—	—
Musicians	(15)	1	1	—	—	—	—	2	—	—	1	1	2	—	—
Teachers	(19)	12	1	1	—	—	2	12	—	12	—	—	11	3	—
Nursing		—	1	—	—	—	—	1	—	—	1	—	1	—	—
Total		30	14	1	1	—	10	36	1	24	10	1	41	5	—

* All now British (1952)

257

TABLE XV

LONDON BOARD OF JEWISH RELIGIOUS EDUCATION CLASSES[1]

Age and Sex

TYPE OF CLASS	BOYS						GIRLS						TOTAL CHILDREN
	Under 13	Per Cent	Over 13	Per Cent	Total Boys	Per Cent Boys	Under 13	Per Cent	Over 13	Per Cent	Total Girls	Per Cent Girls	
Synagogue ...	4,805	(93%)	358	(7%)	5,163	61%	3,086	(95%)	167	(5%)	3,253	39%	8,416
Talmud Torah..	1,463	(97%)	52	(3%)	1,515	80%	368	(96%)	14	(4%)	382	20%	1,897
Total (per cent).	6,268	(96%)	410	(4%)	6,678	65%	3,454	(95%)	181	(5%)	3,635	35%	10,313
Withdrawal ...	843	(57%)	629	(43%)	1,472	52%	755	(56%)	594	(44%)	1,349	48%	2,821
Total (per cent).	7,111	(87%)	1,039	(13%)	8,150	62%	4,209	(84%)	775	(16%)	4,984	38%	13,134

[1] Classes held under the auspices of the London Board of Jewish Religious Education have 13,134 pupils enrolled—approximately 70% of the total number of Jewish children receiving religious instruction in Greater London—See Table XVII, p. 257

TABLE XVI

LONDON BOARD OF JEWISH RELIGIOUS EDUCATION CLASSES

Enrolment and Attendance at Synagogue and Talmud Torah Classes

TYPE OF CLASS				NO. ENROLLED	ATTENDANCE			
					Sundays (per cent)		Weekdays (per cent)	
Synagogue Classes	...	...	...	8,416	6,019	(72%)	3,737	(44%)
Talmud Torahs	...	...	...	1,897	1,249	(65%)	1,313	(69%)
Total (per cent)	...	...	...	10,313	7,268	(70%)	5,050	(49%)

TABLE XVII

RELIGIOUS INSTRUCTION IN GREATER LONDON

FULL-TIME SCHOOLS.

Jewish Secondary Schools Movement ...	1,210
North-West London Jewish Day Schools	265
Stepney Jewish School	358
Solomon Wolfson School	352
Hillel House School	90
Ahavas Torah School	30

2,305

RELIGIOUS CLASSES

London Board of Jewish Religious Education

Synagogue Classes	8,416
Talmud Torahs	1,897
Withdrawal Classes at non-Jewish Schools	2,821

13,134

Union of Orthodox Hebrew Congregations	1,090
Union of Liberal and Progressive Synagogues	875
Association of Synagogues	[750]
Sephardi Synagogues	240

Other Classes :

Tree of Life College	68
Law of Truth Talmud College ...	45
Golders Green Beth Hamedrash ...	50
Teesdale Street Talmud Torah ...	24
Enfield & Winchmore Hill Hebrew Congregation	20
L.C.C. Classes	[40]

247

16,336

Estimated Total 18,641

APPENDIX II

ESTIMATED JEWISH POPULATION GROWTH IN GREAT BRITA

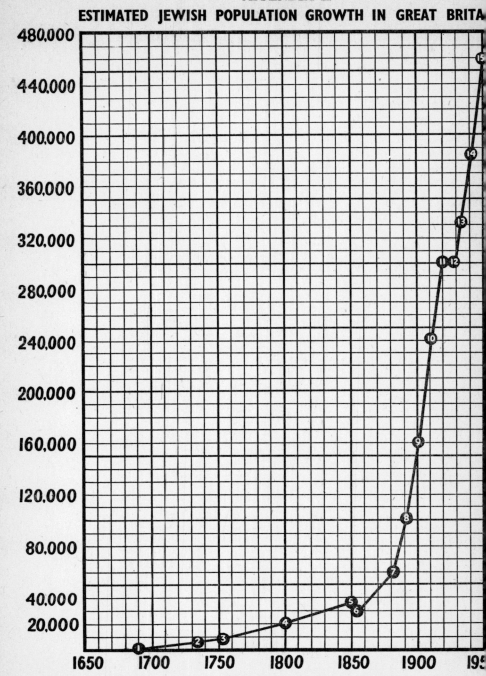

NOTES

1. 350: V. D. Lipman *Social History of the Jews in England, 1850-1950*, pp. 5 and 8, quoting the Petition of the Jews against the Aliens Tax in 1690.

2. 6,000: *Ibid.*, pp. 6 and 8, quoting d'Blossiers Tovey *Anglia Judaica*, p. 302.

3. 8,000: *Ibid.*, pp. 6 and 8.

4. 20,000: *Ibid.*, pp. 6 and 8. According to James Picciotto, *Sketches of Anglo-Jewish History* (1875), p. 152 (quoted by Lipman), the figure may have been as high as 26,000.

5. 35,000: *Ibid.*, pp. 7 and 8. Lipman points out that contemporary estimates vary. F. H. Goldsmid *Remarks on the Civil Liberties of British Jews* (1830), pp. 69-71, puts the figure at about 27,000 in 1830, which Lipman thinks had increased by a further 8,000 20 years later. Egan, on the other hand, puts the number in 1849 at "about 40,000." In 1851 Mayhew wrote that a statistical inquiry carried out by the Chief Rabbi in August, 1845, had arrived at an estimate of 35,000, of whom 18,000 were resident in London. This figure is supported by the tables of "*Baale Batim* (householders), seatholders, and individuals" published in *The Jewish Chronicle* of July 23rd, 1847, and assumed by Lipman to be based on the Chief Rabbi's 1845 inquiry. It is also supported by the Board of Deputies' annual return of 1848 for births, marriages, deaths, and seatholders at individual congregations, and likewise by the synagogal returns of the number of seats let and Sabbath attendance on the census Sabbath of March, 28-29th, 1851. By contrast, Mill, writing two years after Mayhew, said that though the number "generally calculated" was 30,000 his own reading of the annual death-rate of 560 reported in the Board of Deputies' returns was that the number of Jews in Britain was 25,000.

6. 30,000: *The Jewish Chronicle*, September 17, 1954.

7. 60,000: *The Jewish Year Book 1897*, p. 26.

8. 101,189: *Ibid.* This figure is arrived at by extrapolation from estimated Jewish death- and marriage-rates and rates for the general population in relation to the 1891 census of the British Empire.

9. 160,000: *The Jewish Year Book 1901-1902*, p. 178. The Editor, the Rev. Isidore Harris, points out that though the *American Jewish Year Book 1900* gives a figure of just over 100,000, this is almost certainly an underestimate. He recalls that *The Jewish Chronicle* of March 9th, 1900, published an article by the former editor of *The Jewish Year Book*, Joseph Jacobs, estimating London's Jewish population as being 96,000 in that year, and natural increase as 1,000 per year. Accordingly, argues Mr. Harris, London's population in 1901 could be put at 97,000. As for the rest of the United Kingdom, returns sent to *The Jewish Year Book*, plus an element for those provincial centres which sent no replies to the editor's inquiries, give a grand total of about 160,000, including the 3,771 (851 in Ulster) in Ireland returned by the Registrar-General in Dublin.

10. 242,525: *The Jewish Year Book 1911*, p. 267. Greater London is quoted as having 150,000 Jews. *Ibid.*, p. 273.

NOTES

11. 300,000: *The Jewish Year Book 1920*, p. 165, quoting Davis Trietsch. The editor, the Rev. Isidore Harris, however, doubts whether the figure is higher than 286,000 (*ibid.*, p. 170). *Cf.* Dr. Redcliffe Salaman's figure of 300,000 as early as 1914, referred to on p. 73 above.

12. 297,000: *The Jewish Year Book 1929*, p. 292. The editor appears to have hardened in his doubts concerning Trietsch's figures in 1920 (see Note 11 above). On p. 291 he quotes figures from Jakob Lestschinsky's article " Die Gesamtzahl der Juden auf der Erde," *Blätter für Demographie, Statistik und Wirtschaftskunde der Juden*, No. 5, 1925, which repeat his own 1920 estimate (286,000).

13. 333,000: *The Jewish Year Book 1935*, p. 364.

14. 385,000: *The Jewish Year Book 1940*, p. 334. The figure of 385,000 is stated to include about 35,000 refugees.

15. 450,000: *The Jewish Year Book 1952*, p. 313. And see pp. 73-76 above.

LIST OF WORKS CITED

In English

Books

ABRAHAMS, ISRAEL: *Jewish Life in the Middle Ages,* London, 1932.

ADLER, ELKIN: *History of the Jews in London,* Philadelphia, 1930.

ADLER, HENRIETTA: " Jewish Life and Labour in East London," *The New Survey of London Life and Labour,* Vol. VI, London, 1934.

AMORY, CLEVELAND: *The Proper Bostonians,* New York, 1947.

BARNETT, LIONEL D.: *Bevis Marks Records. Being Contributions to the History of the Spanish and Portuguese Congregation of London,* Part I, Oxford, 1940.

BARON, S. W.: *The Jewish Community; its history and structure to the American Revolution,* 3 vols., Jewish Publication Society of America, Philadelphia, 1942.

COHEN, A.: *An Anglo-Jewish Scrapbook, 1600-1840,* London, 1943.

COON, C. S.: *The Races of Europe,* New York, 1939.

COUNT, E. W.: *This is Race,* New York, 1950.

EYSENCK, H. J.: *The Uses and Abuses of Psychology,* Penguin Books, 1953.

GINSBERG, MORRIS: *Reason and Unreason in Society,* London, 1947.

GODBEY, ALLEN H.: *The Lost Tribes: a Myth,* Duke University Press, 1930.

GOLDSMID, F. H.: *Remarks on the Civil Liberties of British Jews,* London, 1830.

HARTMANN, GRETHE, and SCHLESINGER, FINI: *Physical and Mental Stress and Consequential Development of Arterio-Sclerosis,* Copenhagen, 1952.

HENRIQUES, H. S. Q.: *The Jews and the English Law,* Oxford, 1908.

HUGHES, EVERETT C. and HELEN M.: *Where Peoples Meet,* Glencoe, 1952.

LIPMAN, V. D.: *Social History of the Jews in England, 1850-1950,* London, 1954.

LITTLE, K. L.: *Negroes in Britain,* London, 1948.

MACCRONE, L. D.: *Race Attitudes in South Africa,* London, 1937.

MATTUCK, ISRAEL I.: *The Essentials of Liberal Judaism,* London, 1947.

MENCKEN, H. L.: *American Language,* 4th ed., New York, 1946.

MIKES, GEORGE: *How to be an Alien,* London, 1946.

MULLALLY, F.: *Fascism inside England,* London, 1946.

MYRDAL, GUNNAR: *An American Dilemma,* New York, 1944.

PARKES, THE REV. DR. JAMES: *The Jew in the Medieval Community,* London, 1938.

PICCIOTTO, JAMES: *Sketches of Anglo-Jewish History,* London 1875.

POTTER, BEATRICE: " The Jewish Community (East London) ": in Booth, C. (ed.): *Life and Labour of the People in London,* Vol. III, 1892.

263

LIST OF WORKS CITED

REITLINGER, GERALD: *The Final Solution: The Attempt to Exterminate the Jews of Europe 1939-45*, Vallentine, Mitchell & Co., London, 1953.

RICHMOND, A. H.: *Colour Prejudice in Britain*, London, 1954.

RIESMAN, DAVID *et al.*: *The Lonely Crowd*, Yale, 1950.

RIESMAN, DAVID *et al.* and GLAZER, NATHAN: *Faces in the Crowd*, Yale, 1952.

ROBSON, R. J.: *The Oxfordshire Election of 1754*, London, 1949.

ROSENBERG, LOUIS: *Canada's Jews: A Social and Economic Study of the Jews in Canada*, Canadian Jewish Congress, 1939.

ROTH, CECIL: *A History of the Jews in England*, 2nd ed., Oxford, 1949.

ROTH, CECIL: *The Rise of Provincial Jewry*, London, 1950.

ROTH, CECIL: (ed.) *Anglo-Jewish Letters*, London, 1938.

RUPPIN, A.: *The Jews in the Modern World*, London, 1934.

RUSSELL, BERTRAND: *Power—a New Social Analysis*, London, 1948.

RUSSELL, C. and LEWIS, H. S.: *The Jew in London: A Study of Racial Character and Present-day Conditions*, London, 1900.

SELTZER, C. C.: "The Jew—His Racial Status" in: *This is Race*, ed. by E. W. Count, New York, 1950.

SLOTKI, DR. I. W.: *Jewish Education in Manchester, 1928*, Manchester, 1928

WIRTH, LOUIS: *The Ghetto*, Chicago, 1929.

ZBOROWSKI, MARK, and HERZOG, ELIZABETH: *Life is with People*, New York, 1952.

ARTICLES IN PERIODICALS

BANTON, MICHAEL: "Negro Workers in Britain," *Twentieth Century*, January, 1952.

BARON, RAYMOND V.: "Jewish Students: a Survey," *The Jewish Chronicle*, February 16th and 23rd, 1951.

BENTWICH, NORMAN: "A Jewish Corner of Kent," *The Jewish Chronicle*, September 26th, 1952.

BRAW, STANLEY R.: "Sampling Jewish Marriage Data," *Jewish Social Studies*, Vol. X, No. 1, 1948.

BURGESS, E. W., and WALLIN, P.: "Homogamy in Social Characteristics," *American Journal of Sociology*, Vol. XLIX, No. 2, 1943.

COLLINS, S. F.: "Social Processes Integrating Coloured People in Britain," *British Journal of Sociology*, Vol. III, No. 1, 1952.

GREENBERG, M.: "The Reproduction Rate of the Families of the Jewish Students at the University of Maryland," *Jewish Social Studies*, Vol. X, No. 3, 1948.

JAFFE, A. J.: "The Use of Death Records to Determine Jewish Population Characteristics," *Jewish Social Studies*, Vol. 1, No. 2, April, 1939.

KANTOROWITSCH, MIRON: "On the Statistics of Jewish Marriages in England and Wales," *Population*, Vol. II, No. 2, November, 1936.

KANTOROWITSCH, MIRON: *"Estimate of the Jewish Population of London in 1929-1933," Journal of the Royal Statistical Society*, Vol. XCIX, Part 2, 1936.

LIPMAN, V. D.: Address to the Jewish Historical Society of England, *The Jewish Chronicle*, July 21st, 1950.

LIST OF WORKS CITED

METHORST, H. W.: "Differential Fertility in the Netherlands, *Population* (Special Memoir), Vol. I, April, 1935.

MONTEFIORE, C. G.: "Dr. Wiener on the Dietary Laws." Being a review of: "Die Jüdischen Speisegesetz nach ihren verschiedenen Gesichtspunkten . . . etc.," by Dr. A. Wiener, *Jewish Quarterly Review* (old series), Vol. VIII.

OLSOVER, L.: "A Social Survey of Newcastle Jewry," *The Watchman*, Newcastle, September, 1951.

PELA, DAVID: "Storm over Refugee Report," *The Jewish Chronicle*, February 22nd, 1952.

PRAIS, S. J.: "Social Survey of Birmingham Jewry," *The Jewish Monthly*, February, 1949.

RICHMOND, A. H.: "Social Scientists in Action," *Science News*, No. 27, Penguin Books, 1953.

ROSENTHAL, ERICH: "Trends of the Jewish Population in Germany, 1910-1939," *Jewish Social Studies*, Vol. VI, No. 3, July, 1944.

ROSENTHAL, ERICH: "The Size of the Jewish Population in Chicago, 1930," *Jewish Social Studies*, Vol. VII, No. 2, April, 1945.

ROTH, CECIL: "The Collapse of English Jewry," *Jewish Monthly*, July, 1947.

SALAMAN, REDCLIFFE N.: "Anglo-Jewish Vital Statistics," *The Jewish Chronicle Supplement*, Nos. 4, 5, 6, 7, and 8, 1921.

SALAMAN, REDCLIFFE N.: "Jews in the Royal Society; a Problem in Ecology," *Notes and Records of the Royal Society*, Vol. XVII, No. 1, 1947.

SHAPIRO, LEON, and STARR, JOSHUA: "Recent Population Data Regarding the Jews in Europe," *Jewish Social Studies*, Vol. VIII, No. 2, April, 1946.

SLATER, ELIOT: "A Biological View of Anti-Semitism," *Jewish Monthly*, November, 1947.

SLATER, ELIOT: "A Note on Jewish-Christian Intermarriage," *Eugenics Review*, Vol. XXXIX, No. 1, April, 1947.

SLOTKI, I. W.: "The Jewish Population of Manchester," *The Jewish Chronicle*, November 3rd, 1950.

SOREF, HAROLD: "A Demographic Revolution," *The Jewish Chronicle*, March 14, 1952.

SPIEGELMAN, MORTIMER: "The Reproductivity of Jews in Canada, 1940 to 1942." *Population Studies*, Vol. IV, pt. 3, December, 1950.

TRACHTENBERG, H. L.: "Estimate of the Jewish Population of London in 1929," *Journal of the Royal Statistical Society*, Vol. XCVI, Part 1, 1933.

ZANTEN, J. H. VAN, and BRINK, T. VAN DEN: "Population Phenomena in Amsterdam," *Population*, Vol. III, No. 1, January, 1939.

"The Conscience Clause," *The Jewish Chronicle*, June 9th, 1950.

"Holy-day Appeals in Synagogues," *The Jewish Chronicle*, October 6th, 1950.

"An Inquiry into Anglo-Jewish Youth," *Jewish Observer*, May 2nd, 1952.

"Study of Church-goers," carried out by Mass Observation, *The British Weekly*, January 6th, 13th, 20th, 27th, February 3rd, 10th, 1949.

T

LIST OF WORKS CITED

PERIODICALS, ANNUALS, ETC.

American Jewish Year Book, 1900.

The Grocer and Oil Trade Review. Various issues.

The Jewish Chronicle, London. Various issues.

The Jewish Chronicle Supplement, London. Various issues.

The Jewish Chronicle Travel Guide, 1954.

The Jewish Year Book. Various years.

Whitaker's Almanack. Various years.

REPORTS, ETC., OF GOVERNMENT AND PRIVATE ORGANISATIONS

Central Council for Jewish Religious Education: *Report of Inspector,* year ending October, 1953.

Home Office: *Naturalisation of Aliens : White Papers.* Various years.

London Board of Jewish Religious Education: *Fourth Report,* May, 1952-December, 1953.

Registrar-General:
   Births, Marriages, and Deaths, in England and Wales. Annual Reports for 1904 and 1905.

   General Report of 1911 : Census of Population.

   Report of Royal Commission on Population, 1949.

   Royal Commission on Population: *Report on Family Limitation,* 1949.

   Statistical Review of England and Wales, 1938, 1942, 1948, 1949.

Trades Advisory Council:
   Monthly Bulletins.

   Annual Reports.

   The Jews in Work and Trade, by Dr. N. Barou, 1945 ; 3rd ed., 1948.

University Grants Committee: *Return from Universities and University Colleges in Receipt of Treasury Grants, 1949-50.*

World Jewish Congress: *Reports* for various years.

In Foreign Languages

ARONIUS, J.: *Regesten zur Geschichte der Juden in Deutschland,* Berlin, 1902.

NEUMARK, F.: " Betrachtungen zur gegenwärtigen Bevölkerungsgliederung Deutschlands," *Population,* November, 1935.

LESTCHINSKY, JAKOB: " Die Gesamtzahl der Juden auf der Erde," *Blätter für Demographie, Statistik, und Wirtschaftskunde der Juden,* No. 5, 1925.

TEILHABER, F. A.: *Der Untergang der deutschen Juden,* Munich, 1911.

Unpublished Material

BROTZ, HOWARD M.: *An Analysis of Social Stratification within Jewish Society in London.* Thesis for Ph.D. of University of London. (London School of Economics), 1951.

ROBB, J.: *A Study of Anti-Semitism in a Working-class Area.* Thesis for Ph.D. of University of London, 1950. See *Quarterly Bulletin of the British Psychological Society,* Vol. III, No. 16, April, 1952.[1]

RUMYANECK, J.: *The Social and Economic Development of the Jews in England, 1730-1860.* Thesis for Ph.D. of University of London, 1933.

[1] Published as *Working-class Anti-Semite : A Psychological Study in a London Borough,* Tavistock Publications, London, after the completion of this book.

INDEX

A

Abrahams, Israel: 30
Acculturation and assimilation, inter-action of: 202f., 227ff., 240
Action against Jewish misconduct: 219
Adjustments of British social life to Jewry: 241
Adler, Chief Rabbi Dr. Nathan Marcus: 24, 26
Adoption societies for Jewish children: 151
Age groups of Jewish population: 68
Age structure, influence of birth-rate on: 97
Age structure of Anglo-Jewry, London: 97
    England and Wales: 97
Aliens Immigration Act, 1905: 45
Alliance Israélite Universelle: 34
Ambivalence in Jewish attitude: 167
    towards Jewish élite: 187
    towards non-Jewish world: 179
American Jewish Committee: 36
American Jewish Congress: 36
Amsterdam, marriages of necessity in: 88
Anglo-Jewish Association: 30, 32, 33, 35, 142, 159, 165, 196, 207
Anti-Jewish accusations: 212
Antisemitism: xiv, 49 *et seq.*, 202 *et seq.*, 223 *et seq.*, 241
    dualism in attitude: 224
    economic motivation: 215
    extent of: 224, 225
    need for study of: xiii
    reaction to: 223
Antwerp, Jews in: 9
Anxieties arising from minority position: 209
Army and Navy, Jews in: 41
Ashkenazim and Sephardim: 21 *et seq.*, 164
    and reform: 29
    first cemetery: 21
    in England: 12, 13, 15, 19, 20 *et seq.*

preponderance among immigrants, 1911: 109
    synagogue, 1690: 21
Assimilation:
    as complete merger: 227
    as equal status with other religions: 228
    by intermarriage: 233
    counter-action to: 181
    effect of: 65
    impossible for Orthodox: 227
    in economic field: 129
    interaction with acculturation: 240
    meanings of: 227 *et seq.*
    numerically considered: 110
    process of: 108
    struggle for: 41
    varying criteria of: 202
Association for Jewish Youth: 119-20, 142
Association of Jewish ex-Service Men and Women: viii, 66, 125, 208, 223
Association of Jewish Friendly Societies: 142
Association of Jewish Refugees: viii, 131
Association of Synagogues in Great Britain: 31
    membership of: 233
Attitude to Jews, non-Jewish: 49

B

Bachad (Hechalutz B'Anglia) figures of immigration to Israel: 124
Balfour Declaration: 35, 51
Barmitzvah: 117
Belfast: 65, 79, 104
Berkshire, Earl of: 48
Beth Din: 26-7, 142, 207-8, 210, 231
Bevis Marks: 18, 30, 31, 142
Bill for abolition of Civil Disabilities, 1830: 40
Bill for Naturalisation of the Jews, 1753: 39, 40, 49

INDEX

Birmingham: 16, 26, 44, 66, 75, 77, 89, 98, 99, 100
Birth control,
  affected by religion: 86
  affected by social class: 86
  effect of war on Jewish: 85
  general, in Great Britain: 84-5
  percentage of women of various religions using: 85
Birth, definition of Jew by: 151
Birth-rate, decline in England and Wales, 1921-31: 82
  decline in Jewish: 69, 80, 82
  estimate of Jewish: 83
  influenced by age structure: 97
  Jewish, affected by social class: 84, 86
  reasons for decline in: 71
Black marketing: 213, 217
Board of Deputies: 22, 28, 30, 31 *et seq*, 34, 63, 112, 142, 158, 165, 180, 196, 207, 209, 213, 215-6, 219, 261
  Defence Committee: 36, 217, 223
Board of Guardians: viii, 28, 33, 45, 127, 142, 159, 186
Board for Shechita: 114
Book, objects of: vii, ix, x
Born Jew, attitude to convert: 152
Bristol: 16, 44
Britain, Jewish admiration for: 166, 167
British criteria applied to Jews: 203
Brodetsky, Dr., esteem for as senior wrangler: 178
Brodie, Rabbi Israel, Chief Rabbi: 24, 34
Broker, first Jewish: 11
  licensed to act as: 38
Brotz, Dr., theme of his essay: xi
Burial figures, male and female Jewish: 103, 104
Burton, Sir Montague: 129

C

Callings, limits to the diversification of Jewish: 222
Cambridge: 69
Canada,
  decline in Jewish birth-rate: 80
  reproduction rate of Jews: 106
Canterbury: 16, 78
Cemeteries: 17, 21
Cemetery in community life: 17
Central British Fund: 36

Central Council for Jewish Religious Education: 117, 120
Central London, Jewish return to: 140
Charitable activities (see also various societies): 25, 33, 42
Charity as cohesive force: 186
Charles II and Jews: 11, 12, 210
Charter for British Jewry, absence of: 17
Chicago, Jewish population of: 67
  reproduction rate among Jews in: 106
Chief Rabbi: 24, 28, 34, 172, 207, 208, 231, 238, 261
Chmielnitzki, Bogdan: 12
Christianity: 205, 228
Church, percentage of British population attending: 111
Citizenship, achievement of full: 39
Civil disabilities, Bill for abolition of: 40
Civil Marriages, Jewish: 90, 91
Clichés, Jewish, about Jews: 163
Closed society, Anglo-Jewry considered as: 169, 188, *et seq*.
  extent to which it has been modified: 192-3
  extent to which it has survived in Anglo-Jewry: 191-2
  prestige values in: 189
Cohen, Lord Justice: 162
Cohesion of Jewish society,
  based on internal culture: 182
  not due solely to hostile environment: 186
Cohesive force of charity: 186
Colour bar: 202, 225
Communal representation as reason for Jewish esteem: 171
Communion, sacrament, essential to British citizenship: 39
Communities (Jewish),
  growth of provincial: 44
  nature of: 23-6
  outside London: 15, 22-3
  study of local: xiii
  (See also various towns)
Community (Jewish),
  as centripetal force: 182
  control over individuals: 13
  co-ordination, illusory nature of: 207
  economic bases of: 42-44
  economic differentiation in: 43
  London (see also districts): 42
  organisation of: 65

270

E

F

G

INDEX

Germany,
  decline in Jewish proportion of population before 1939 : 80
  decline of Jewish birth-rate in : 80
  intermarriage in : 96
Ghetto,
  not abolished but transferred : 149
  a " closed " society : 165
Gideon, Sampson, Sheriff and Alderman of City of London : 39
Glasgow,
  death-rate, male to female : 104
  Jewish population in, 1950 : 75, 77
Goebbels : 50
Golders Green.
  " a homely place " : 148
  " tone going down in " : 149
Grammar schools, proportion of Jews to total scholars in Manchester : 132
Great Britain, immigration into : 59
Great Synagogue : 21, 31, 33
Grocery trade, Jewish practices in : 213, 214
Grouping in Anglo-Jewry, voluntary nature of : 209

H

Hambro Synagogue : 21, 23, 25, 31, 33
Hampstead, superior social status of : 147
Hatikvah, Jewish attitude to : 157
Hebrew, pronunciation in Great Britain : 238
Heine, Heinrich : 61
Hendon, "like the East End was" : 147
Henriques family, attitude to : 156
Hertz, Dr., Chief Rabbi : 27
Hirschell, Rabbi Solomon, first Chief Rabbi : 24
Homogeneity of Anglo-Jewry, growing : 153
" Hope of Israel " : 10, 11
Houtzmann, Rudiger, Bishop of Speyer : 6
Hull, Representative Council of : 66, 125

I

Immigrants,
  number of Jewish, 1914-50 : 73, 261
  characteristics of, 1933-39 : 110
Immigration, effect of, on trades : 128

Indianapolis, birth-rate in, by religions : 82
Inferiority complex among Jews : 176
Inglis, Sir Robert : 48
Institute of Jewish Affairs : 56
Intermarriage,
  as process of assimilation : 233
  as revealed by questionnaire : 92
  by social groups : 95
  changes in attitude of Jewish social strata : 234
  difficulty of ascertaining facts : 92
  disdain for : 153
  in Berlin prior to 1914 : 92
  in Germany : 96
  in various countries : 95, 96
  increase of : 93
  religious obstacles to : 234
  results if continued : 94, 97
  status of offspring of : 234
International affairs, activities of Anglo-Jewry in : 22
Inter-University Federation of Jewish Students : 65, 116
Ipswich : 16
Israel,
  a source of Jewish self-respect : 237, 238
  and Anglo-Jewry : 235
  Embassy of : viii
  immigration into from Britain : 58
Israel, Menasseh ben : 9, 10, 164, 191, 193

J

Jewish National Fund : 122
  „   judgments of fellow-Jews distorted : 177
Jewish Memorial Council : viii
  „   Historical Society : 112
  „   Refugee Committee : 64, 104
  „   Religious Union : 30, 233
  „   Representative Councils (see under various towns),
Jewish Schools and Zionism : 238
Jewry, a civilisation : 4
  „   not a homogeneous racial group : 4
Jews and non-Jews : 241
Jews' College : 34, 120-1, 141
Jews, definition of : see "Definition"
Jews' Free School : 34
Jews, geographical distribution of : 77-8
Jews in Britain, no serious problem : ix

273

Jews not unique : 202
" Jews' poker " : 241
Joint Foreign Affairs Committee of
  Board of Deputies and Anglo-
  Jewish Association : 32, 35, 165
Joint Palestine Appeal : 236
Judaism : 204, 227ff., 230ff.
  and Christianity : 205

K

Kasher Customer registration, figures
  for : 113
Kasher butchers and poulterers, Lon-
  don : 114
Kashrut Commission : 62
King's Lynn : 16

L

Land, right of Jews to acquire : 38
Lauderdale Road Synagogue : 142
Leeds : 29, 47, 65, 75, 77
Levi, Phineas, a Navy agent, 1830 : 44
Levy, Benjamin, of Hamburg : 21
Liberal Jews, attitude to Jewish law :
  175
Liberal Synagogues, distribution in
  Greater London : 233
  objects of : 232
Liverpool : 16, 29, 32, 47, 75, 77, 128
London,
  birth control in : 85
  compared with provinces : xii
  Jewish population of Greater :
    66-7, 75, 77, 261
  Jews in : xii
  kasher butchers and poulterers
    in : 114
  male to female deaths : 104
  samples of Jewish population of
    66
  " secret communities " in : 9
  (see also East End, and other
    London districts)
London Board of Jewish Religious
  Education : 117, 118
London, City of, restrictions on Jews
  in : 49
London Jewish Hospital : viii, 66
Louis the Pious, passports issued by : 6
Lyons, Hart : 24
Lyons, Sir Joseph : 29

M

Maccabi Associations, Union of :
  119
Macher, the, or " pusher " : 211
Mahamad : 17, 18, 29, 190
Manchester : 19, 26, 29, 47, 66, 71, 72,
  75-9, 128, 132
Maria Theresa expels Jews from
  Bohemia : 22, 48
Marks and Spencer : 129
Marranos : 9, 14
Marriage,
  age of Jewish men at : 86
  age of Jewish women at : 86 *et seq.*
  increase in civil, 1884-1934 : 89
    et seq.
  influence on birth-rate : 86
  of necessity, in Amsterdam : 88
  proportion of, to total British
    and Jewish populations, by age-
    groups,
      Females : 91
      Males : 90
      Percentages : 91
  rate in Birmingham : 89
  rate in England and Wales by
    religious ceremonial, general
    and Jewish, 1934 : 88
Maryland, University of,
  ratio of foreign- to native-born
    mothers of Jewish students at :
    111
  University of, family composition
    of Jewish students at : 106
Mass Observation, study of church-
  goers : 111
Mattuck, Dr. Israel : 30
Medina, Sir Solomon de : 15
Members of Parliament : 41
Merchants, Jews as : 6, 7, 14, 15, 42
Merthyr Tydfil, birth-rate in : 69
Middle ages, privileges of Jews in : 6
Middleman, difficulties of the Jewish :
  220
Migration, characteristics of Jewish :
  13
Mikes, George, *How to be an Alien,*
  quoted : 204
Milieu, flight from Jewish : 148
Ministers, shortage of : 120
Minority community based on religion
  and extra-national activities : 208
Minority societies, " closed " and
  " open " types of : 180

S

T

Tone in Jewry set by non-Jewish world : 149
Trade, retail : 47
Traders and business men, estimated number of Anglo-Jewish : 221
Trades Advisory Council : viii, 36, 128, 213, 216 *et seq.*, 223 *et seq.*, 227
Trades, percentage of, worked by Jews : 128
Transmigration, works both ways : 149

U

U.S.A.,
    Intermarriage in : 96
    Reproduction rate of Jews in certain areas : 106
Union of Orthodox Hebrew Congregations : 27, 28, 174, 230, 232
United Synagogue : viii, 24, 25, 26, 28, 30, 174, 238
    and Zionism : 122
    attacked by more Orthodox bodies : 174
    consulted by Ministry of Food : 166
    death-rate : 101-3
    distribution in Greater London : 230, 231
    fashionableness of : 175
    female, and vote : 87
    female death-rate : 105
    membership in Greater London : 230
    membership, burials of : 101
    male to female deaths : 105
    place of in Anglo-Jewry : 231
Urbanisation of Jews : 84
    special form among Anglo-Jewry : 79
Usury, Jews and : 7, 14

V

Value system, affected by immigration : 194
    exaggerated emphasis on wealth in : 193
    schizoid quality of Anglo-Jewish : 193
Van Oven : 210

Vicksburg, U.S.A., intermarriage in : 96
Victoria, Queen : 48

W

Waley-Cohen, Sir Robert, attitude to : 156, 162
War, its effect on Jewish occupational distribution : 127
Wealth a cause of differentiation : 155-6
Weizmann, Dr. Chaim : 158
West London Synagogue : 29-31, 233
Wiener Institute and Library : viii, 36
William III : 48
William IV : 48
Witriol, J. : 28
Woburn House : 142
Women at home : 125
World Jewish Congress : 33, 35, 56
World Union : 31
World Zionist Organisation : 123

Y

Yamey, B. : 214n.
Yeshiva: 159
Yiddish,
    among East End Jews : 139-40
    extent to which used, 1911 : 63, 109
    in Poland : 167
" *Yom Kippur* Jews " : 242
Yom Kippur method of determining Jewish population : 167
York : 111
Youth and Israel : 123
Youth, attitude to Judaism : 119-20
Youth leaders, shortage of : 120
Youth organisations : 119 *et seq.*

Z

Zionism : 35, 207, 208, 229
    and Anglo-Jewry : 121 *et seq.*
    and assimilation : 235
    and Board of Deputies : 32
    and divided loyalties in Anglo-Jewry : 236

and problem of Jewish affinity : 150
attitude of élite to : 157-8
attitude to : 157
British supporters of : 236
conflict over : 195-6
in Anglo-Jewry a form of charity : 237
influence among children : 238
its ideas permeating modern Judaism : 238

its significance in Anglo-Jewry : 235
largely misplaced fear of : 237
not co-terminous with Judaism : 238
Zionist Congress : 123
Zionist Federation of Great Britain : 35
Zionist Federation Synagogue Council : 122
Zionist Youth Movement : 119